Land Rover
90, 110 & Defender
Restoration
Manual

THE STEP-BY-STEP GUIDE TO THE
ENTIRE RESTORATION PROCESS

First published in August 2014, reprinted 2016, 2017, 2019,
2020 (twice), 2021 (three times), 2022, 2023, 2024 and 2025

A catalogue record for this book is available from the British Library.

ISBN 978 0 85733 479 4

Library of Congress control no. 2014930860

Published by Haynes Group Limited,
Sparkford, Yeovil,
Somerset BA22 7JJ, UK.
Tel: 01963 440635
Int. tel: +44 1963 440635
Website: www.haynes.com

Haynes North America Inc.,
2801 Townsgate Road, Suite 340
Thousand Oaks, CA 91361

While every effort is taken to ensure the accuracy of the information
given in this book, no liability can be accepted by the author or
publishers for any loss, damage or injury caused by errors in, or
omissions from, the information given.

Printed in India.

The manufacturer's authorised representative in the EU for product safety is:

HaynesPro BV
Stationsstraat 79 F, 3811MH Amersfoort, The Netherlands
gpsr@haynes.co.uk

Land Rover
90, 110 & Defender

Restoration Manual

THE STEP-BY-STEP GUIDE TO THE ENTIRE RESTORATION PROCESS

Lindsay Porter

■ BUYING ■ PROJECT PLANNING ■ STRIPDOWN AND REFIT ■ STRUCTURAL REPAIRS
■ BODYWORK, PREPARATION AND PAINT ■ INTERIOR REFURBISHMENT ■ MECHANICAL OVERHAUL

Contents

Introduction

During my decade or more as technical editor of a leading Land Rover magazine, I created many thousands of workshop photographs, compiled masses of information and absorbed some of the very best specialist advice available – which has all helped to make this all-new *Defender Restoration Manual* pretty much what I want it to be, and, more importantly, all that I hope you, the reader, need it to be.

The first edition – black-and-white photographs, and covering earlier models only – was a great success, but Haynes Publishing have encouraged me to go so much further with this new edition. Not only does it cover many more restoration jobs and in much more detail than before, but it also covers Defenders right up to the end of the five-cylinder, TD5 era.

But Land Rover repair, restoration and ownership aren't just about nuts and bolts, as any enthusiast will know. They're about a passion for the character, foibles, faults and fun in owning a Defender and, most of all, in sharing that passion with other enthusiasts. I can honestly say that there's nothing else, either on-road or off-road, that matches up to a Defender. And there's no one else quite like the community of Land Rover owners. You're a great bunch; among the best there is – and I hope you feel that this book is right for you.

Acknowledgements

It would be easiest to say that all the people I need to thank appear in the photographs in the pages of the manual, but it wouldn't quite be true. First, I'd like to thank my wife Shan for her shared enthusiasm for our Defender and her unfailing encouragement with the huge amount of work that went into the vehicle and this book. Things don't always go smoothly. In fact, they all too often don't. But when you've got someone alongside who smoothes out the bumps – in life as well as in book production – it doesn't half help! Shan also takes some cracking photographs when required.

Next I'd like to thank Zoë Palmer, who's been my assistant for over 20 years, at the time of writing, and who knows more than most people about the mechanics of putting a book together – and a fair bit about putting Land Rovers together, too. She's put a lot of invaluable work into this book and, as always, has made a real difference.

My grateful thanks are also due to the great crowd I worked with at *Land Rover Monthly* magazine, from founding editor Richard Thomas, to 'young' Richard Streeton, who went on to work for Land Rover themselves, to the great ol' characters such as Frank Elson, Charlie Thorn and all the other stalwarts. It was there that much of this material appeared in its original, magazine-orientated form. On which subject, my editor at Haynes, Steve Rendle, has done a great job of working with me and Zoë to carve my stuff into a suitable form for this manual. Steve really knows his stuff – and he's a great bloke to work with, too!

On the workshop side, Ian Baughan at IRB Developments has been my 'main man' for unrivalled technical expertise, while the folk at MM 4x4 have been really great in every way. You'll see for yourself just what an excellent job was carried out by a number of other specialists named in the pages of this manual, and my thanks go to them all. Thanks are especially due to Dave Bradley-Scrivener, who works for me a day or two per week, and whose efforts have gone above and beyond the call of duty with the workshop work for this book. He's a great bloke to work with, he always gives of his very best, and Shan and I greatly enjoy having him work with us.

Also, it's not too much to say that you, the Defender enthusiast, are to be thanked for your unwitting assistance. I've heard from many Defender owners, and met a good number at shows, and every single one I've come across has been a good-hearted enthusiast and, in short, an utter nutter for Defenders, just like myself. Thanks to you all!

CHAPTER 1

Buying a 90, 110 or Defender

TIMELINE

- The Land Rover One Ten was introduced in 1983, and the Land Rover Ninety followed in 1984. The Land Rover 127 was available from 1985. In 1985, the 2.5-litre petrol engine was introduced. At the same time, the 114hp (85kW) V8 was also made available in the Ninety – the first time a production short-wheelbase Land Rover had been given V8 power. The V8 on both models was now mated to an all-new five-speed manual gearbox.
- A lightly turbocharged version of the existing 2.5-litre diesel (the Turbo Diesel, or TD engine) was introduced in 1986. It had a reputation for poor reliability. A revised block and improved big end bearings (1988) and a redesigned breather system (1989) made it less bad. The V8 engine was upgraded in 1986.
- From 1991, the Ninety and One Ten were renamed the Defender 90 and Defender 110. The Land Rover 127 became the Defender 130 (although the wheelbase remained unchanged). A V8 petrol engine was still available. The new,

massively improved turbo diesel 200 Tdi engine was inherited from the Discovery, boasting an alloy cylinder head; improved turbocharging; intercooling; direct injection; and an oil separator filter to remove oil from the air in the system, solving the Diesel Turbo's main weakness of breathing in its own sump oil.

- In 1993 the Defender was introduced into the United States and Canada. To comply with US regulations, North American Specification (NAS) Defenders were extensively modified and were fitted with the 3.9-litre V8 petrol engine. In the final year of US production the engine was improved, designated 4.0, and mated to a four-speed automatic transmission. In 1998 US regulations changed, and since the Defender could not be adapted it was withdrawn from the North American market.
- In 1994 the 300 Tdi engine was introduced in non-US markets; it was virtually all-new, quieter and (relatively) more refined. This engine continued to be fitted where stringent emission

controls were not enforced (until 2005). It is generally considered to be the most 'bomb-proof' Defender engine.

- In 1998/9 the UK Defender was fitted with the Td5 engine, an all-new, 2.5-litre, five-cylinder inline turbo diesel unit, and the last in-house Land Rover engine. It used electronic control systems and was more refined and powerful. For the 2002 model year further refinements were made to the Td5 engine, while there were also many detail improvements to dash, instruments and general comfort levels and options. In 2003/4 all-steel front doors were fitted, with excellent corrosion resistance, to replace the corrosion-prone steel/aluminium doors. A one-piece steel station wagon rear door was introduced.
- From spring 2007 the Td5 engine was replaced by Ford's DuraTorq engine, the 'Puma' engine, a version of the 2.4-litre four-cylinder unit also used in the Ford Transit. It was mated to a new six-speed gearbox. There were major changes to the interior, heater and ventilation.

With Ian Baughan of IRB Developments

Here's a short, sharp buyers' checklist of what to look out for when buying a Defender for restoration or improvement. As a Land Rover-trained engineer, restorer and tuner of considerable repute, Ian's comments are words of wisdom!

IDENTITY CHECKS

Hybrid Land Rovers made from a mixture of different models can be fraught with problems. In the UK there is a DVLA points system that, at the time of writing, works as follows:

To keep its original registration number, your vehicle must have eight or more points from the table below. Five of these points must come from an acceptable chassis, monocoque bodyshell or frame.

Part	Points
Chassis, monocoque bodyshell (body and chassis as one unit) or frame – original or new and unmodified (eg direct replacement from the manufacturer).	5
Suspension (front and back) – original.	2
Axles (both) – original.	2
Transmission – original.	2
Steering assembly – original.	2
Engine – original.	1

You won't be able to keep your vehicle's original registration number if any of the following apply: it has fewer than eight points; it has a second-hand or altered chassis, monocoque bodyshell or frame; or there's evidence that two vehicles have been welded together to form one – sometimes known as 'cut and shut'. In these cases, you'll have to gain DVLA type approval for your vehicle. If it passes, you can register it and it will receive a 'Q'-prefix registration number.

Land Rovers that have been altered to make them appear to be older than they are (by screwing on a false VIN plate, for instance) so that they can be imported into the USA or to qualify for lower road tax in the UK, are liable to be impounded and crushed without recompense. (It does happen!)

NUMBERS GAME
■ Look for the chassis (VIN – vehicle identification number) plate in the engine bay. If it's not there, don't touch the vehicle unless you can have a specialist firm check it over for you.

■ Double-check the chassis number, on the chassis rail just ahead of the left-hand front wheel position. Of course, on older vehicles the number can be made invisible by rust, and a changed or repaired chassis won't necessarily show the number you're looking for.
■ Also, check the engine number against the VIN plate and/or registration document.

Be aware that Defenders have many ways in which their true age can be checked. According to Ian Baughan, these include:

■ The TD5's ECU can be interrogated (with the correct diagnostic tester) to reveal the vehicle's VIN.
■ A riveted plate (1994 on) on the dash top, visible through the windscreen. (If it's not there, why not?)
■ Chassis four-digit date stamps on the chassis, facing outwards, below the left-hand footwell and on the top of the adjacent outrigger.
■ Doors (2004 on) have the last three digits of the VIN written in permanent marker on door cards and water shedder.
■ From circa 2000 on, the VIN number stamp should be made up of dots, not solid, stamped numbers.
■ Engine, transmission, gearbox and transfer box numbers.
■ Finally there are three more hidden locations that Ian won't reveal, but could check for you if you suspect a vehicle's provenance.

DON'T SUCK A LEMON
The following is information from the DVLA website 'Checks when buying a used car' (https://www.gov.uk/checks-when-buying-a-used-car):

You can reduce the risk of buying a stolen vehicle by following these steps.

Before you see the vehicle
1 Ask the seller for the registration number, make and model, tax disc details and MOT test number.
2 Use DVLA's online vehicle enquiry service to check that the details you've been given match their records.
3 Check that the vehicle's MOT is up to date, and the MOT history matches the details you've been given.

When you go to see the vehicle
1 Ask the seller to show you the V5C vehicle registration certificate (known as the 'log book'). Make sure it has a 'DVL' watermark, and the serial number isn't in the range between BG8229501 to BG9999030, or BI2305501 to BI2800000. If it is, the V5C might be stolen – contact the police as soon as it's safe to do so.
2 Make sure the details in the log book match the details you've been given.
3 Check the vehicle identification number and engine number. Make sure these match the details on the log book.

Engine, transmission, running gear

ENGINES

Looking at the condition of the engine oil might give you a few clues to maintenance on petrol-engine vehicles, although on diesels, the engine oil is black even when it's relatively fresh. Look out for oil leaks on all engines.

Early, pre-200 Tdi turbo diesels are prone to creating crankcase pressure, which blows oil out of the seals. Look out for the top of the engine and the air filter and pipework being covered in oil. Take off the oil filler cap with the engine running and look for heavy oil mist blowing out.

Untoward diesel engine noises are very difficult for the untrained ear to pick out (because of the general cacophony that goes on with a diesel engine!), but listen for tappet noise on a V8 engine, which will be very expensive to put right. Do bear in mind that oil pressure is congenitally low on V8 engines and doesn't really signify very much.

Avoid a Defender with an engine conversion using non-Land Rover (or Land Rover-related) engines. As well as potential parts availability problems, it will almost certainly devalue the vehicle and could lead to problems with insurance and with selling on in the future. Vehicles fitted with Land Rover-derived Jaguar engines and 300 Tdi-derived 2.8 TGV engines don't suffer in this way.

Find out the last time the cam belt was changed on a Tdi diesel engine. (TD5s have a chain, not a belt). If there's no invoice to prove that the cam belt has been changed within the specified time, allow for adding the cost of fitting a new one on to the purchase price of the vehicle. You must

not, under any circumstances, run the vehicle beyond its specified cam belt change because, if the cam belt breaks, the engine will almost certainly be scrapped.

On TD5 models, Ian says you should check the red plug on the ECU for signs of engine oil ingress. The injector harness seals can leak where it sits inside the cylinder head, and this allows oil to pass down the loom. According to Land Rover the loom should be replaced, but Ian says that a

new harness at the head, combined with a thorough clean-out of the loom with brake cleaner, should do the trick. (The problem persists, Ian says, even though later harnesses have two seals in place of the original single seal.)

Check the condition of the radiator, which can be quite expensive to replace, especially on Turbo diesel and Tdi models with a built-in oil cooler. On Tdi and TD5 models, there's also an air intercooler (for the turbocharger) that should be checked. Carefully check all pipework.

For further specific information on potential engine faults, see Chapter 5.

TRANSMISSION

Most Defender gearboxes seem to leak a bit, but check the oil level, because if it's been allowed to fall the gearbox could be damaged. Backlash can be expensive to put right, especially if it's between the output shaft on the 'box and the input shaft on the transfer box. On the other hand backlash can be confused with worn universal joints, or rear suspension bushes.

To check for a badly worn clutch, Ian suggests applying the parking brake, putting the vehicle in second gear and, with the engine ticking over, gently letting in the clutch. The engine should stall. If the vehicle moves, the parking brake is poor, so try again with your right foot on the brake pedal. If the clutch slips, it's desperately in need of replacement! Also, the clutch should not start to 'bite' right at the top of its travel – another wear symptom.

Select low range on the transfer box and ensure that it's OK. Check for noise or an inability to engage low ratio. To check the diff lock, apply and check that the light comes on. A Land Rover specialist could test the operation by jacking one wheel off the ground with a trolley jack, on a smooth surface with the trolley jack wheels facing the same direction as the vehicle wheels. With diff lock engaged, the vehicle should ease forward. If the raised wheel spins, the diff lock isn't working. This test should only be carried out by a qualified mechanic who's familiar with the procedure.

Differentials are tricky to assess and it's difficult to ascertain free play by moving the propshafts – and it can't be done at all with the handbrake on because this locks the transmission. Listen for droning from the differentials, especially on the over-run.

You can also check each wheel bearing in turn by raising each wheel, diff lock disengaged, and spinning each wheel (to the extent that it's possible to 'spin' a Defender's wheels) while checking for noise, roughness or undue play. Again, previous experience is necessary in order to know what to look for.

Check the condition of the swivel housings. Earlier ones were chrome plated but later versions are Teflon coated. They must be clean and free from pitting. If badly pitted they'll be useless, and costly to replace. Some leakage from the housing seal is to be expected, but signs of excessive oil loss could mean worn swivel pins. Some movement in the swivel pins is acceptable, but if it's excessive the bushes or bearings will need to be replaced. See the relevant section of this manual.

STEERING AND SUSPENSION

Check for severe corrosion. In extreme cases badly corroded suspension parts have been known to break, with catastrophic consequences. Steering is checked for wear at the joints in all the usual ways, but note that a power steering box is very expensive to replace. As well as checking for wear, you must check for leaks – a leaking box or pump invariably needs replacement.

Leaking shock absorbers invariably need replacement, and broken (or, far more likely, worn) springs will be indicated by a vehicle that's down at one corner.

CHASSIS AND BODY

With the bodywork on a Land Rover, what you see is generally what you get. But do note that you can't get rid of oxidation in aluminium, especially in the pre-steel doors, which corrode like nobody's business! The front of the bulkhead can also rot.

All the common rot-spots can be seen in Chapter 4. Use the photographs there as a guide, and look out for evidence of (a) poorly welded repairs, (b) repairs with lots of underseal (especially fresh underseal) to disguise poor workmanship, and (c)

evidence of filler, which, especially if found on a chassis or other structural components, suggests that something dodgy is going on. It's OK for an older vehicle to have had the rear crossmember or other chassis components replaced – provided it's been done properly and there are no other rot-spots on the chassis.

Check around each seat-belt anchorage point, especially behind the seats where the inertia reel mountings can be found.

If there's any corrosion, welding will be needed – see Chapter 4. Also, seat belts tend to get caught, become frayed and will need replacing in order to pass an MoT. And they're quite expensive!

Don't rely on a UK MoT certificate, especially if it's a few months out of date. Many MoT testers are excellent, but some don't seem to be as well informed as they should be! In other words, don't rely on what the MoT certificate says.

CHAPTER 2

Choosing power tools and equipment

This chapter is about how to choose the most suitable equipment for your workshop. Product adverts won't tell you the whole story – you'll need to dig a little deeper...

MIG WELDER

You won't be able to do much serious restoration without a MIG welder. Don't think that all are equal, however. An inverter-based welder will be lighter and (usually) produces smoother welds than transformer-based sets. My choice is the i-TECH MIG170 from Inverter Fusion. It's built to work for its living so can be depended on for full restoration projects. The heavy-duty cycle means this machine won't keep cutting out if worked hard. There's enough max-power for up to 5 or 6mm of weld penetration, while unusually it also goes right down to 25A, so you can weld thinner metal without blow-through.

You can also add a TIG attachment for welding even thinner steel. You have to fit the torch to the positive terminal on the i-TECH MIG170 and flick the position switch. The gas must be pure argon, because CO_2 destroys the tungsten tip.

The position switch is also flipped 'up' when the set is used as a conventional arc-stick (or gasless MIG) welder. You can't normally MIG-weld outside because wind blows away the shielding gas, but you can stick-weld or even use gasless wire with the i-TECH MIG170. So versatile!

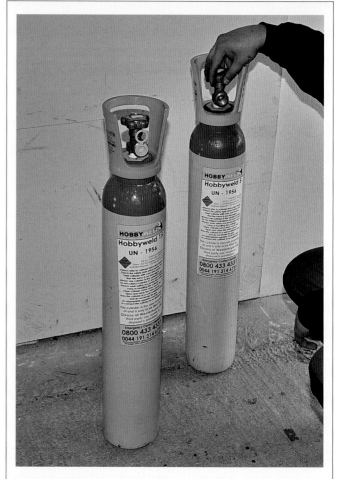

GETTING THE GAS

For most enthusiasts, using disposable welding cartridges or paying rental on a gas cylinder for occasional use adds up to a lot of dosh. An alternative is HobbyWeld's rental-free, refillable welding gas system. You buy the cylinder outright (about the cost of a decent tyre), and when you need a refill you just order a delivery or take the cylinder to your local stockist. Oxygen and acetylene are also available.

SELECTING A PLASMA CUTTER

Plasma guarantees less distortion or collateral damage, lower fire risk, lower running costs, less edge-cleaning and greater speed, as this test shows. But be aware that the cheapest plasma cutters won't cut as 'clean' as this superb i-TECH cutter from Inverter Fusion. You'll need an air compressor producing 4.5–5.0 bar pressure and a decent-sized tank (see the ABAC compressor here), but no other gas.

I selected an i-TECH CUT40 inverter plasma cutter, and here's what to look for:

- 230V, single-phase current.
- A decent duty cycle – this has 60%.
- At maximum thickness, cuts tend to be messy, but this 40A tool cuts steel up to 12mm thick while a 25A tool might manage 6mm.
- DON'T buy a cheap tool that requires you to 'strike' an arc. Buy one where you just push a button to start the arc.
- Two or three amperage positions aren't enough. It's best to have a variable control.
- Look for a machine with an integral regulator and pressure gauge.

Maximum quoted cutting thickness is invariably for mild steel; it'll be less for aluminium and stainless steel (neither of which can be cut with oxy-acetylene, by the way).

CHOOSING A COMPRESSOR

When working out what you'll need from a compressor, my advice is to go for 230v, single-phase power, single-stage pump, and belt drive for quieter operation and greater longevity. Also, do you want a cheap, use-it-and-chuck-it compressor or one that will last?

My choice is an ABAC A29B 90 CM3. It's belt-drive, 3hp, with a 90-litre tank, and produces 11.2ft^3 per minute (CFM). This is a high-end or semi-pro machine, and there are lower horsepower and smaller tank-capacity versions from ABAC – as well as larger, of course!

TIP
In order to compare manufacturers, you often need to convert between differing mixtures of metric and imperial units.

This ABAC compressor can power many tools by adjusting the pressure, including (low to high):

Pneumatic (air) tool	Air consumption (CFM)
Spray gun (20–45psi)	0.5–3.5
Tyre inflator	2
Dust gun	3
Body polisher, drill or impact driver (½in)	4
Random orbit sander	6–9
Sand blaster	10–100s

In general, go for a top-notch manufacturer and avoid the High Street 'specials', which are invariably of the cheap'n'nasty variety and try to match the compressor's capacity to your needs. But be aware that cheap compressors usually quote high (fictional?) CFM outputs. These are only approachable by running the motor and pump at excessive speeds. They won't last – and they'll be *so* noisy! ABAC also produce this very convenient hose reel attachment.

PLENTY OF POWER
Many heavy-duty tools, such as welders and compressors, can push the limits of a UK 13A domestic power supply. The best solution is to have a dedicated 16A supply fitted. Here you can see a stand-alone circuit breaker (left) for those without any spaces in their main supply board, plus a 16A socket and plug. They must be connected (in UK law) by a qualified electrician.

SELECTING ELECTRIC CORDLESS TOOLS

For convenience and safety, I hardly ever use corded tools. But how do you choose the best cordless ones available? In my case, I saw a cabinet-maker named Matt using his Makita kit and was so impressed that I went out and got my own, and now, five years on, most of my power tools are Makita. In front of my well-used Makita tools are the newer versions, with brushless motors giving much longer battery life and an invaluable battery meter on the drill (inset).

The Makita DTD129 18V impact driver might seem an unusual vehicle workshop tool, but mine is used all the time! With a hammer action and maximum fastening torque of 160Nm, it releases all sorts of seized fixings. When fitted with a socket adapter, it zips bolts, screws and nuts swiftly on and off.

BATTERY CHARGER CHOOSING

It's essential to use a 'smart' charger with modern vehicle batteries. Batteries allowed to sit discharged and those used with 'old-style' chargers will invariably die prematurely. The Ring SmartCharge Maintenance Charger will maintain all types of lead-acid batteries

quality producers, such as 3M and UPOL, but probably none with the same range. The Würth Group is world market leader in assembly and fastening materials, with about 64,000 employees, over 100,000 products and annual turnover of around €10 billion.

People don't always know that Würth also produce top-quality hand tools under the Zebra label. Once again, this is an enormous range of top-quality German tools with a much longer lifespan than cheaper alternatives. As Würth says, 'Every product is subjected to endurance tests for days and sometimes weeks at our testing laboratories. These tests are always practice-oriented and

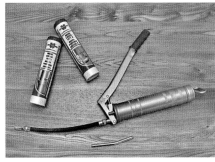

are usually even tougher than practical use itself.' In my experience with these tools, it shows!

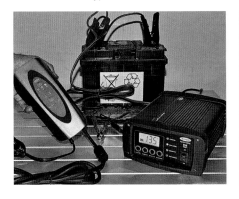

in optimum condition. For recharging flat batteries, the heavy duty Ring Smart Pro 25 Charger has a pulse charge facility designed to break down the build-up of lead sulphate. It can also be left permanently connected.

CONSUMABLES AND HAND TOOLS

Cheap consumables are almost always false economy. Since I discovered Würth I use little else, even though the up-front cost is sometimes higher than lower-quality materials. There are some other high-

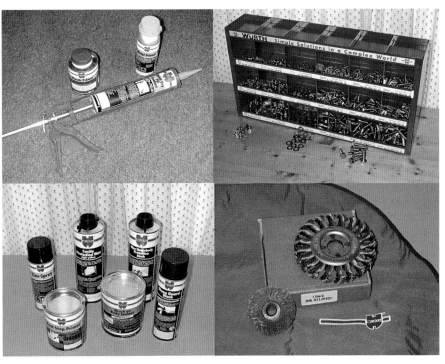

Essential safety

Professional motor mechanics are trained in safe working procedures, whereas the onus is on home mechanics to find these out for themselves and act upon them. However enthusiastic you may be about getting on with the job in hand, do take the time to ensure that your safety isn't put at risk. A moment's lack of attention can result in an accident, as can failure to observe certain elementary precautions.

There'll always be new ways of having accidents, and the following points don't pretend to be a comprehensive list of all the dangers; they're intended rather to make you aware of the risks, and to encourage a safety-conscious approach to all the work that you carry out on your vehicle.

Be sure to consult the suppliers of any materials and equipment you may use, and to obtain *and read carefully* the operating and health and safety instructions that they may provide.

PREPARATIONS
You'll need to go out and buy yourself a set of basic safety gear such as Würth disposable overalls, ear defenders, goggles, face mask, disposable gloves and hand cleaners.

ESSENTIAL DOS AND DON'TS
- DON'T rely on a single jack when working underneath the vehicle. Always use reliable additional means of support, such as axle stands, securely placed under a part of the vehicle that you know won't give way.
- DON'T attempt to loosen or tighten high-torque nuts (eg wheel hub nuts) while the vehicle is on a jack; it may be pulled off.
- DON'T start the engine without first ascertaining that the transmission is in neutral (or 'Park' where applicable) and the parking brake applied.
- DON'T suddenly remove the filler cap from a hot cooling system – cover it with a cloth and release the pressure gradually first, or you may get scalded by escaping coolant.
- DON'T attempt to drain oil, automatic transmission fluid or coolant until you're

sure it has cooled sufficiently to avoid scalding you.
- DON'T grasp any part of the engine, exhaust or catalytic converter without first ascertaining that it's sufficiently cool to avoid burning you.
- DON'T allow brake fluid or antifreeze to contact vehicle paintwork.
- DON'T siphon toxic liquids such as fuel, brake fluid or antifreeze by mouth, or allow them to remain on your skin.
- DON'T inhale brake lining dust – it may be injurious to health.
- DON'T allow any spilt oil or grease to remain on the floor – wipe it up straight away before someone slips on it.
- DON'T use ill-fitting spanners or other tools which may slip and cause injury.
- DON'T attempt to lift a heavy component that may be beyond your capability – get assistance.
- DON'T rush to finish a job, or take unverified short cuts.
- DON'T allow children or animals in or around an unattended vehicle.
- DON'T park vehicles with catalytic converters over combustible materials such as dry grass, oily rags etc, if the engine has recently been run. As catalytic converters reach extremely high temperatures, any such materials in close proximity may ignite.
- DON'T run vehicles equipped with catalytic converters without the exhaust system heat shields fitted.
- DO wear eye protection when using power tools such as electric drills, sanders, bench grinders etc, and when working under the vehicle.
- DO use a barrier cream on your hands prior to undertaking dirty jobs – it will protect your skin from infection as well as making the dirt easier to remove afterwards; but make sure your hands aren't left slippery. Note that long-term contact with used engine oil can be a health hazard.
- DO keep loose clothing (cuffs, tie etc) and long hair well out of the way of moving mechanical parts.
- DO remove rings, wristwatch etc, before working on the vehicle – especially the electrical system.

- DO ensure that any lifting tackle used has a safe working-load rating adequate for the job, and is used precisely as recommended by the manufacturer.
- DO keep your work area tidy – it's only too easy to fall over articles left lying around.
- DO get someone to check periodically that all is well, when working alone on the vehicle.

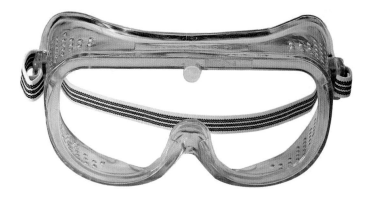

- DO carry out work in a logical sequence and check that everything is correctly assembled and tightened afterwards.
- DO remember that your vehicle's safety affects your own, and that of others. If in doubt on any point, get specialist advice.

If, in spite of following these precautions, you're unfortunate enough to injure yourself, seek medical attention as soon as possible.

FIRE

Remember at all times that fuel, and especially petrol (gasoline), is highly flammable. Never smoke or have any kind of naked flame around when working on the vehicle. A spark caused by an electrical short-circuit, by two metal surfaces contacting each other, by a central heating boiler in the garage 'firing up', or even by static electricity built up in your body under certain conditions, can ignite petrol vapour, which in a confined space is highly explosive.

Always disconnect the battery earth (ground) terminal before working on any part of the fuel system, and never risk spilling fuel on to a hot engine or exhaust.

It's recommended that a fire extinguisher of a type suitable for fuel and electrical fires is kept handy in the garage or workplace at all times. *Never* try to extinguish a fuel or electrical fire with water. If you do have a fire, DON'T PANIC. Use the extinguisher effectively by directing it at the base of the fire.

Never use petrol (gasoline) to clean parts.

Use a biodegradable, purpose-made, non-flammable parts cleaner such as Terralus Viroclean Biodegradable Cleaner from Morris Lubricants.

FUMES

Certain fumes are highly toxic and can quickly cause unconsciousness and even death if inhaled to any extent. Petrol (gasoline) vapour comes into this category, as do the vapours from certain solvents such as trichloroethylene and those from many adhesives. Any draining or pouring of such volatile fluids should be done in a well ventilated area.

When using cleaning fluids and solvents, read the instructions carefully. Never use any materials from unmarked containers – they may give off poisonous vapours.

Never run the engine of a motor vehicle in an enclosed space such as a garage. Exhaust fumes contain carbon monoxide which is extremely poisonous.

Inspection pits: never drain or pour petrol or run the engine, while the vehicle is over it. The fumes, heavier than air, will concentrate in the pit with possibly lethal results.

THE BATTERY

Always disconnect the battery earth (ground) terminal before working on fuel or electrical systems.

- Never cause a spark or allow a naked light near the vehicle battery. It gives off highly explosive hydrogen gas. Always switch off the power supply before charger leads are connected or disconnected.
- If possible, loosen the filler plugs or cover when charging the battery from an external source.
- Use a modern charger with electronic controls to prevent overcharging.
- The acid electrolyte, even when diluted, is very corrosive and should not be allowed to come into contact with the eyes or skin.
- Battery terminals should be shielded to prevent a spark.

MAINS ELECTRICITY

When using mains electric equipment:

- Ensure the appliance is correctly connected to its plug and is properly earthed (grounded).
- Don't use such appliances in damp conditions.
- Beware of sparks or excessive heat near fuel vapour.
- Always use an RCD (residual current device) circuit breaker.

WELDING AND BODYWORK REPAIRS

It's so useful to be able to weld when carrying out restoration work, and yet there's a good deal that could go dangerously wrong for the uninformed –

in fact more than could be covered here. Consequently:

■ You're strongly recommended to seek formal tuition before welding.
■ All of the information and instructions produced by equipment and materials suppliers must be obtained and studied carefully.

In addition, it's strongly recommended that the author's *Classic Car Bodywork Repair Manual* should be purchased and studied before carrying out any welding or bodywork repairs.

COMPRESSED GAS CYLINDERS
There are serious hazards associated with the storage and handling of gas cylinders and fittings, and standard precautions should be strictly observed in dealing with them. Ensure that cylinders are stored in safe conditions, properly maintained and always handled with special care, and make constant efforts to eliminate the possibilities of leakage, fire and explosion.

It's vitally important that you obtain manufacturers' and suppliers' storage and safety instructions and follow them to the letter. Keep the suppliers' safety data to hand. In the event of an accident, notify the police and fire services and hand the safety data to them so that they can see what substances they're dealing with.

HYDROFLUORIC ACID
This is an extract from a document entitled 'Examination of Burnt Out Vehicles' issued in 2002 by the Police Service of Northern Ireland:

(i) In the manufacture of motor vehicles, some components such as gaskets, 'O'-rings, seals, some cables and wiring looms are made of certain synthetic rubbers which are classed as fluoroelastomers. These components are usually located within the engine compartment.
(ii) Under normal conditions these products are safe to handle and pose no risk to health and safety. However, if exposed to temperatures in excess of 400 degrees centigrade, the material decomposes forming hydrofluoric acid, which is extremely corrosive to the skin. Components, which have decomposed, may appear black and charred or sticky.
(iii) Any member of the police or police staff who is required to inspect or examine a burnt out vehicle to establish its identity [or anyone who chooses to work on one or to use parts removed from one – *author's note*] should be aware of the risks associated with the task and the protective measures required.
(iv) Hydrofluoric acid may present health hazards in two forms:

(a) as a gas it is highly irritating to the eyes and highly irritating to the respiratory system.
(b) in solution form it can cause burns if it goes untreated. In some instances when it comes into contact with the skin, pain may not be felt immediately, but many hours later. Contamination can cause severe skin problems, sometimes requiring surgery.

First aid information can be found by going to the www.hse.gov.uk website and searching for indg307.pdf.

WORKING WITH PLASTICS
Working with plastic materials brings additional hazards into workshops. Many of the materials used (polymers, resins, adhesives and materials acting as catalysts and accelerators) readily produce very dangerous situations in the form of poisonous fumes, skin irritants, risk of fire and explosions. Don't allow resin or two-pack adhesive hardener, or that supplied with filler or two-pack stopper, to come into contact with skin or eyes. Read carefully the safety notes supplied on the tin, tube or packaging.

GENERAL SAFETY NOTES
■ Take care not to inhale any dust, especially brake dust, which may contain asbestos.
■ Wipe up oil or grease spillages straight away. Use oil granules (cat litter will do the same job!) to soak up major spills.
■ Use quality tools – an ill-fitting spanner could cause damage to the component, your car and, of course, to yourself!
■ When lifting heavy items, remember: bend your legs and keep your back straight. Know your limitations – if something is too heavy, call in a helper.
■ Time is a vital element in any workshop. Make sure you've allowed sufficient time to finish a job, and if you haven't, leave it until later. Rushed work is rarely done right.
■ Children and pets are naturally inquisitive. Don't allow them to wander unsupervised round or in your car, especially if it's jacked up or when antifreeze is around.

ENGINE OILS
There is some danger from contaminants present in all used oil – and diesel engine oil is worst of all. Prolonged skin exposure can lead to serious skin disorders, and even cancer. Always use barrier cream on your hands and wear plastic or rubber gloves when draining oil.

OIL DISPOSAL
Never pour your used oil down a drain or on to the ground. Environmentally, it's very unfriendly, and will render you liable to legal action by your local council. In most EU countries, including the UK, local authorities must provide a safe means of oil disposal. If you're unsure where to take your used oil, contact your local Environmental Health Department for advice.

PAINT SPRAYING
Paint spraying safety is too large a subject for this book. See the author's *Classic Car Bodywork Repair Manual* for further information.

RAISING YOUR LAND ROVER – SAFELY!
■ NEVER work beneath a vehicle held solely on a jack.
■ Don't jack-up the vehicle with anyone on board, or when a trailer is connected (it could pull the vehicle off the jack).
■ Before raising the vehicle with a jack, engage the differential lock (note that the warning lamp will only illuminate if the ignition switch is in the 'on' position).
■ Pull the handbrake on, engage first gear (main gearbox) and low gear in the transfer box.
■ Unlike most vehicles, the Land Rover's handbrake works on the transmission and NOT on the rear wheels. It's important therefore to follow the procedures outlined here in order to be totally safe, for if one front and one rear wheel were to be raised at the same time, it's possible for there to be no braking effect at all.
■ Wheels on the ground should be chocked at all times when the vehicle is raised.

USING RAMPS
■ First, make sure the ramps you're using are rated for the weight of the Land Rover you'll be working on, and that they're in sound condition.
■ Make absolutely certain that the ramps are parallel to the wheels of the car and that the wheels are exactly central on each ramp.
■ Always have an assistant watch both sides of the car as you drive up.
■ Drive up to the end 'stops' on the ramps but never over them!

- Apply the handbrake firmly, and put the car in first or reverse gear.
- Chock both wheels remaining on the ground, both in front and behind, so that the car can't move in either direction.
- TIP! Wrap a strip of carpet into a loop around the first 'rung' of the ramps and drive over the doubled-up piece of carpet on the approach to the ramps. This prevents the ramps from skidding away (as they're inclined to do) as the vehicle is driven on to them.

USING A TROLLEY JACK

- An SWL (safe working load) of at least two tonnes is required. Ensure that the floor is clear and smooth so that the trolley jack wheels can roll when raising and lowering.
- Ensure that the handbrake is off and the gearbox is in neutral, so that the vehicle can move as the jack is raised. Reapply brake and gear after the raising is complete. Remember to release them before lowering again.
- Axle stands also need to be man enough for the job – those with an SWL of three tonnes are widely available.
- At the front, position the jack so that the head engages the front axle casing below the coil spring. It should be positioned between the bracket to which the

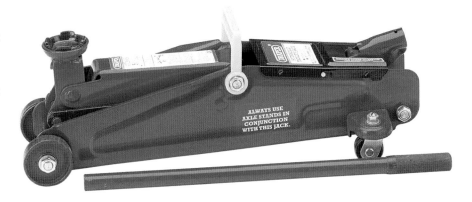

suspension members are mounted and the flange at the end of the axle casing.
- At the rear, position the jack so that the head engages the rear axle casing below the coil spring, as close to the shock absorber mounting bracket as possible.

MORE SAFETY NOTES

- Whenever you're working beneath a car, have someone primed to pop out every quarter of an hour or so to see how you're getting on; it could save your life!
- Be especially careful when applying force

to a spanner or when pulling hard when the car is supported off the ground. It's all too easy for the vehicle to topple off the axle stands.
- In general, a vehicle will be more stable when only one wheel is removed and one axle stand used. Don't work on the vehicle with all four wheels off the ground – it would then become dangerously unstable.
- Before lowering the Land Rover to the ground, remember to remove the chocks, release the handbrake and place the transmissions in neutral.

CHAPTER 4

Bodywork restoration

More than almost any other vehicle on the road, each chassis-based Land Rover is just a giant kit of parts. It was deliberately made to be a vehicle that can be unbolted and bolted together at will, and although the outer panels are difficult to repair by virtue of the fact that they're made of aluminium, they couldn't be simpler to remove.

At least, that's the theory. In practice, the body panels on any older Land Rover will be held in place with nuts and bolts that are well rusted in, so the first step in bodywork repair is to soak with releasing fluid all the threads that you know you're going to have to undo. If you really want the releasing fluid to have a beneficial effect, carry this out several days before you intend to start

work and then do the same thing again the day before. Even so, you'll have to face up to the fact that some fixings will undoubtedly have to be drilled out. Equip yourself with a centre punch and a set of new, sharp drills. Take care not to slip the drill sideways when drilling one of the obstinate fixings, because the drill bit will cause severe damage in the soft aluminium panelling. Panels themselves are unlikely to be corroded unless they're of steel (see later parts of this chapter), but they're quite likely to be damaged.

Almost all Land Rovers seem to have been treated roughly at some point in their lives. However, you can take heart from the fact that replacement 90, 110 and Defender panels are available 'off the shelf' in most cases.

For further technical advice, it's strongly recommended that a copy of the author's *Classic Car Bodywork Repair Manual* is purchased and studied. Consisting of 283 pages and around 1,000 illustrations, this book picks the brains of specialists from a variety of fields and covers arc, MIG and 'gas' welding, panel beating and accident repair, rust repair and treatment, paint spraying, glass-fibre work, filler, lead loading, interiors and much more besides. Alongside a number of projects, the books describes in detail how to carry out each of the techniques involved in car bodywork repair with safety notes where necessary. As such, it's the ideal complement to this book.

Fuel tank removal and replacement

SAFETY FIRST! Always have the correct type of fire extinguisher containing foam, CO_2, gas or powder easily accessible when handling or draining fuel or dismantling fuel systems and in areas where fuel is stored.

FUEL TANK TYPES
There are two types of tank fitted to these vehicles: the side-mounted type, fitted to earlier 90 models; and the rear-mounted type fitted to later 90s and the 110. Some 110s are fitted with twin-tanks – one of each type – with interconnecting pipework and two separate fillers.

SAFETY
■ Before carrying out any major body repairs, it makes good sense to drain and remove the fuel tank to a place of safety.
■ First, disconnect and remove the battery from the vehicle. Never drain a fuel tank indoors or where the highly flammable vapours can gather, such as over a pit. Store petrol drained from the tank in safe, closed, approved containers. If the empty tank is to be stored, have it steam-cleaned to remove the petrol vapour. For very short-term storage place a damp rag in any openings and keep the tank outdoors. Keep all sparks and flames away from the fuel system whilst working on it.
■ On earlier models there's a drain plug for the fuel tank or tanks well away from either of the tank positions. Look underneath the vehicle, towards the front, beneath the bulkhead and to the left of the vehicle's centre-line. You'll find a bowl with a drain plug on the bottom of it.
■ Some fuel tanks also have a drain plug on the bottom of the tank itself – check your vehicle to see which type you have. Buy a new drain plug sealing washer and fit it before refilling the tank.

■ Soak all of the mounting bolts with releasing fluid well before starting work.

DRAINING A TD5's FUEL TANK
Draining the TD5's fuel tank can be difficult – there's an anti-siphon device on the fuel filler and there's no drain tap. Ian Baughan of IRB Developments uses the following system for emptying the tank:

■ Remove the hose in the engine bay that feeds the regulator and put the end of the hose into a suitably large container.
■ Turn on the ignition and pump the throttle pedal five times – each pump

must be a complete stroke from top to bottom. This will override the limitation on the pump cycle.
■ The engine management light on the dash will flash and the pump will run on an extended cycle.
■ If there's more fuel in the tank than can be drained by one extended cycle, Ian says that it should be OK to use two full pump cycles without overheating the pump. After that, the pump should be turned off for a period to allow it to fully cool down again.

1 These are the components of a side-mounted fuel tank. (Illustration © Lindsay Porter)

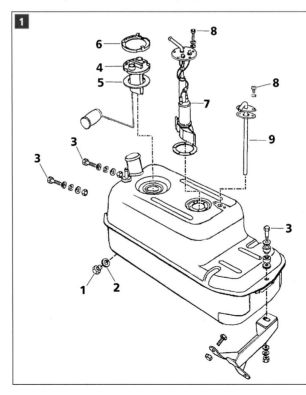

1 Drain plug.
2 Sealing washer.
3 Mounting bolt.
4 Level sender unit.
5 Sealing washer.
6 Fixing ring.
7 Fuel pump.
8 Securing screw.
9 Return pipe.

2 After disconnecting the battery negative terminal and draining the tank...

3 ...take off the front seat cushion and the seat base cover from above the tank. The level sender unit, pump and return pipe are all there.

PRE-TD5 MODELS

4 After removing the wiring from the sender unit, you can remove it by drifting the lugs (arrowed) anticlockwise until the locking ring is free.

5 Disconnect the fuel hoses from the fuel tank, and wrap masking tape around their ends to stop dirt from getting in. Be sure to close off the fuel 'flow' pipe (from the tank) to stop fuel running out of the pipe. Remove the pump by taking out the five screws.

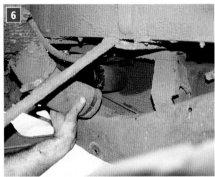

6 On all models, take off the breather pipe from the filler pipe, where it connects to the tank, and disconnect the filler pipe itself.

TD5 MODELS

7 Although this isn't the tank being removed, it indicates the component locations. Electrical and fuel-to-engine connections are all unplugged at the tank.

8 The undertray holding the rear-mounted tank has to be unbolted. Bolts frequently shear and captive nuts may have to be re-welded later.

9 Two nuts are accessed through the crossmember and these are especially prone to rusting around their heads.

10 You may need a special socket with sharp, spiralled flutes to grip on to rounded or corroded nuts, though the length of threads sticking through these nuts makes them tricky to use unless you can find a long-reach version, or fabricate your own by sacrificing a long-reach socket and welding it on to the special removal tool.

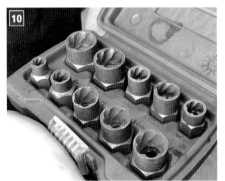

11 After the undertray has been manoeuvred away...

12 ...the tank itself can be removed from the tight space inside the mounting brackets.

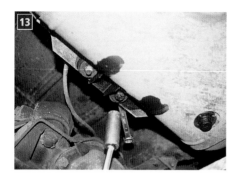

PRE-TD5 MODELS

13 In the case of a metal tank, it may help to place a trolley jack or stand beneath the tank (with a piece of wood over the head) to support it as it comes free, and remove the two front mounting nuts and bolts, followed by the rear nuts and bolts, in each case taking care not to lose washers or packing materials. Remove the three nuts and bolts holding the mounting bracket to the chassis and lower the tank.

If you want to remove the tank sender unit, tap the retaining ring anticlockwise with a drift until the ring and then the sender unit can be removed. Always fit a new sealing ring when replacing the sender unit.

END-MOUNTED FUEL TANK

14 The procedure for the end-mounted tank, shown here, is essentially the same as for the side-mounted tank, with the following extra points to bear in mind:

- a If an anti-roll bar or a towing hitch drop plate with support bars is fitted, the anti-roll bar

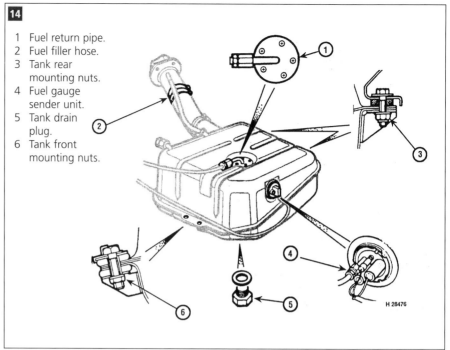

1 Fuel return pipe.
2 Fuel filler hose.
3 Tank rear mounting nuts.
4 Fuel gauge sender unit.
5 Tank drain plug.
6 Tank front mounting nuts.

H 28476

or drop plate support bars will first have to be removed. On all models, you'll gain better access if you remove the left-hand lashing eye from the chassis.

- b The fuel return hose connection on the top of the tank cannot be removed until the tank has been disconnected from its fixings and carefully lowered a small way on a trolley jack.
- c The sender unit is on the side of the tank, as shown.

FUEL TANK REPLACEMENT – ALL MODELS

Remember to refit the return hose to the tank on the early model, end-mounted tank before fully raising it into position – otherwise 'strong words' will ensue! With all types, fit all of the mountings but don't tighten any of them until all are in place. Similarly, fit the filler pipe, but don't tighten it until you've checked that there are no kinks, twists or other obstructions in the pipe.

15 This is a new, replacement chassis for a 300 Tdi Defender, and these are the positions of the fuel tank's rear mounting points.

16 The bolts for the front mounting are held on to a tab plate…

17 …with tabs knocked over on both bolt heads and chassis mounting.

18 Mark, at MJA Land Rover, methodically arranged all of the nuts, washers and rubber buffers before…

19 …offering the fuel tank into the allotted space in the chassis.

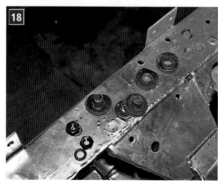

20 An empty plastic tank is easy to hold up with your knees…

21 …while loosely fitting all of the fixings.

22 Finally, all fixings can be tightened.

23 The sender unit for this earlier tank is accessed from the side…

24 …and Mark fitted it before tapping the locking ring in a clockwise direction to hold it in place.

25 On the later type of tank the sender unit is on the top of the tank and can (theoretically) only be accessed after lowering the tank. The sender unit is held in with a large, knurled plastic nut.

26 There may be different types of fuel connectors, depending on year or model, but the least obvious to remove are these push-on connectors with tabs that need to be pushed in as the pipe is removed. It's essential they go back in their original locations!

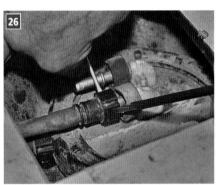

Bonnet removal

1 To remove the bonnet, you open it, lift it so that it's vertical and then, with one person on each side, lift it out of its hinges (arrowed).

2 To replace the bonnet, turn the bush in the hinge bracket on the bulkhead so that the slot (arrowed) is facing upwards…

3 …then, with the bonnet in the same vertical position as when it was removed, lower the bonnet hinge at the point shown (arrowed) into the bush and lower the bonnet back into position, carefully checking that the hinges are properly aligned.

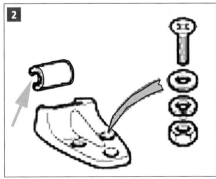

Having pranged my Defender and needing to change a wing outer panel, I decided to convert to ABS outer wings at the same time. ABS plastic is flexible and in most ways superior to the original aluminium panels (including being cheaper). Its initials stand for acrylonitrile butadiene styrene, a plastic compound used in many products, including pipework. It's resistant to being damaged by being sharply hit or from pressure – it bends rather than breaks – and is normally semi-flexible, though less so as the temperature drops.

The fitting procedure is almost exactly the same as for aluminium wings, and they've got several advantages over aluminium. The weight doesn't seem to be much different, the price is lower, the appearance is virtually the same, and whereas an aluminium wing will dent, an ABS plastic one will usually spring back into shape. The exception would be a severe bump, especially in very cold weather, when the ABS will break.

Incidentally, ABS can be repaired, either cold with suitable adhesives or hot by welding it (though I've always found this to be very tricky to get right). Also, before painting it has to be prepared with a plastic primer, otherwise regular paint won't bond to it.

First we'll explain how a Defender front wing is removed, stripped and rebuilt. If you're not going to be following 'factory' procedure by spot-welding aluminium, a bit of creativity is called for! All the work here was carried out by Land Rover ace Ian Baughan at IRB Developments.

FRONT WING REPLACEMENT AND REBUILD

1 Push centre pins from studs so you can remove the wheel arch liner and wheel arch extension. Remove radiator grille and release bonnet lock cable (inner and outer) at bonnet lock.

2 IRB Developments' Ian Baughan removed the snorkel and grilles from the top/side of the wing. Disconnect all the lighting plugs. Remove components from the inner wing such as (where appropriate) EGR solenoid, expansion tank pipe and PAS reservoir.

3 Remove the air cleaner (from engine) and remove the four screws fixing the air intake elbow to the wing, plus two bolts securing the heater air intake bracket to the inner wing (a). Remove the heater air intake (b) and seal.

4 Remove the four top bolts holding the outer wing to the inner wing – two through the vent hole and two more further forward, reached from under the wing top.

5 Remove the nuts and bolts securing the support stay to the wing, leaving it loosely attached to the vehicle.

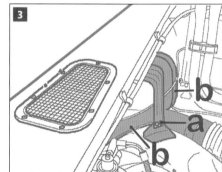

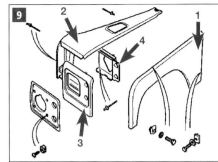

6 If you're removing the wing liner with the wing, remove the four bolts fixing the radiator mounting bracket to the wing – some of these are also accessed from inside the engine bay.

7 Remove the bolt securing the inner and outer wing panels to the chassis. Slacken the bolts securing the wing to 'A' post via slotted holes. See picture 33.

8 Remove the top bolt securing the wing to the bulkhead (arrowed) and remove wing from the vehicle. It's best to have assistance if you're not practised, as you can easily scratch other bodywork.

9 These are the individual components of the Defender front wing, not including the liner – galvanised steel on early versions, plastic on later models.

10 There are several Defender wing variants – with the vents, for example, popping up on different sides, according to model. Be sure to buy the correct panels!

11 A lot of the wing components can be dismantled by unbolting the fixing screws. Ian started to remove the damaged outer panel by taking out the line of screws along the wing top...

12 ...and those that screw through the flange on the outer wing to the front panel. All screw into clipped-on spire nuts and, because of the type of fixing, are rarely rusted solid.

13 Having taken off the outer panel (picture 9, part 1), Ian next set to work on separating the front panel (part 3) and headlamp box (part 4) from the wing top (part 2).

14 You now get to the stage where Land Rover decided that bolts weren't complicated enough, and so added a few pop-rivets and loads of spot welds for good measure.

15 Ian used a small twist drill to take off all the pop-rivet heads and a spot-weld drill (though a regular drill is fine in aluminium) to drill out the spot welds.

16 Half the difficulty is actually finding all the spot welds! This is the mounting panel (not in the parts drawing), which has to come off when replacing the front panel...

17 ...which Ian removed after quite a bit of careful tweaking of the remaining spot weld joints in order to actually find them. Rubbing the paint surface with abrasive...

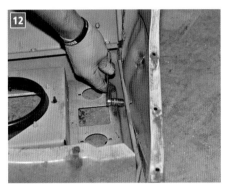

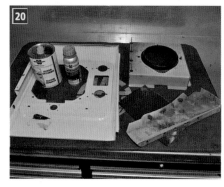

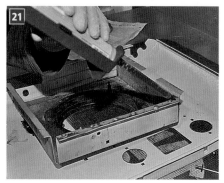

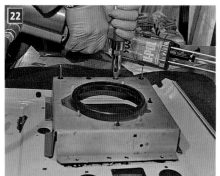

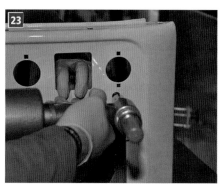

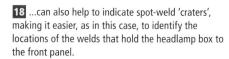

18 ...can also help to indicate spot-weld 'craters', making it easier, as in this case, to identify the locations of the welds that hold the headlamp box to the front panel.

19 Once again, there was a bit of careful levering and investigation to identify every last spot weld. Don't just try wrenching them apart – you'll distort the panels.

20 Left of the box and bracket shown being removed, is the new front panel from MM 4x4, which I'd had painted. There's also abrasive, Würth panel wipe and metal primer...

21 ...which prepared the surfaces for the application of U-POL Stronghold 903, an amazingly strong vehicle body adhesive for steel, aluminium and GRP, which starts to set in 15 minutes.

22 Ian used his pneumatic pop-rivet gun through the holes he'd already drilled to hold the headlamp box to the bracket on the inside of the front panel.

23 Where the headlamp box had been spot-welded to the old front panel, Ian drilled and riveted once again. The pop-rivet heads will be covered by the surround trim.

24 It's worth noting that U-POL recommend a smooth layer of Stronghold, which Ian followed up with a mazy bead, just to make sure there'd be no gaps.

25 This time pop-rivets couldn't be used, so a weight – placed on a plastic bag to prevent it from sticking to the Stronghold – held the parts together while the adhesive went off.

26 When fully set, it was time for Ian to introduce the fully assembled front panel to the remainder of the existing wing. Because he'd reassembled everything with precision...

27 ...it proved simple to reattach those parts of the wing that were originally bolted together, using the bolts that were taken out during the dismantling process.

28 Once again, some of the joints had originally been pop-riveted, while most of them were spot welds. Because each new pop-rivet has similar strength to a spot weld...

29 …no bonding was required. However, Ian specially chose pop-rivets with large, flat heads to cover existing spot-weld holes while not standing out too far and causing wider panel gaps.

30 At this stage you need to decide whether to fit the outer wing now or after the wing top and front are in place on the vehicle. Ian chose the latter approach.

31 You reuse the existing spire nuts – but we hit a small snag. On this ABS outer wing, the thickness of the plastic prevented the spire nuts (left) from going on fully…

32 …until the ends had been cut off with shears. Ian could then push them on far enough to align with the pre-drilled holes in the outer wing panel.

33 This wing took a lot of fiddling to get the bolts to line up correctly. Perhaps, in retrospect, it would be best to fully assemble the wings off the vehicle whenever possible.

34 These are the three slotted holes (arrowed) that slide under the loosened bolts and washers still in the bulkhead.

35 When everything was back together it all looked as good as new. The ABS outer wings look great and I'm really pleased with them.

REPLACING JUST THE OUTER WING PANEL

36 After removing the road wheel, Ian Baughan disconnected the wiring connectors for the indicator light…

37 …after unclipping the light unit from the wing. Next he started to remove the wheel arch extension. It's held in place with plastic rivets (part number AFU1075)…

38 …which are removed by driving out the centre pin, then, if tight, removing the main body of the rivet with a trim removal tool. If possible, retrieve the pins later.

39 In the previous picture you can see the rivet locations. After removing them, the wheel arch extension comes free. TIP: you're sure to lose or destroy some rivets, so buy extras.

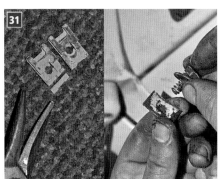
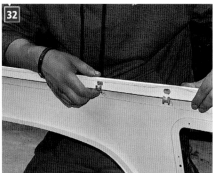

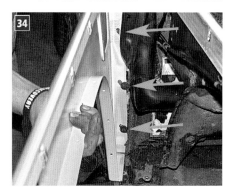

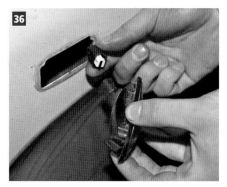
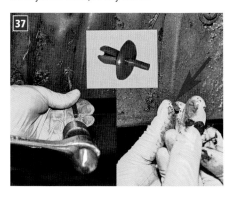

40 Ian knew he was going to need extra access to the inside of the wing so he unscrewed and removed the vent from the wing top.

41 The chequer plate wing tops had been fitted with screws and nuts, so Ian had to reach inside the wing liner with a spanner to grip the nuts,…

42 …(which had, of course, rusted themselves on) while taking out the countersunk fixing screws with a screwdriver from above. Once free, he lifted off the chequer plate.

43 Next the two screws holding the wheel arch liner in place – one at the front and one at the back of the vent aperture – were removed…

44 …which kind of allowed Ian to move the liner to one side. But only 'kind of', because there were various accessories bolted to the inner wing that needed to be dismantled first.

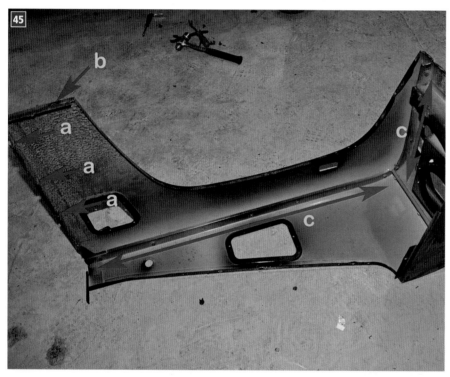

45 Just for reference, here is another wing viewed from the inside, showing the three slotted holes for the A-post bolts (a), the hole for the support stay (b)…

46 …and the line of holes for the coarse screws holding the outer panel to the front and top panels (c). This is the lower of those coarse threaded screws…

47 …while these are the positions of those higher up (arrowed). A ratchet ring spanner is ideal for getting into the restricted space alongside the wheel arch liner.

48 Next, Ian started work on the equally coarse threaded screws that pass through the holes in the top and front panel flanges, holding the outer wing panel in place.

49 Aluminium has enough 'give' to allow you to check that all the screws are out, but don't risk damaging it, especially if, as in this case, you have a perfectly reusable panel.

50 Ian now turned his attention to the four screws holding the back of the outer wing panel to the A-post (bulkhead), bearing in mind that only the top bolt…

51 …has to be fully removed, because the holes for the bottom three are slotted so that you should be able to lift the wing away after loosening their screws.

52 It's quite unusual to see a wing in this state, showing the locations of four holes in the front panel and seven more across the top.

53 Those coarse threaded screws shown being removed earlier don't screw into the aluminium wing panel, but instead screw into special clips that have to be removed from the old wing…

54 …and transferred to the new. These clips are known variously as spire nuts, spring-clip nuts or J-clips. The good news is, they do fit over the thicker ABS.

55 When refitting, Ian offered the slotted holes in the new wing over the bolt heads on the A-post.

56 When fitting panels, you need a different mindset to fitting mechanical parts. You don't just bolt them up; you make sure they fit! There's almost always some adjustment required.

57 That's why the holes are oversize, allowing the spire nuts to slide. These MM 4x4 ABS plastic wings turned out to be a fantastically good fit!

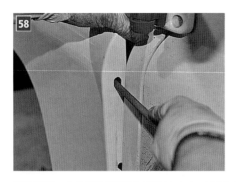

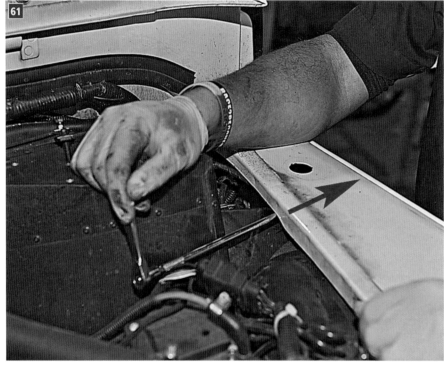

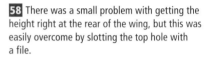

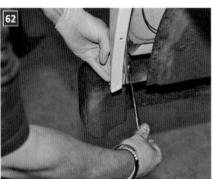

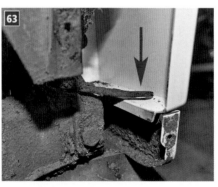

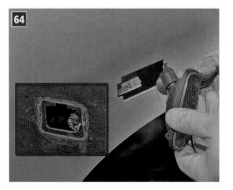

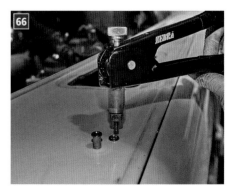

58 There was a small problem with getting the height right at the rear of the wing, but this was easily overcome by slotting the top hole with a file.

59 IAN's TOP TIP: when you need to use a ratchet extension to install a screw, put a nut in the socket so the screw doesn't go all the way in.

60 Put insulation tape around the head of the screw so it doesn't drop out of the socket. And if you need to use a universal joint in a place that you can't reach,…

61 …wrap more insulation tape around the UJ so that it doesn't flop about as you offer up the screw. There will still be enough movement for the UJ to work.

62 Of course, the spire nuts also had to be transferred to the front of the new ABS panel, allowing the front fixing screws to be fitted.

63 And at the back, where the stay bracket had been left in position, we were surprised to find that the hole in the ABS panel lined up perfectly.

64 These wings come without cut-outs for the side-marker lights. You have to measure, mark and cut them out yourself, measuring from top and rear of the wing. (Earlier type, inset.)

65 After a good half an hour of careful fitting but without stressing the wing (because it could later crack), Ian deemed the fit of the new flexing wing a success.

66 Before refitting the chequer plate, we drilled out and fitted Würth aluminium rivnuts, which allow one-side access for a threaded bolt and won't react with either the aluminium wing top or the stainless screws.

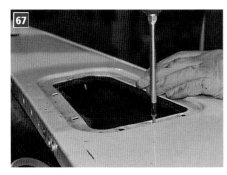

67 Don't forget to fit the two screws holding the inner wing liner in place! Also, don't over-tighten: remember that you're screwing into plastic.

68 Now, Ian reused the original countersunk stainless screws. The small gap produced by the rivet-nut tops is filled by the foam gasket on the back of the chequer plate.

69 At this point I became aware of the only very small blemish in these wings – a very slight rippling, which you literally don't see unless you look very hard.

70 Ian started to refit the wheel arch extension, offering it up to the wing and checking the alignment of the pre-drilled holes in the wing panel.

71 Several of the holes didn't line up and had to be re-drilled, but Ian tells me this isn't at all uncommon, even with original equipment Land Rover aluminium panels.

72 We're all used to panel variations in our Defenders, after all! The trick when refitting those plastic rivets is to push the centre pin just a millimetre or so…

73 …into the head of the rivet, push the rivet fully home with thumb or pliers, then use a hammer to tap the pin flush with the head, spreading and locking the rivet legs.

74 Neither of us had used or fitted ABS wing panels before and we were both impressed by the overall quality of these MM 4x4-supplied parts.

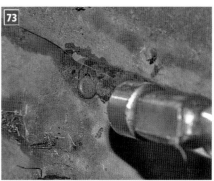

Defender 90 sill panel replacement

This work was carried out and the parts supplied by Ronnie Maughan Jr of YRM Metal Solutions Ltd. (Pictures are © YRM Metal Solutions Ltd.)

1 On one of their Land Rover show stands, Ronnie Maughan Sr demonstrates one of YRM's replacement sill panels (left). Interestingly, although it looks identical when fitted it's far stronger than the original, flimsy item (right) – and also much less expensive.

2 Any replacement sill will come with the fixing brackets, complete with adjustment slots, welded on.

3 This is the plastic clip (arrowed) to be removed from the trim.

4 These are the locations of the original fixings (Defender 90) – the bolts need removing, and it may be quicker to cut them off.

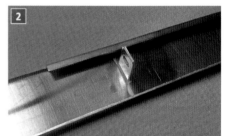

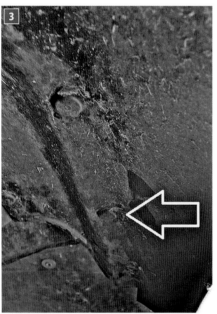

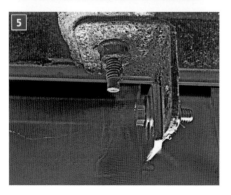

5 The new sill panel has been fitted in place using the stainless steel fixings provided. You must ensure the cleats fit to the rear of the sill, to allow easy fitting, and the holes must, of course, line up with the body panels. Use the 35mm long bolts for the front and rear wing stays. The cup square bolts are used in fixing the sill to the wheel arch and the 20mm long bolts are used to fix to the sill rail.

6 When painting, don't forget that you'll first need to use an etch primer, because regular paint won't bond to aluminium.

Front grille panel removal

1 Though this is a KBX aftermarket grille, the principle is the same as for the standard one – you remove the screws from the periphery.

2 After removing the grille, the surround's bottom bolts were removed...

3 ...followed by the top ones.

4 The grille surround was then removed.

5 With the surround out of the way, the bonnet slam panel and supports can be unbolted, if required.

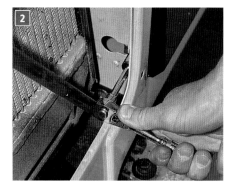

Front and rear side-door removal and replacement

1 Start by disconnecting the check strap from the door. Front doors have a rod or flat plate check strap, held to the door with a clevis pin. Open out the split pin and remove it with pliers, making sure you 'save' the washer from above. Pull out the clevis pin.

Rear door check straps are held to the doors with lock-nuts and plain washers. So that you don't lose the parts, reassemble the clevis pin, washers and split pin (or the nut and washer) on to the door stay, or the stay bracket itself.

2 If you're working by yourself, close the door so that it's held securely and take out the bolts holding the door hinge to the door pillar. There are captive nuts inside the door pillar. If you're carrying out a restoration, don't be tempted to disconnect the bolts from the door itself in the hope that you won't disturb the captive nuts in the door pillar, because you'll invariably have to carry out some restoration work to the bottom of the steel door pillars themselves.

Be sure to retain the gaskets that fit between the hinges and the body. Remember to refit them when refitting the doors. Note, when refitting the doors, that there's a certain amount of adjustment available when the hinge fixing bolts are loose.

3 From about 1998, hinge screws have had TORX heads.

4 You're recommended to replace the standard screws with stainless steel ones, such as from Stig Fasteners. Those that screw into the bulkhead go into J-nuts, and new ones are supplied as part of

the kit. Earlier Defenders have imperial threads, and on those you must fit the new replacement J-nuts. On later Defenders, the originals can be reused if they're metric, provided they're in good condition. Use copper grease on the threads to

provide a barrier between stainless screws and mild or plated steel nuts. The screws that go into the door are very similar to those used on the rear doors – see the section on Rear side-door removal, replacement and rebuild.

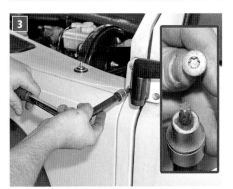

STRIPDOWN

If your Defender's door frame has rotted beyond repair, then a complete replacement may be the answer. Most manuals show how to remove door gear with the door in situ, but if you're replacing a door you'll strip the door when it's off the vehicle.

The only way of building up a Land Rover Defender's door to new-vehicle standard is by being meticulous with every detail and being prepared to identify and purchase every last one of the multiplicity of clips and fixings that Land Rover's designers once seemed to take a delight in making as varied as possible. But once you've finished the work, and especially with the use of modern anti-corrosion waxes and treatments, there's no reason why you shouldn't have a door that will last much longer than the original one did.

Stripping out a rotten door frame (or 'shell') won't be as easy as it looks in a workshop manual. Fittings may have been botched, and it'll certainly be rusty and generally horrible to work on. The main sequence here shows a second-hand Defender door being stripped ready for rebuilding into a new frame. The work was carried out by Britpart's Adrian Longstaff.

1 It's a good idea to disconnect the check strap before starting to detach the door-hinge fixings. It's so annoying to have the door hanging loose but for the fiddly check strap that you'll need to disconnect with your third and fourth hands while supporting the door!

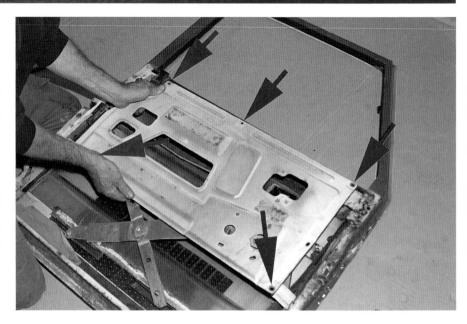

2 It'll be amazing if a twist with a large cross-point screwdriver actually slackens the hinge fixing screws! Try soaking with releasing fluid the day before – and hope some soaks past the paint and rust. Tap the end of the screwdriver while twisting hard. You could try a screwdriver bit in a ratchet via an adaptor. Better still, use an impact screwdriver and a heavy hammer.

3 If you really have to you can sacrifice the hinge when cutting through the head of the screw. Removing the stub will still be difficult, but at least

you can get at the thread after the door hinge has been removed.

4 Defender doors are really heavy – it takes two people to lift them away safely.

5 Start the stripdown by removing the window winder handle. Prise out the round finisher, remove the retaining screw and take off the handle and bezel.

6 The door latch trim is removed by unscrewing the screw (arrowed), lifting the latch and sliding out the trim.

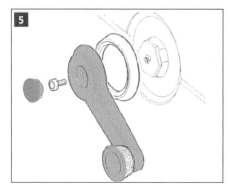

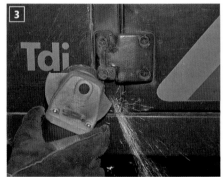

7 The door-pull is held with two screws – simple, when you know there are two hinged trim flaps that have to be flipped open first with a very small screwdriver.

8 You need to remove the door lock trim by levering it up so that the clip (inset) clears the door card.

9 At last, the door card can be removed, as well as the waterproof sheet from behind it. You may need to replace the door card...

10 ...you'll almost certainly need to replace the plastic barrier, to prevent moisture from damaging the door card in future.

11 Release the spring clip and disconnect the control rod from the latch mechanism.

12 For reference, here's how many of the clips fit on to their operating rods. Lever and hinge the spring off the rod.

13 Next, release the control rod from its plastic clip in the mounting panel.

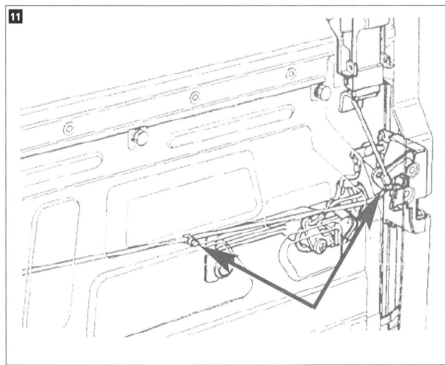

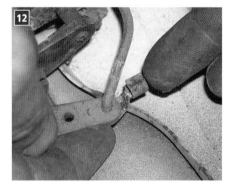

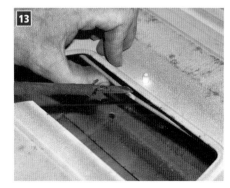

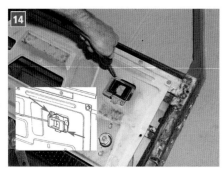

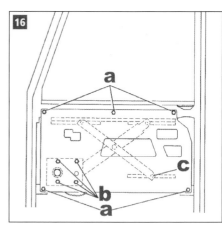

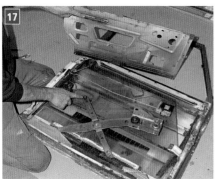

14 Remove both screws securing the remote control lever to the mounting panel – remove the lever and control rod together.

15 Adrian continued to remove the subframe or mounting panel.

16 The order of work is:
  a Remove five screws (a) securing the mounting panel to the door frame.

b Remove four screws (b) securing the window regulator to the mounting panel.
c Slide the window regulator arm from the mounting panel (c) while removing the latter.

17 The panel is shown being lifted away, with Adrian pointing to the regulator arm where it's been slid from its runner.

18 The window regulator mechanism was removed next.

DOOR ON VEHICLE

19 If you were trying to replace the regulator and/or glass with the door still in situ:
  a Wind the window half open and support with a length of timber.
  b Remove the two lower screws to the mounting panel.
  c Slacken the three upper screws.
  d Remove the four screws holding the window regulator to the mounting panel.
  e Slide the operating arms from the channels attached to the glass and mounting panel.
  f Remove the regulator.

20 To remove the glass:
  a Push the glass up to the top of its travel and support it with a suitable length of timber.
  b Remove (a) the two self-tapping screws securing the window glass runner on the latch side of the door and the single screw from the hinge side.

21 Lever the exterior waist weather strip from the door, remove the timber support and carefully lower the glass to the bottom of the door.

22 Ease the runner from the glass at the hinge-side of the door...

23 ...then manoeuvre the glass over the bottom of the door.

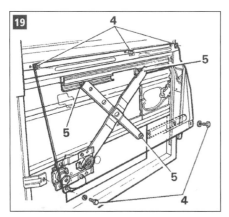

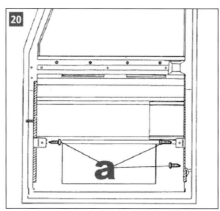

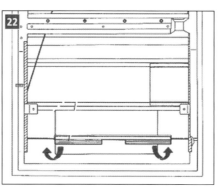

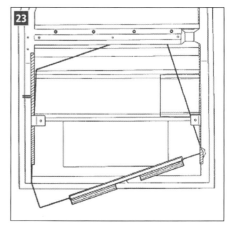

DOOR REMOVED

24 No such problems with the door on the ground as Adrian lifted out the window glass.

25 To remove the door lock, you take out the two screws (a) and disconnect the operating rod at (b).

26 Or, You could leave the rod attached and waggle the button away from the top end of the rod.

27 To remove the exterior door handle with door in situ, you would first need to remove the mounting panel as shown earlier and support the glass with timber (a), then disconnect the operating rod (b) from the handle mechanism, and rod (c) from the locking barrel lever.

28 Then there's the easy bit – provided they come undone OK and haven't seized or stripped – the two screws (picture 25, c)...

29 ...holding the exterior handle to the door.

30 Just a general restoration point: with a well-rusted door, there are sometimes occasions when things just won't come undone, and then it's time for drastic action. A Dremel-type tool will get into small spaces.

31 After detaching all relevant rods, the locking latch is held with three screws through the outside of the door.

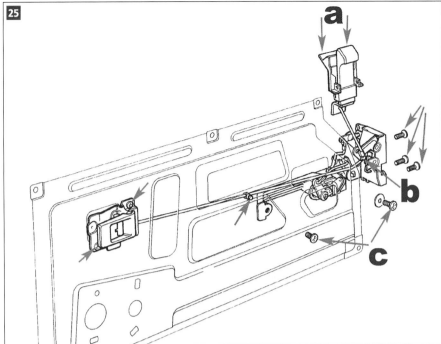

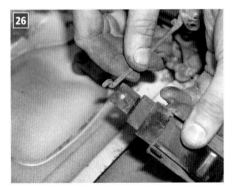

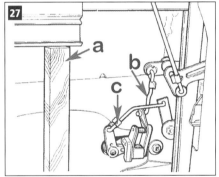

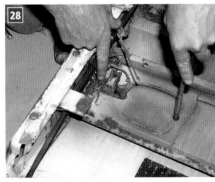

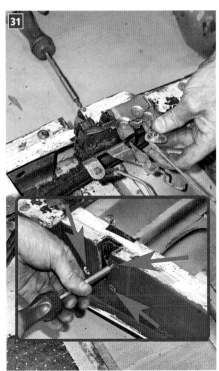

32 Start to take out the glass runner by removing the two self-tapping screws on the latch side of the door and the single screw from the hinge side (picture 20, a). Then, remove the screws holding the channel to the door frame – you'll need to search for these.

33 Sometimes, carefully lifting and pulling will tell you where the channels are held by screws.

34 Here, Adrian removes the three separate lengths of channel and the door is now totally denuded.

The trouble with a really old, corroded door is that many of the interior fixings won't be reusable – but you won't know that for sure until you've completed the stripdown.

REBUILD

It's essential that the new door is painted before you start putting it all back together, though you may not want to apply wax-based rust-proofer until after you've finished building the door up. Otherwise, the job would become a very messy one!

35 Before starting to rebuild the door, Adrian meticulously cleaned, de-rusted and painted all of the components from the old door that were reusable.

36 He'd already temporarily fitted the subframe, to make sure that all holes lined up and that none of the threads were clogged with paint.

37 If you use copper grease on threads, even those as notoriously prone to rusting as hinge mounting screws…

38 …will last far longer before any rust sets in. Note that Adrian used new gaskets…

39 …behind each leaf of the hinge. None of the fixing screws should be tightened fully until door adjustment has been completed – or at least enough for now to prevent damage caused by the door crashing against the bodywork. The reason is that the door will certainly need to be readjusted once it's been fully loaded up with all the glass and door gear.

40 These are the new glass runners as illustrated in the parts manual. Note the glass guide, coloured red

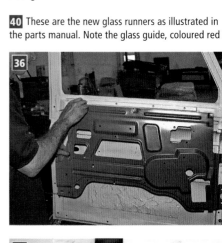

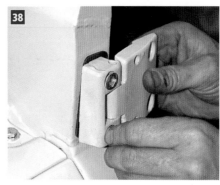

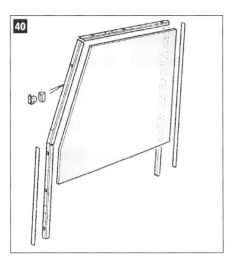

here (though not in reality, of course) and referred to later on.

41 Each section of channel has cut-outs where folding has to take place.

42 The locations of the window colleagues are handed, left and right, because the guide must be on the outside of the glass.

43 Adrian started off by offering up the window channel and making a small mark where fixing screw holes were to be drilled.

44 He ensured the marks could be clearly seen, then drilled the channel in readiness.

45 Note the thin aluminium strip that fits between the channel and the door. It really is very thin and flexes easily into position.

46 Next Adrian drilled tapping size holes through the door channel hole and into the door…

47 …and fitted the correct self-tapping screws. Note the position of the glass guide mentioned earlier.

48 The runner for the top and rear of the door comes in one section. Adrian offered it up…

49 …folding it at the appropriate point and checking for fit. He then marked the screw fixing holes' positions, drilled the door and fitted the self-tapping screws just as he did with the front channel section.

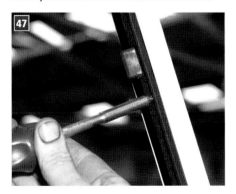

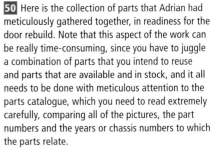

50 Here is the collection of parts that Adrian had meticulously gathered together, in readiness for the door rebuild. Note that this aspect of the work can be really time-consuming, since you have to juggle a combination of parts that you intend to reuse and parts that are available and in stock, and it all needs to be done with meticulous attention to the parts catalogue, which you need to read extremely carefully, comparing all of the pictures, the part numbers and the years or chassis numbers to which the parts relate.

51 One particular case in point is the gaskets that are meant to be fitted to the door lock/latch mechanism. This is the smaller side-piece…

52 …and this is the larger, having the backing paper removed from its self-adhesive surface…

53 …before being stuck down to the latch.

54 Adrian found it easiest to introduce the mechanism almost the wrong way round and turn it until it located in position inside the door frame.

55 He fitted it with three new screws, though this is an area where you can save a little money if you have plenty of time by cleaning up screws and painting the screw heads.

56 Door-handle mechanisms do wear, and it's likely that a scrap door will have a handle that's also best suited to the scrapheap. Note that once again there are essential gaskets that will make the mountings waterproof and prevent damage to the paintwork.

57 After introducing the handle at an angle so that the operating lever passed through the hole first…

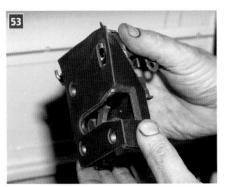

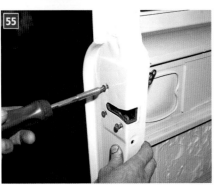

58 …Adrian used screws and spring washers to fit the handle to the door.

59 You can't always fit parts in the sequence ordained in the workshop manual for a variety of reasons, one of them being that parts aren't always in stock precisely when you need them. And so it was that Adrian fitted the glass seals…

60 …to the top of the door after fitting part of the door gear. Not that it mattered, of course. In some cases you can't fit certain components if others have been fitted first, but in this case it really didn't matter.

61 After ensuring that the three screws holding the bottoms of the glass runners in place were loose, Adrian eased them apart and inserted the glass. There's a bit of a trick involved in this.

62 You have to insert the glass into the runners at the angle illustrated then, while lifting the glass, position it squarely in the runners and raise it to the top of travel and hold it there using duct tape or by inserting a timber support.

63 Now you can secure the hinge-side glass runner with a single screw, ensuring that the packing strip is in position. Then, again locate the packing strip and secure the runner on the opposite side with the two screws fitted there. Ensure that all the fixing screw heads are well below the bottoms of the runners, to prevent damage to the glass. Slide it carefully up and down by hand in order to check that it's clear.

64 Now, the door lock button (A) and opening lever (B) have to be screwed to the door frame…

65 …so that the operating rods, the pivot bushes and the clips holding the rods in place can be fitted.

66 Here's an example of one of the pivot bushes being pushed into its hole in the bare latch lever.

67 The relevant rod end is pushed into the bush complete with its fixing clip.

68 Note that there are slightly different types of fixing clips, but all operate on the same principle of being turned around and clipped to the rod to hold it in position.

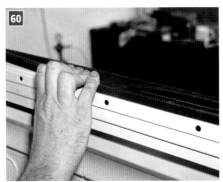

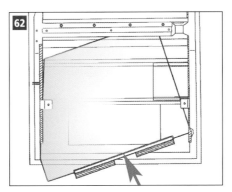

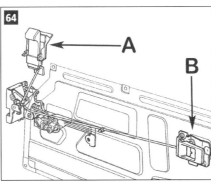

A

B

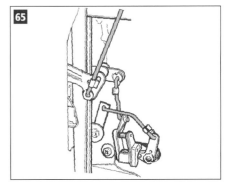

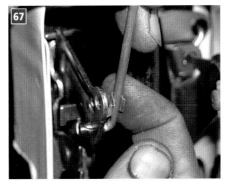

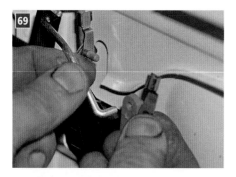

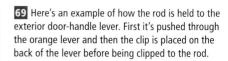

69 Here's an example of how the rod is held to the exterior door-handle lever. First it's pushed through the orange lever and then the clip is placed on the back of the lever before being clipped to the rod.

70 Note that the other end of the rod had already been fitted to the latch lever, where there Is no fixing catch required.

FITTING A NEW DOOR

You can repair Defender door frames, but if the rot's too far gone you'll be better off with a new one. Here's what's involved in building up a bare Defender front door.

71 This is the subframe or mounting panel, as Land Rover call it, being offered up to the bare door.

72 Only five bolts, around the periphery, attach the mounting panel to the door frame. As always when fixing a large component in place, fit all of the bolts loosely before tightening any of them, otherwise some of the holes probably won't align.

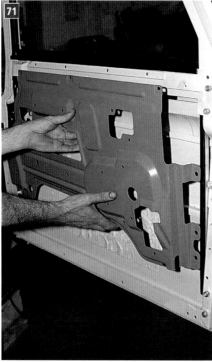

73 There are several types of nylon insert designed to take screws and other fixings to the mounting panel. Adrian had spent quite some time going through the parts book identifying them before ordering the relevant packs of inserts. If you're fitting a new mounting panel you've simply got to bite the bullet and identify all of them from the parts list. Even if you're reusing your old one, there'll almost certainly be several inserts that are missing or unusable. There's no getting away from the amount of time you need to spend at the planning stage!

74 Bearing in mind that the glass had already been slid into the runners and secured at the top of the frame, Adrian now inserted the window winder gear…

75 …sliding it into position until the winder handle spline poked through the hole in the mounting panel and, once the four fixing points (arrowed) were aligned, he loosely attached the mounting bolts.

76 At the outer end, the window gear attaches to the mounting panel with two more bolts, but once again, neither is to be fully tightened at this stage. It's here that the window angle can be adjusted.

77 If you haven't already fitted the door latch mechanism, you may have to fit more, different types of nylon insert…

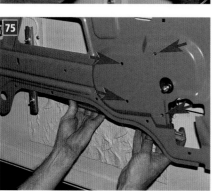

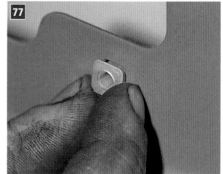

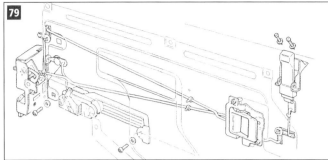

78 ...to take the fixing screws.

79 Here, for reference, is the layout of the door lock/latch gear.

80 It's just worth mentioning that most of the rods are fitted into place with special clips, but some of them simply hook into position, such as this lock-operating rod.

81 With the relevant door gear in place, Adrian removes the tape holding the glass up and slides it down to meet the door winder gear.

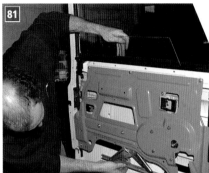

82 There are two keyhole slots, one at each end of the winder gear. These slots pass over the screws fitted to the channel that's mounted on the bottom of the glass. Once the slots are in place and slid along to the narrowest point...

83 ...the fixing screws can be tightened using an open-ended spanner to get into the slightly restricted space available.

84 Würth's aerosol copper grease really came into its own as Adrian gave all the mechanisms a good blasting with lubricant.

85 It's all too easy to overlook the mountings for the rods that run from the interior door handle to the back of the door. These rods are meant to be supported by plastic clips. If you're fitting new ones, the bush – held in Adrian's right hand – is first inserted from the back and into the hole in the mounting panel. The rod carrier then clips into the bush.

86 You can now see the rod – or at least part of it (arrowed) – being clipped into the plastic carrier.

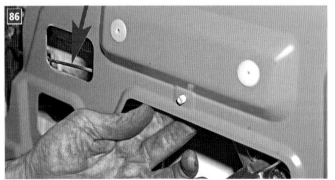

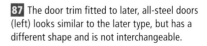

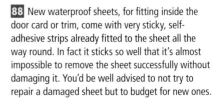

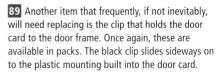

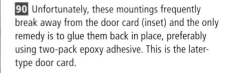

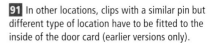

87 The door trim fitted to later, all-steel doors (left) looks similar to the later type, but has a different shape and is not interchangeable.

88 New waterproof sheets, for fitting inside the door card or trim, come with very sticky, self-adhesive strips already fitted to the sheet all the way round. In fact it sticks so well that it's almost impossible to remove the sheet successfully without damaging it. You'd be well advised to not try to repair a damaged sheet but to budget for new ones.

89 Another item that frequently, if not inevitably, will need replacing is the clip that holds the door card to the door frame. Once again, these are available in packs. The black clip slides sideways on to the plastic mounting built into the door card.

90 Unfortunately, these mountings frequently break away from the door card (inset) and the only remedy is to glue them back in place, preferably using two-pack epoxy adhesive. This is the later-type door card.

91 In other locations, clips with a similar pin but different type of location have to be fitted to the inside of the door card (earlier versions only).

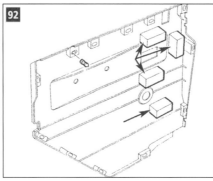

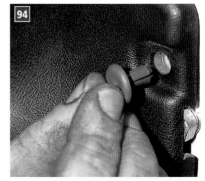

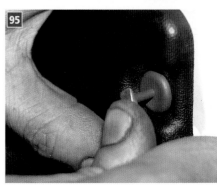

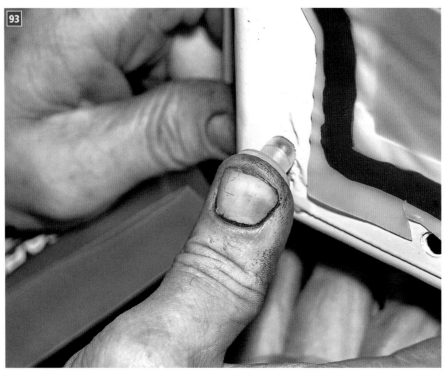

92 The door card should have foam anti-vibration blocks in place, and if they're missing (varying with year of vehicle), it would be a relatively simple matter to make your own and glue them in position.

93 Just in case you thought Land Rover had run out of ideas for different types of clip to use, the new door will need a pack of fixing grommets to be pushed into the relevant holes around the door frame so that when the door card is offered up the fixing clips can be oh-so-carefully aligned with the grommets before pushing – or more likely banging with your hand – so that the clips fit into their respective grommets.

94 And oh joy! Here's yet another different type of fitting, which pushes through the diagonally opposite corners of the door card and into the door frame…

95 …and then the plastic pin in the fixing is carefully pushed home, spreading the legs on the back of the fixing and holding it in place.

96 The bad news is that when you want to get one of these out, you have to push the plastic pin right through the fixing and hope that you can find it later, somewhere inside the door cavity!

97 The door-lock knob surround is a simple push-on (and some would say fall-off) affair.

98 Note the cut-out in the door card. There's a circular plate or boss behind the winder handle and the cut-out locates it to stop it rotating when winding the handle.

99 While earlier types of winder mechanism are held in place with a screw covered with a trim button, later ones use a spring clip that can sometimes be a pig, both to fit and to remove. You need to push the door card back further than the point where the spring has to be clipped into place so that you can see it, reach it and slide it into position. To remove it, you need something with a small hook on the end.

100 Door pull-handles are simply held with a pair of screws whose heads are covered with these hinged caps.

101 The interior door handle surround can only be fitted with the door handle pulled into the open position…

102 …and while in the same position, the single fixing screw can be fitted.

103 As with every job that Adrian Longstaff carries out, the finished door both looked good and worked perfectly. Incidentally, non-standard (but much more robust) GRP door cards are available from LaSalle Trim.

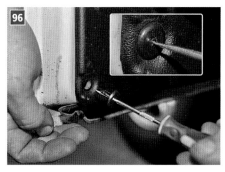

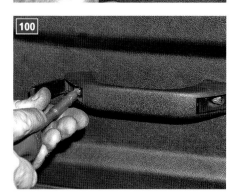

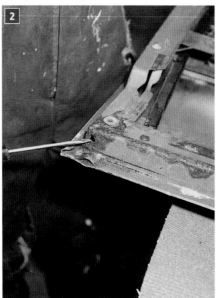

1 Earlier (aluminium-skinned) side doors for 90s, 110s and Defenders are notorious rotters! It has to be said that the basic design is faulty, and if you rebuild the door as it was built at the factory it'll just rot out again. This door shows typical signs of aluminium rot all along the base – when prodded with a screwdriver it just went right through. Later, all-steel doors are much better!

2 And this is the same door viewed from the other side. The steel frame has also started to corrode. Theoretically, aluminium should always corrode before steel when the two are in contact with one another, because aluminium becomes what's known as a sacrificial anode to steel when they're joined together. The aluminium gives up its life in an electrolytic process, one that's greatly encouraged by all the moisture that finds its way to the insides – and especially the bottom – of vehicle doors. Quite why Land Rover have continued to build doors with steel and aluminium in contact with one another is anyone's guess.

3 Before starting to remove the skin, the door must be stripped out as described in the previous section. A single pop-rivet holds the door skin halfway along the window aperture. Drill it out.

4 You now have to work your way all around the door skin, levering up the folded-over edge of the skin from the steel frame.

5 If there's any risk of causing damage to the steel frame, use a packing piece between lever and frame.

6 The door skin is frequently held to the steel frame with mastic (a half-hearted attempt by Land Rover to separate the two metals?), and the two often have to be strongly encouraged to come apart.

7 Lift the door skin off the frame...

8 ...and clean off any traces of rust from the surface of the frame. You'll also have to cut out and repair any rusty sections of frame (most often found near the bottom of the door), and the door frame must be primed and painted.

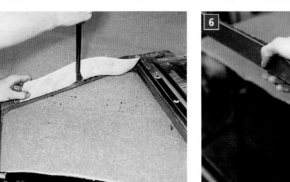

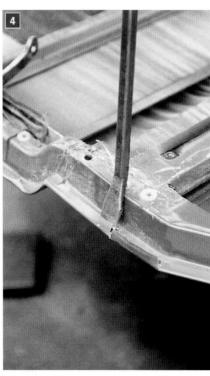

9 And here's one I made earlier! Actually, this is a brand new door frame. These non-Land Rover frames are plastic-coated so that there's no chance of the steel and aluminium coming into contact with each other. Perhaps a similar effect could be achieved by using waterproof plastic tape, available from DIY centres for things like guttering repairs. Alan Agutter shows how a replacement door skin is fitted.

Be sure to go all the way round the outside of the frame, tapping down with a hammer any raised areas of metal. If you don't, they'll show through the soft aluminium skin after it's been fitted.

10 Likewise with the new skin itself. Alan went all the way round with a hammer and dolly, taking out any tiny blemishes. It's worth spending time to get things right at this stage, because you won't be able to get at it later.

11 Alan applied sealer from a roll all the way round the frame and on each crossbar. On the outer frame he applied the sealer to each of the inner raised areas (the door skin will need to be tight against the metal of the outer raised area), and puts a double-thickness strip on the centre crossbar. He explains that a replacement door skin tends to bow outwards fractionally in the centre, come unstuck from the sealer and cause drumming. The double thickness overcomes this tendency.

12 Place the door skin on a work surface with something soft and protective such as cloth or corrugated paper between the aluminium and the work surface. Carefully lower the frame into place...

13 ...and check that the lip is tight against the steel frame in the window aperture. When the lip is right, says Alan, all else will be.

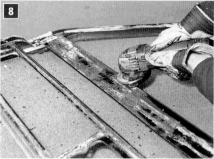

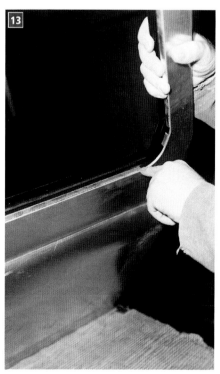

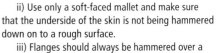

ii) Use only a soft-faced mallet and make sure that the underside of the skin is not being hammered down on to a rough surface.

iii) Flanges should always be hammered over a little at a time, all the way along their length, before going back to the beginning and hammering over a little more. If you try hammering the flange over fully at one end, then work your way along, the metal will stretch and you'll end up with wrinkled metal.

16 Make sure that the top of the door frame is supported with a piece of wood to take account of the fact that it's angled inwards. You'll have to use a drift – the broader the better – to hammer over the flange. A piece of smooth hardwood would be better than steel.

17 Don't forget to fit a new pop-rivet to the centre of the lip in the window aperture.

18 Use a smooth file or medium abrasive paper to round off each of the sharp corners. If you're concerned about filing right through the aluminium, try rounding off the corner first with your hammer.

19 Drill right through the frame and through the new aluminium door skin to recreate the hinge holes.

20 If your door frame had rotted out, or if you want to purchase a completely rebuilt door such as this one, you can buy new, replacement doors with a plastic-coated frame and ready-primed aluminium skin.

21 Whichever route you choose, it then remains to refit the door components – once again taking great care not to damage the aluminium skin – before refitting the door to the vehicle.

14 You can now go all the way around the frame, pressing it down on to the door skin.

15 You can now start hammering over the door skin flange on to the frame, but bear in mind the following important points:

i) Alan recommends that you start folding the flange over at the top of the curved area halfway up the door. This can be the trickiest part to do, and it also starts you off by holding the skin in place at its centre.

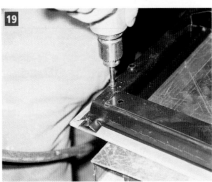

When older-style, aluminium-skinned rear doors are rotten they're usually done for. (Later, all-steel doors are a vast improvement.)This Defender had some corrosion in its rear door and we were anticipating that a replacement would be needed. However, I suddenly remembered another 'used' door I had lying around. When I looked more closely, I realised that the two doors were corroded in different places, all except for the bottom steel channel. The profile of the channel turned out to be exactly the same as the channel at the top of the door, which almost never corrodes, so I decided that we'd build one good door out of two.

Some people seem horrified by this sort of thing (though not Land Rover folk, of course; we know better). But what's wrong with it? Doors and all other vehicle parts are only made up of separate parts anyway, so there's nothing wrong with changing them around a bit, is there?

Mind you, it's important, when you repair a door in this way, that either the aluminium door skin is sound or that it can be repaired successfully. A door with a rotted-out skin as well as corroded steel channels is only repairable if you're really determined to do it. A new replacement would be more cost effective in most cases.

It many be possible to fit all-steel doors to earlier Defenders, but none of the trim or door gear is likely to be interchangeable. Door hinges are different and latches/catches will probably present problems.

1 This rear door looked good from the outside and the skin was sound, but the old frame had corroded badly beneath the door latch assembly, where the vertical frame had also rotted through. One of the vertical centre sections had corroded and the horizontal lower channel had broken right through, while the joint at the other end had disintegrated in a similar fashion.

2 After stripping away the spare wheel support panels we were surprised to see that there was no further corrosion in this area.

3 Meanwhile, I worked on the old door to remove the skin and then cut away the sections that we would need for repairing the original door.

4 Here you can see that the main frame section (a) was in good condition, although the bottom channel had rotted away. This was replaced with the identically shaped top channel (b). You can see where the top of the door frame has been cut away, and it's this that would be used for repairing the bottom end.

5 New door frame sections are available from companies such as YRM Metal Solutions.

6 The flap of door skin, where it fitted around the frame, was carefully levered up with a screwdriver.

7 The corroded section of the old door frame was removed with a thin (1mm) blade on the angle grinder. Note the piece of scrap metal – actually the old door skin from the other door – pushed behind the frame to reduce the risk of the angle grinder damaging the main door skin.

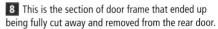

8 This is the section of door frame that ended up being fully cut away and removed from the rear door.

9 The replacement frame was repaired by welding in the section of channel from the top of the old door to the base of the door frame, producing one that was as sound as new.

10 The scrap section of frame was then placed against the replacement frame so that we could work out how to cut out our repair section.

11 This was marked as carefully as possible, once again planning to cut slightly oversize.

12 This meant that the replacement could be offered up and trimmed until it fitted perfectly. You have to be prepared to do this several times until you get it right.

13 After wire brushing all traces of aluminium corrosion away from the inside of the skin and painting the surface with weldable zinc-rich primer, we applied Würth Bond and Seal to those areas where the replacement frame would be fitted. Note the bracket shown in the bottom left of the picture, which was still sound and was left attached to the old door, ready for the new frame to be welded up against it.

14 The replacement frame had also been cleaned back to bare metal and primed. It was offered up, clamped into place…

15 …then tack-welded into position.

16 When it was properly aligned, the flap of the door skin was coated in more Würth Bond and Seal for two reasons: one to strengthen the joint where the door skin flap folds around the frame, and the other to try to isolate the aluminium from the steel.

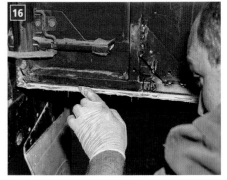

It's this close proximity between steel and aluminium that causes so much trouble on earlier Land Rover Defenders' bodywork.

17 Now it was time to fold the flap of metal back over the door frame. You can see that a clamp had been used to hold the two close together at the base and a large block of wood was used as a dolly against which to hammer.

18 The most important point to bear in mind is that the flap must be bent over a little bit at a time as you go along. If you try to bend over one end of the flap entirely and then work along the flap, it will stretch and you'll end up with wrinkles all along it and some distortion on the outside of the door skin. Start by folding the whole of the flap over as level as possible no more than about a quarter of the way over, then go all the way along the flap once again – and then again several times more, until it lies flat.

19 The flap finally has to be hammered completely flat against the frame and it's best to hold the dolly in place with something heavy, such as a lump hammer, so that you've got something solid to hammer against. Bond and Seal will go everywhere but that can't be helped. It's best to clean it off straight away with panel wipe, otherwise it will be the very devil to remove when it's gone hard.

20 Next, the welding was completed, making sure the new frame was securely welded into place.

21 The final result was even better than I'd hoped for and the rear door had been given a completely new lease of life.

REAR DOOR GLASS REPLACEMENT

When a Defender is only a few years old the rubbers will be soft and flexible, but when aged they harden and must be replaced, otherwise the seal will leak and will also be extremely difficult to fit.

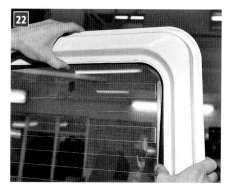

22 After disconnecting the heated screen terminals (which incorporate the terminals for the high-level brake light, when fitted) you can start by pushing the rubber from inside-out…

23 …until the glass is sufficiently free to lift away. Those rear glasses are all worryingly simple to remove, and a definite security weakness.

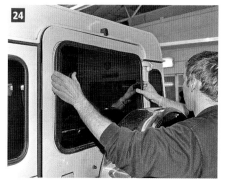

24 Replacement is a matter of offering up glass and rubber from the outside…

25 …while on the inside you can use the crossed-over length of cord that had previously been inserted into the groove on the screen rubber, to pull the rubber over the lip on the door…

26 …working all the way around and paying particular attention to the corners while pushing and persuading carefully, so that the rubber slides into position.

1 Depending on year, you'll need a large cross-head screwdriver or one with a Torx bit for the hinge screws.

2 It's a good idea to replace the standard mild steel bonnet bolts with stainless ones, such as those from Stig Fasteners.

3 As well as being completely corrosion-resistant, they're more secure than standard screws because the Nyloc nuts can't be undone without opening the door first.

4 Adrian Longstaff from Britpart prepared this gasket before fitting the lock handle so that there would be no water ingress once the lock is fitted.

5 The lock is held to the door with these two fitting plates (aluminium doors only): on this version, one is a stud plate (bottom) and the other a nut plate (top). Later steel doors don't use them.

6 It's worth using these stainless bolt plates from YRM Components. Mild steel ones will cause corrosion in the aluminium; these won't!

7 To demonstrate the point, Adrian holds a screwdriver on the screw going into the top plate and a spanner on one of the nuts that fit on the stud plate.

8 The finisher for the lock is fitted to the outside of the door once the lock and handle are in place.

9 Adrian initially bolted the door catch loosely on to the door shut pillar.

10 As always with traditional Land Rovers, there are adjustments to be found in lots of places: the door itself, the door lock and the door catch.

11 Final adjustments can only take place after the rubber seals have been fitted, and even the up-and-down adjustment may need to be reset once the door is finally kitted out with all of its equipment.

12 Part of the equipment in this case was a spare-wheel carrier. These reinforcing channels are pop-riveted on to the inside of the door.

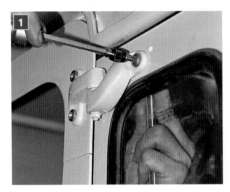

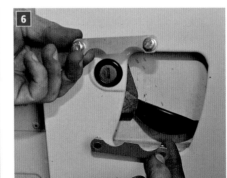

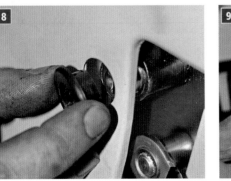

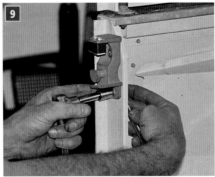

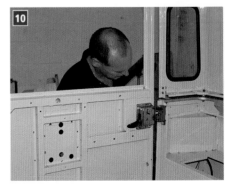

13 The wheel carrier itself is bolted on to the door with a large plate on the inside, to help spread the load. We used butyl sealing strip to keep the joint watertight.

14 Before sliding the door stay into the channel on the Defender door, Adrian slipped the rubber buffer (arrowed) into the channel first.

15 This backing plate, with captive nuts, is placed on the other side of the bodywork to provide a secure mounting point.

16 This is a selection of parts that Adrian had assembled before we began: door seals and the correct Land Rover pop-rivets for fitting them.

17 Sometimes, even when using original parts, you need to show some ingenuity. Adrian used a socket to punch holes in the rear door lower seal where it went over hexagon head bolts.

18 This enabled him to screw down the seal retainer as it should be.

REAR THRESHOLD TRIM

Removal of old threshold trim is also covered in 'Station Wagon rear tub removal, rebuild and replacement' in Chapter 4.

19 Replacing the threshold trim can be slightly complicated if there are sheared-off screws. You can try removing sheared screws with a self-grip wrench when the old threshold trim has been removed, but any that can't be removed may have to be ground off flush. In this case you'll have to shift the threshold trim slightly to one side and drill fresh tapping holes to be drilled for new screws. This YRM threshold plate differs from the original in that it's of stainless steel, as are the supplied fixing screws – so no more reaction with aluminium. The new screws are slightly larger than the originals so they'll be sure to grip, but if a screw is overtightened it may shear, so be prepared to lubricate any tight ones and 'work' them back and forth to cut a new thread (stainless screws shear more readily than mild steel).

20 Defender door seals are pop-riveted to the bottoms of the doors. The Clarke compressed-air-powered pop-rivet gun was useful because it enabled me to apply the rivets one-handed while using the other for holding the seal – or, as in this case, taking the photograph!

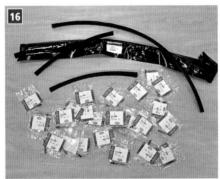

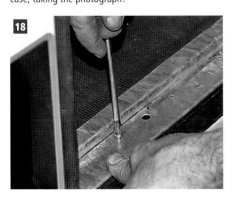

the removal of the separate components, such as the window winder gear, and it's only this that's covered in the Land Rover manual. After all, when they wrote it Defender doors were never going to rot, were they? Not much! I found our 'donor' doors advertised by someone breaking a Defender Station Wagon. The door had already been stripped of its large trim panel when I received it.

1 The trim panel is simply levered off, taking care not to damage the fixing clips, after removing the catches and surrounds shown here. Adrian also removed the screws holding the interior latch to the door frame. See picture 5.

2 Release the spring clip and disconnect the locking button control rod from the latch mechanism (1) and the actuating rod from the door lock mechanism (2).

3 Adrian shows how the rod has to be disconnected from its spring clip. There's more than one type of clip in use.

4 The lock knob is unscrewed from the door frame, and Adrian had the bright idea of leaving the operating rod in its plastic pivot (arrowed) and unclipping the pivot from the door. It will be needed later.

5 For reference, these are the relevant components: (a) fixing screws; (b) rod clip; (c) fixing screws; (d) plastic rod guides.

6 Another plastic pivot is removed from the door by careful pushing or drifting out.

Defender Station Wagons were fitted with pretty much the same rear side doors for around 20 years from about 1986, so there's a fair few of them about. When they rot – and they do – you'll have to strip them down. This is true whether you want to replace the door bases (an extremely tricky job to carry out successfully unless you're a 'proper' panel beater) or, more plausibly, replace the doors, as Adrian Longstaff demonstrates. Later, all-steel doors are much less prone to corrosion.

STRIPDOWN
Stripping the door down isn't the same as

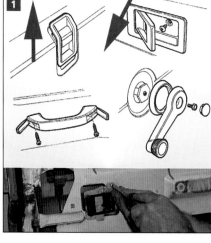

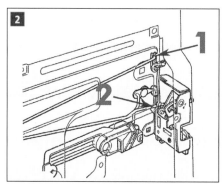

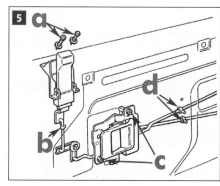

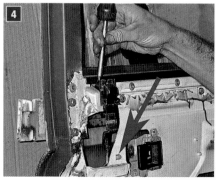

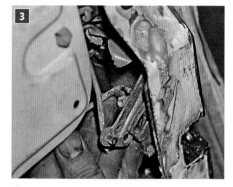

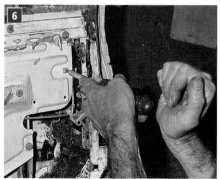

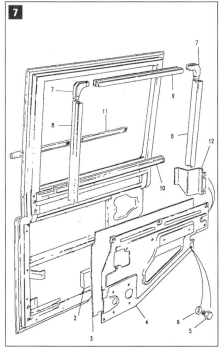

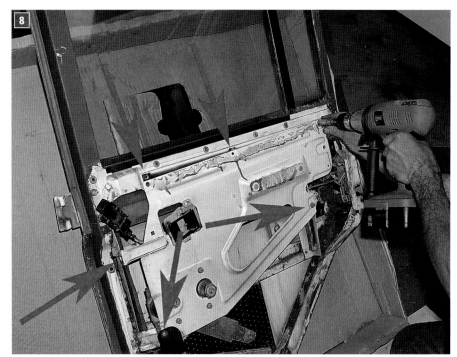

7 For reference again, these are the main door components that Adrian will be attacking later: (2) pad, sound deadening; (3) water shield; (4) inner panel; (5) screw; (6) washer, plain; (7) filler, corner; (8) filler, vertical; (9) filler, top; (10) seal, waist inner; (11) seal, waist outer; (12) deflector.

8 There's a separate carrier to which the door winder gear is attached. A rechargeable drill makes a fine power wrench to spin the fixing screws out.

9 The winder gear is disconnected from the glass and the remaining lock controls taken off with the frame.

10 The lock control rods are so much easier to disconnect when you can actually see the darned things!

11 This is one of the plastic guides seen in picture 5. Adrian carefully uses side-cutters to lever it free.

12 Adrian zipped out the bolts holding the winder mechanism to the frame...

13 ...then put it to one side to decide whether to reuse it later or replace it with a new one if it's worn.

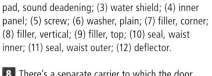
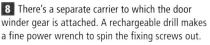

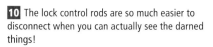

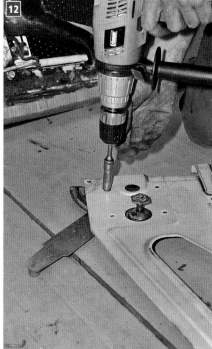

14 On the main door frame, this plate and rusty rod are part of the door stay mechanism...

15 ...and the exterior lock is disconnected from its operating rod by flipping off another of those spring clips.

16 Adrian unscrewed the exterior door handle from the door casing...

17 ...and removed it. You can see the door lock mechanism disconnected in the background.

18 With the door tipped up on end, Adrian removed the screws holding the door latch to the frame. These are sometimes over-tightened, and you might need to use an impact screwdriver. Doesn't matter if you dent the door, does it? IF it's being replaced!

19 The latch assembly was lowered away.

20 Adrian then set about removing the water deflector plate, only to find that the screws were rusted solid. He decided to leave them and come back to them later, grinding and/or drilling as necessary when all the glass was removed.

21 He freed the base of the rearmost window glass channel....

22 ...then slipped the glass down the channel and out of the door.

23 The sealing strip is pushed on and levered off.

24 Adrian started to remove the runner from the door but then it dawned on him that, though the bottom can be freed, the top end can't unless you remove the other channels first.

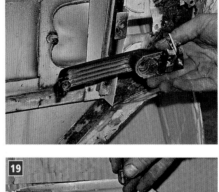

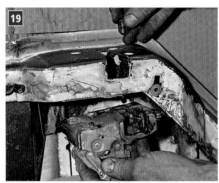

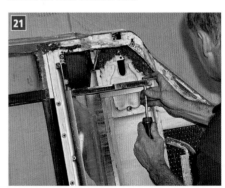

25 Out came the screws holding the channel to the door frame (you have to hunt for them)...

26 ...out came the channel...

27 ...followed by the corner section of the window channel.

28 Once again, Adrian played hunt-the-retaining-screw then removed the channel guide from the top of the frame. Remember that the door is on its side!

29 The guide was unscrewed and levered free from the steel front channel – slightly easier to do with the bottom fixing screw removed, but you have to take care not to distort the steel channel if you're going to reuse it.

30 Adrian lifted the guide away...

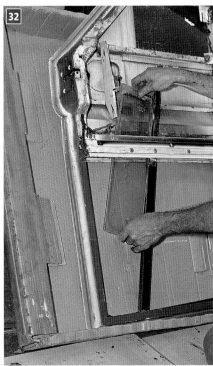

31 ...then removed the screw holding the top of the guide rail to the door frame. The door is fully upside-down now, by the way.

32 There was now enough free space to remove the section of auxiliary glass.

33 The guide channel was removed...

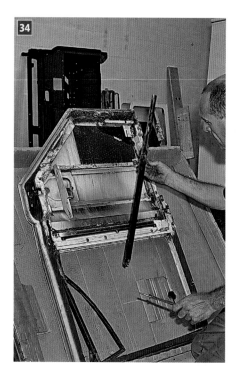

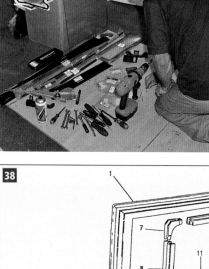

34 ...followed by the steel channel itself.

35 Adrian demonstrates the top guide strip and the rear corner section.

36 These are Defender doors that were fitted to a Series 3 Station Wagon, but the doors themselves are exactly the same.

37 Many owners would want to salvage as many parts from the old doors as possible, painting and fettling them to make them as good as they could be.

REBUILD

38 These are the Defender Station Wagon rear side door's components. The red arrows will be referred to later.

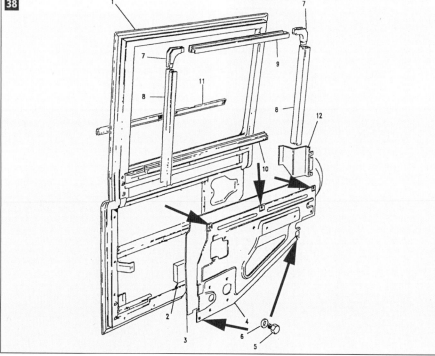

DEFENDER REAR SIDE DOOR, 1987 ON		
Part no	Description	Covering vehicles...
1	Rear side door	
2	Pad, sound deadening	
3	Curtain, water	
4	Panel, inner RH	Up to VIN EA
	Panel, inner LH	Up to VIN EA
	Panel, inner RH	From EA up to LA932486
	Panel, inner LH	From EA up to LA932486
	Panel, inner RH	From LA932487
	Panel, inner LH	From LA932487
5	Screw	
6	Washer, plain	
7	Filler, corner	
8	Filler, vertical	
9	Filler, top RH	
	Filler, top LH	
10	Seal, waist inner RH	
11	Seal, waist outer RH	Up to LA937709
	Seal, waist outer LH	Up to LA937709
	Seal, waist outer RH	From LA937710
	Seal, waist outer LH	From LA937710
12	Deflector, RH	
	Deflector, LH	

39 In the heading picture, you can see Adrian holding the seal for the quarter-light before he folded it into the shape shown here.

40 Before fitting the quarter-light with its seal, Adrian fitted that part of the door seal (see picture 38, parts 7, 8 and 9) that goes behind it.

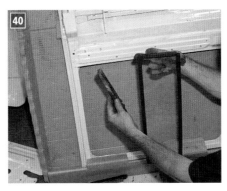

41 Next, as you can see, Adrian put the quarter-light to one side and started to install the rear glass runner. The inset shows how it has to slot into the space provided in the upper door seal.

42 Next, Adrian inserted both the quarter-light and the runner, together.

43 This semi-hidden mounting bracket fits behind the rail on the door frame...

44 ...and is bolted in place with these small screws and nuts with lock washers.

45 This deflector plate is fitted next. Note that it has cut-outs where the mounting bracket nuts and bolts go. The deflector plate is fitted with self-tapping screws after first drilling pilot holes.

46 With the runner frame pressed reasonably tightly against the quarter-light, Adrian drills through the bracket in the top of the frame and into the top of the door frame. Of course, the door is still upside down at this stage.

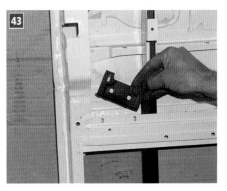

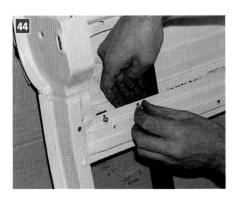

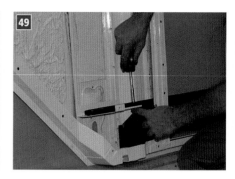

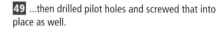

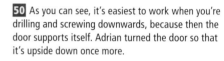

47 Another self-tapping screw fixes the top of the runner frame into place.

48 Next, Adrian installed the glass runner...

49 ...then drilled pilot holes and screwed that into place as well.

50 As you can see, it's easiest to work when you're drilling and screwing downwards, because then the door supports itself. Adrian turned the door so that it's upside down once more.

51 This is the seal for the top of the frame being offered up and marked up so that the fixing holes line up with those in the frame.

52 Adrian drilled into the door frame with a pilot drill.

53 These are the correct, slotted screws for holding the runner seals in place.

54 Once again, you can see that Adrian has turned the door so that he's working downwards. This is the runner for the rear end of the door.

55 After drilling his usual clearance holes in the runner, pilot holes in the door frame and screwing the runner into place with self-tapping screws...

56 ...Adrian started to fit the door glass. Because of the tightness of the new runners, the glass was held firmly in place without falling to the bottom (or, in reality, the top) of the door frame. When glass is being fitted to a door that's in situ it has to be propped up with a piece of wood or taped up with gaffer tape.

57 In an ideal world the door latch assembly would have been fitted before the glass, but in reality...

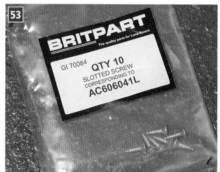

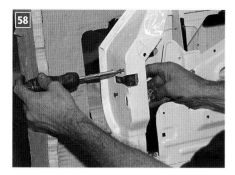

58 ...Adrian screwed the latch assembly to the frame now, which is better than trying to do it after all the winding gear's in place.

59 Adrian took a new window winder mechanism and started to prepare the mounting panel.

60 After bolting the mechanism to the panel, but before fitting the panel to the door – most important, this! – the plastic clips that carry the door latch operating rods have to be clipped into place on the inside of the panel.

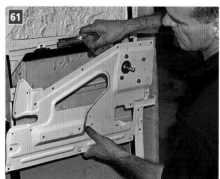

61 Remember that the door is still upside-down. Adrian offered up the winder mechanism panel...

62 ... and bolted it to the door.

63 The operating arm on the bottom of the winder mechanism is held to the plate bonded to the bottom of the door glass with two bolts and washers.

64 At the front-bottom corner of the door (still upside-down, here), this is the loose stud plate which has to be slid behind the slotted plate mounted on the door.

65 The steady catch is screwed into place using two nuts and spring washers.

66 These are new plastic clips into which self-tapping screws can be inserted. Note that the door's the right way up again here.

67 The interior handle and its operating rod can be threaded into the space inside the door frame.

68 It then has to be attached to the lock mechanism...

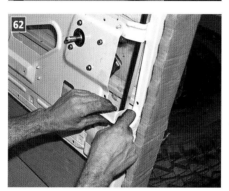

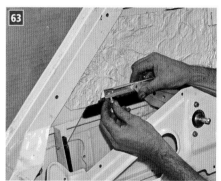

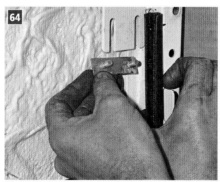

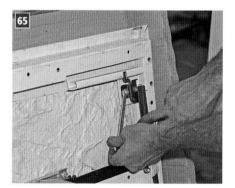

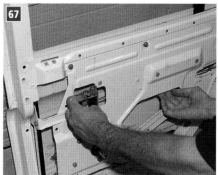

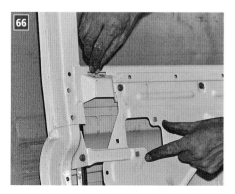

69 ...before being screwed to the door panel.

70 The lock knob mechanism also has to be connected via its operating rod (see picture 1) and can then be screwed to the door frame.

FINISH AND FIT

71 Adrian previously built up most of the door gear, including fitting the separate panel held on with the five bolts (a) which carries the window winder gear. He also started to fit the door latch and lock mechanisms, and you can see the operating rods here, coloured red.

72 Adrian had already connected up the upper rod before fitting the interior pull-handle into place. This is the lower rod, which comes with swivels and extensions on each end.

73 The left-hand swivel clips into its receiving hole...

74 ...as does the right-hand swivel. They both go into the square receiving holes seen here.

75 As each swivel clip is held into its retaining hole, the plastic spreader pin is pushed through the centre of it to grip it firmly into place.

76 On this end, the vertical extension rod pushes into the plastic grommet (a) while the clip (b) is snapped on to the rod.

77 At the lock-button end, the rod is pushed through the hole in the base of the plastic and then the clip snapped into place.

78 To fit and seal successfully, the door handle should be fitted with both of its seals.

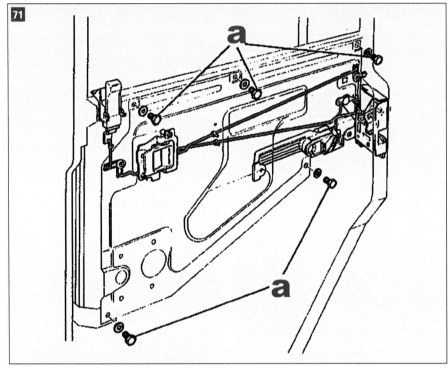

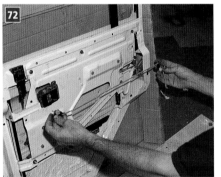

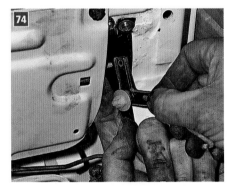

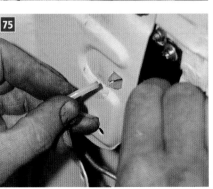

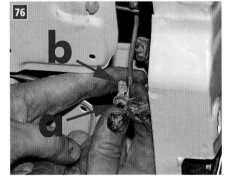

79 The seals are pushed on to the handle before it's offered up to the door...

80 ...which is then held in place as the screws are offered up from the inside.

81 Adrian tightened the two fixing screws while checking again that both seals were in place.

82 The vertically 'hanging-down' operating rod is pushed into the hole provided on the inside of the doorknob and then the spring clip is snapped over both of them. Here you can see that Adrian wangled the clip into place with his screwdriver (arrowed).

83 It's a simple matter to clip the window seal to the inside of the door...

84 ....and the water seal to the outside of the door.

85 Before closing off the inside of the door, Adrian sprayed all of the operating mechanisms and linkages with Würth aerosol copper grease.

86 These white, round, plastic clips are the retainers for the door trim panel. They're simply pushed into the holes on the inside of the door frame.

87 This is the correct damp barrier. You could make up your own sheet out of plastic but, as you'll see, the correct part has many advantages.

88 One of them is that the barrier comes with its own self-adhesive strip all the way around the outer edge. You must make sure that all traces of grease or rust inhibitor have been cleaned off the surface of the paint.

89 Another advantage is that the barrier is shaped to fit around the door stay mechanism.

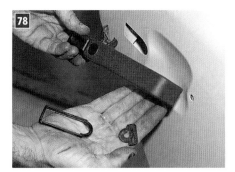

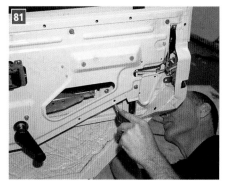

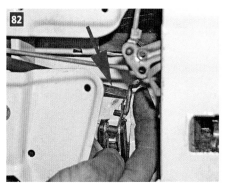

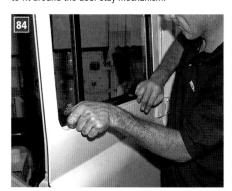

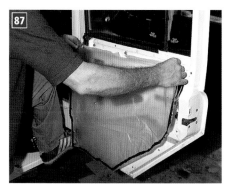

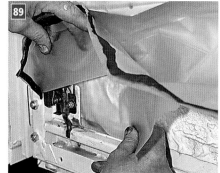

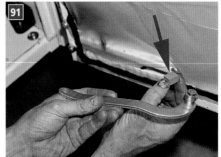

90 Here you can see how Adrian has fitted the barrier correctly at the bottom of the door, effectively sealing out any moisture while still allowing the door stay mechanism to work properly.

91 Before sliding the stay into its runner, however, you must first insert the rubber buffer that protects the stay from the shock of being opened fully.

92 Adrian unwrapped the new door trim from the sealed bag in which it came from the Britpart inventory.

93 Defender door trims come with holes in the back of the trim, but the clips for fitting the trims to the doors have to be fitted to the trims first. The clips are pushed into their retaining holes and then slid sideways, using the end of a screwdriver as shown here.

94 The fixing clips aren't all that sturdy, so you have to be sure that each one lines up correctly with its hole before pushing it, or even banging it, into place. If you don't, you'll probably ruin the clip and have to renew it.

95 Adrian next pushed the doorknob trim into place.

96 The trim surrounding the interior door pull-handle has to be fitted with the pull-handle in its 'out' position, at which point the fixing screw can be inserted and tightened.

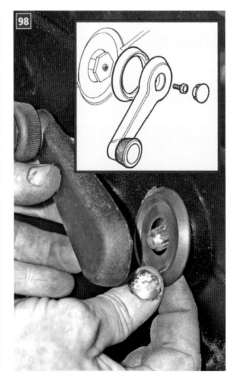

97 The handle for pulling the door closed is held on with a pair of concealed screws, accessed (or concealed) by means of the two plastic flaps seen here.

98 The type of window winder knob that attaches with a screw (see inset) is easier to fit than the one with the hair grip-type clip, which needs to be pushed into the back of the knob. In some cases you have to leave the bezel off entirely.

99 Adrian screwed the door catches to the C-posts and had to use lots of packing pieces to get the catches to line up properly. Remember that this vehicle had been built up out of so many different spare parts it was a wonder that the doors closed at all, never mind that they fit as brilliantly as they do!

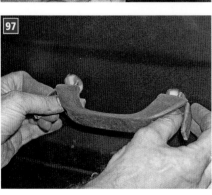

100 The excellent fit is augmented by the use of all the correct door seals...

101 ...and the correct pop-rivets for holding the seals in place.

102 I got roped in to fitting the seals and found that the Clarke air-powered riveting gun made fitting so many rivets a doddle, and also reduced the risk of scratching that you get when using a hand-operated pop-rivet gun.

103 Although nothing strictly to do with the door, while on the subject of sealing things off this is the butyl strip used behind the C-post capping. It's extensively used in the caravan trade and is superb for making leak-proof joints that don't go brittle or dry out with age. You can also get them undone again in the future, if you need to.

104 The door seals did an excellent job of sealing between the doors and the door seal rubbers, but water could still get in around the edges of the door seals between the seals and the bodywork. I gunned in some Würth Bodywork Sealant and, so far so good, this has done the trick and no more water leaks in – not from this source, at least!

105 When refitting the door, you might want to use some of these Stig stainless steel screws, available in door or complete-vehicle sets. They eliminate electrolytic reaction with aluminium and won't rust. On these doors there were nut plates on the insides of the door pillars, but they were replaced with the stainless washers and Nyloc nuts supplied by Stig. They are, in effect, security fixings, because they can't be removed without opening the door to put a spanner on the nuts.

106 The screws into the doors are similar...

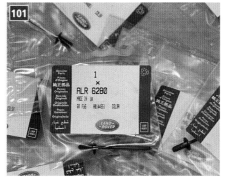

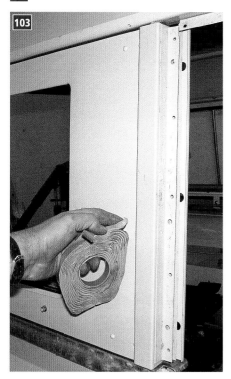

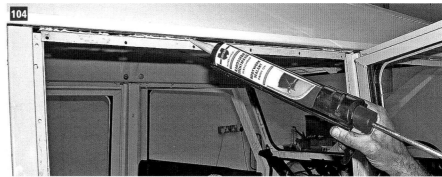

107 …except that they're into nuts on the insides of the doors. (Originally plain nuts – the stainless replacements are the much more secure Nylocs.) You can just get in with a spanner by pulling part of the door trim away.

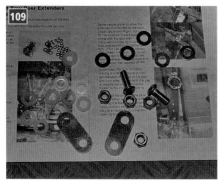

108 For no apparent reason, Defender rear doors don't open as far as they might, making it more difficult to gain access.

109 The answer is to fit a pair of X-Tendoor second-row door extenders, from X-Engineering – the least expensive, easiest-to-fit Land Rover improvement there is, in my view.

110 You unbolt the original door stay from the bracket on the seat box and discard the original nut and washers.

111 There are several options for how you fit the bolt and washers, depending on how thick your carpets or floor mats are. When a vehicle is fitted with floor mats, it may be necessary to turn the bolt upside down to provide clearance, though not if the stay is rigid. The X-Tendoor can articulate as the door closes or it can be bolted rigidly in line with the door stay. If you want it to be rigid, use the stainless washers and tighten the bolt. If not, use the Nylon, tighten then loosen a quarter-turn. The nut on the seat box bracket should use Nylon washers plus one stainless washer and be tightened, then backed off a quarter-turn.

112 The door, when open, will leave a small gap (a couple of millimetres) between the edge of the door and the door pillar (though gaps may vary – it's a Land Rover!). The size of the gap is determined by how thick the rubber buffer inside the door is. If the door hits the pillar, either replace the buffer or, using the stainless washers, rigidly bolt the X-Tendoor to the door stay at an angle, to slightly limit the door opening.

Lock barrel

As shown in the front side door rebuild section, remove the door card, the plastic sheet and the mounting panel.

1 Now raise and support the glass so that you can access the latch mechanism. Disconnect the single screw at the lock operating lever (arrowed) and remove the lock lever assembly.

2 Withdraw the lock barrel complete with locking sleeve (a) from the exterior door handle. To remove the barrel from its plastic retaining sleeve, depress the spring-loaded button (b) and withdraw the sleeve. NOTE: If a new barrel is being fitted, ensure that the numbers on the barrel and the key are the same!

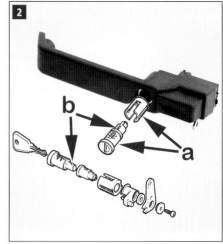

Tailgate removal

On the different types of pick-up model, tailgates are simply bolted to their hinges.

Door mirror replacement

1 The first step is to support the door, because the screws you'll be removing also attach the door to the top hinge. Next, ease out those horribly brittle clips holding the door trim to the top corner of the door. This provides you with access to the nuts on the insides of the two machine screws holding the hinge to the door.

2 Hold a screwdriver in the screw head while fully removing the hinge nuts and washers from the other side.

3 These are the two screws and plastic lock washers, being held adjacent to the new mirror. Note the threaded holes in the mirror bracket.

4 Insert each screw in turn, through the semi-detached door hinge and into the threaded holes in the mirror bracket. The narrow end of each tapered washer faces the hinge. The door can be carefully closed at this stage and will hold itself in place while you work on the mirror. Tighten the two fixing screws evenly – in other words, not by fully tightening one before fitting the other! Then reattach the hinge to the door.

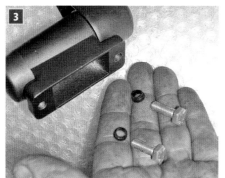

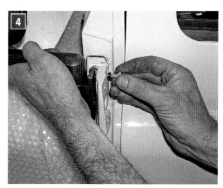

Windscreen removal and replacement

The Defender's front screen glazing owes more to tradition than latest technology – which means it's not rocket science to replace, as IRB Developments demonstrate. However, it's not for the faint-hearted either. Should you do it yourself? Probably not, when bearing in mind the risks from broken glass and the cost of breaking a screen.

SAFETY FIRST! Though he's a professional, windscreen fitter, Dave chose not to wear safety goggles or gloves. This is very unwise – you should always wear protective goggles and gloves when handling and fitting glass.

1 First, remove the A-post trims…

2 …and any stuck-on components, using a sharp blade.

3 No, you're not seeing things! Gently using your foot can be an excellent way of supplying that extra push required to start the glass moving out of the rubber.

4 Once started, it comes away relatively easily and you can work your way all along the top edge of the glass, pushing it free…

5 …until the entire screen can be lifted away.
Next the old rubber can be stripped away, and here, if you're doing the job yourself and you've got plenty of time (not the case when there's a roadside emergency, of course), you can expect to have to sand off rusty metal, apply rust killer and paint before replacing the rubber. The worst-case scenario is that you might even have to carry out weld repairs.

6 The new rubber was eased on to the windscreen surround all the way around.

7 Fresh rubber is far easier to work with than old, brittle rubber, but even so, soapy lubricant makes things far easier.

8 You have to use a string to pull the new rubber into position. An applicator like this (you can make one from a silicone tube dispenser nozzle) isn't essential, but makes it easier to insert the string...

9 ...which is passed all the way round and then overlapped at a convenient spot…

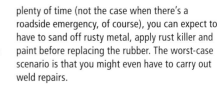

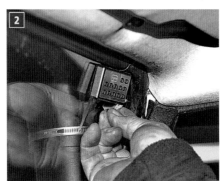

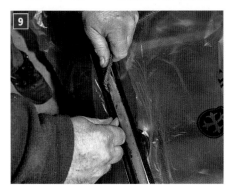

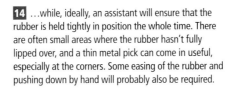

10 …the overlap continuing for about the distance shown here.

11 More soapy lubricant was applied to screen frame and rubber before glass and rubber were lifted into location. It has to be said that this is where experience begins to show. Glass and rubber were eased, pushed, patted and shoved into position...

12 ...before first one end of the string and then the other was pulled…

13 … easing the lip of the rubber over the edge of the frame…

14 …while, ideally, an assistant will ensure that the rubber is held tightly in position the whole time. There are often small areas where the rubber hasn't fully lipped over, and a thin metal pick can come in useful, especially at the corners. Some easing of the rubber and pushing down by hand will probably also be required.

15 With the new rubber in place, not only will the appearance be greatly improved but the risk of water ingress will be significantly reduced.

Removing and replacing a hardtop

1 Although it's rather a large part of a Land Rover's bodywork, the rear hardtop is quite easily moved by two people – being made of aluminium, it's lighter than it looks, and easier still if you want to split it into its constituent parts for any reason! Before starting work, you'll have to remove the rear door and the trim where relevant.

2 The hardtop is held to the windscreen and lower bodywork with lines of nuts, bolts and washers. On models with four side doors, remove the bolts securing the hardtop to the door pillar.

3 Look out for access slots for locking nuts, where relevant. Then, with all the fixings removed, it's back to strong-arm tactics and the hardtop can be lifted away. Note the positions of any rubber washers or seals as the hardtop is removed.

Earlier Defender hardtop side windows were very much in keeping with the agricultural Land Rover tradition. The frames were held in place with nuts and bolts or pop-rivets, covered by a strip of trim. This meant that not only were they time-consuming to assemble in the factory, but they're also something of a security risk, because pulling off the trim strip and drilling out the pop-rivets is a quick and easy task. However, from about 2005 onwards Land Rover went over to a fully bonded-in system: quicker, easier and cheaper to install, a stronger, more secure and watertight fit, and an absolute so-and-so to get out again!

EARLY TYPES

1 This assembly is being removed from a side panel detached from a vehicle, but the principle is the same. The first step is to remove the trim rubber covering the pop-rivets…

2 …and then to drill off the pop-rivet heads…

3 …before drifting out any remaining rivets.

4 The glass now lifts out – not very thief-proof!

5 When you come to install the windows, make sure that the drain holes are at the bottom and the opening section at the front. This might be obvious, but it's not unknown for side windows to be incorrectly marked 'near-side' (LH) and 'off-side' (RH) by the manufacturer.

6 The correct way of sealing the window to the roof is by following current Land Rover practice and using butyl tape. It's also used extensively throughout the caravan and van body building industries and, while it doesn't have much in the way of bonding properties, it's excellent at preventing leaks, because it never sets.

7 You'll now need to hold the window temporarily in place, preferably with masking tape to stop it from falling on the floor and shattering all your dreams.

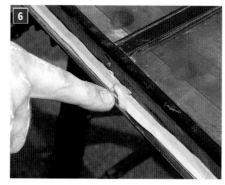

8 Drill four holes, one towards each corner, and push a pop-rivet into each hole as you go, but don't tighten them up. Alternatively, you could temporarily use small nuts and bolts of the same diameter as the pop-rivets. You should then drill all the remaining holes through the body panel on the vehicle using the window as a guide.

TIP! If you temporarily fit the sliding window and drill all the holes before applying the butyl tape you'll prevent swarf from adhering to the tape, which stops a proper seal and looks very unsightly.

9 The job will be a lot quicker if you use a pneumatic pop-rivet gun, such as this inexpensive Clarke unit. Make sure you've purchased the correct size of rivets – these were the 'inches' size of $^5/_{32}$ x ½.

10 You can now push each rivet through the butyl tape and fully into position. You must also ensure that the window is fully bedded home all the way round and pushed tight against the butyl tape.

11 Making certain that the window frame is held down tight by pushing against the inner side of the panel, you can now fit the pop-rivets all the way round.

12 The final step is to ease the rubber covering strip into the channel around the window frame, hiding the pop-rivets. As with the butyl tape, the joint should be at the bottom of the window so that any water will run out rather than in.

13 The sliding side window looking totally original – if a little less leak-prone.

LATER TYPES: REMOVAL AND DISMANTLING

Removing and refitting the later Defender's sliding side windows might not be rocket science, but it's different enough from working on the earlier versions to be a tricky task. Here's how Pentagon Auto-Tint, who have to remove the whole thing when fitting tinted or reinforced glass, go about it.

14 Pentagon's chief Tim Scannell started by removing the interior trim panels. The rear panels unclip first…

15 …followed, after removing the seat belt mountings, by the side panels.

16 Around the perimeter of the side windows there are a number of spacer blocks – typically six or eight of them – that have to be levered…

17 …from between the inner edge of the frame and the body panel, then put to one side for reuse later.

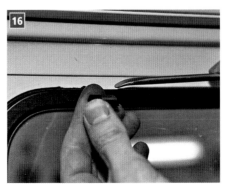

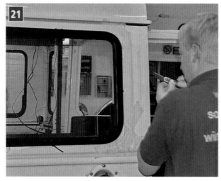

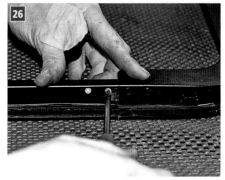

18 At this point, Tim and Co handed over to window specialists Southern Windscreens, whose boss Simon Clark ran a strip or two of protective masking tape all the way around the body, adjacent to the window frame.

19 This was to protect the paintwork from the knife that has to be used to cut into the bonding material around the frame, both on the outside…

20 …and on the inside, where Simon also sprayed screen lubricant to keep the knife moving smoothly through the sealant.

21 Simon transferred his attention from the outside of the Landie to the inside and back again several times, until the frame started to feel loose in the body panel…

22 …at which point more hands are needed to steady the glass and frame before they have a chance to fall out on to the floor.

23 Then it was simply a matter of lifting the frame away and taking it to the work bench.

24 Stray sealant will remain stuck to the bodywork, so Simon Clark returned to the scene of the crime in order to tidy up.

25 Meanwhile, back at the work bench, Tim and Przemo (pronounced 'Shemo') Gramza started to remove the screws holding the frame together. They're in the long top and bottom rails…

26 …in the sides, where the two halves of the frame slot together…

27 ...and in the vertical divider between the front and rear sections of glass.

28 With all the screws out, Tim separated the mortise-and-tenon-type joints at the two shorter, end sections.

29 Though some might prefer to do this lying down – the frame, not the fitter! – Tim lifted out the glass from the semi-dismantled frame.

30 By now, the frame from the other side of the vehicle had been removed and was being thoroughly cleaned to remove all traces of the old bonding material.

31 Similarly, Tim cleaned out the dirt and crud that invariably accumulates on the inside of a sliding window frame.
   The glass itself was now treated to the Pentagon glass reinforcement system, to prevent anyone from being able to smash their way in, while they were also given a medium tint.

LATER TYPES: REASSEMBLY AND REFITTING

32 The edging strip was refitted to the relevant glass, starting at the squared-off end...

33 ...and continuing all the way round, before it was offered up to...

34 ...and reassembled with the frame. Tim started with one end of the frame, popped a couple of screws loosely into position on the upright...

35 ...then held the other end of the frame just sufficiently open...

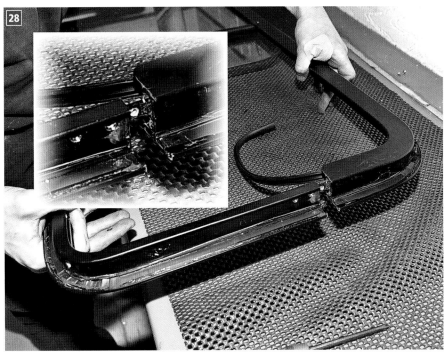

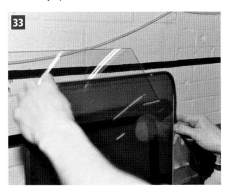

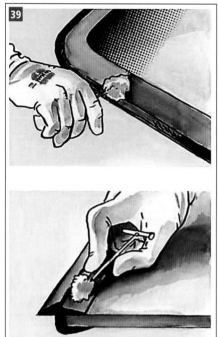

36 …to be able to insert the second section of glass into its runners.

37 With everything in place and an extra pair of hands to assist, Tim fitted the centre bar screws…

38 …then, when he was sure that all the glass was sliding as it should, he went round and fully tightened all of the frame fixing screws.

39 Southern Windscreens stepped back in again at this point and started by applying special primer to the frame and the body panel. This acts as an activator, to set off the sealant. Würth's advice is that, depending on which type of windscreen adhesive is being used, the fitter must bear in mind the drying times of primer (15 minutes) or activator for PU/PVC (at least 5 minutes), and mustn't apply adhesive too soon. This cures chemically throughout the adhesive bead and is independent of humidity and temperature, which gives a guaranteed drive-away time.

40 Apparently, some types of windscreen adhesive can cause long-term corrosion in aluminium.

Würth's Ultimate adhesive is suitable for use with aluminium, magnesium and hybrid bodies, is tested by the German TÜV for crash-strength safety, and meets the requirements of original equipment manufacturers.

41 The windscreen adhesive was applied from a gun in a heavy, even, unbroken bead, all the way around the frame.

42 The frame was lifted carefully into position…

43 …and offered up evenly so that there was no risk of pushing out excess sealant from one particular corner or edge.

44 The frame was then pushed in evenly from the outside while, inside the vehicle, the spacers that were levered out earlier were pushed and tapped back in. They have the job of holding the frame evenly in position until the sealant has gone off.

45 Inevitably, this had the effect of squeezing out the surplus bonding sealant. It had to be wiped off before it went off, because once it's set, it's set!

FIXED REAR GLASS

1 Tim then removed the spreader from the glass rubbers, which allowed the two side glasses to be pushed out.

2 Prezmo used a plastic tool to check that both spreader and rubber were properly seated to fit the finished rear side windows.

ALPINE GLASS

After both Lindsay and Ian Baughan had failed to refit the Alpine lights to Lindsay's Defender Station Wagon, they admitted defeat and called in Autoglass. It turned out that the new, replacement rubbers were incorrect, so the old ones had to go back in – but here's the correct way of fitting the darned things, anyway!

Taking out the Alpine glasses is a lot more straightforward than putting them back in again. You simply have to pull out the spreader by prising one end out and easing it round until it's all out of the channel, then ease the glass retaining rubber away from the body and glass. Mind you, it's easy to drop the glass while removing it, so be sure to have a second pair of hands on the inside of the vehicle while you're carrying out this work.

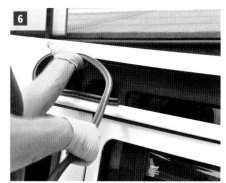

3 We thought we'd done the right thing by buying new rubbers and spreader strips. Theoretically they should be easier to fit, because the rubber is softer and more pliable. However...

4 ...it wasn't until the Autoglass fitter pointed out that the new, Britpart rubber (right) is slightly larger than the original that we realised why we just couldn't get the darned glasses to go in.

5 So, an 'OE' Land Rover rubber was fitted...

6 ...starting at the bottom and pushing it snugly into the curve at first one end...

7 ...and then the other. When fitting a new rubber bear in mind that it'll shrink in time, so cut it off about 25mm (1in) overlength, push the cut ends together and force the rubber back into itself, spreading the compression around the aperture.

8 After squirting on lots of lube (washing-up liquid in water is perfect) the next job is...

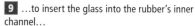 …to insert the glass into the rubber's inner channel…

10 …easing it carefully from both sides and using a plastic or thin wooden tool…

11 …to help encourage the rubber into place without either damaging the rubber or scratching the glass.

12 After squirting on more of the 'magic' lubricant, you can start inserting the spreader strip into the channel in the rubber.

13 This will be far easier to carry out if you use the correct spreader insertion tool. This particular example…

14 …has a loop to open the channel in the rubber (they all seem to have that) but also a convenient little nylon roller…

15 …that helps you to force the spreader strip into the channel as you go along. As you can see from the previous picture, it takes quite a bit of shoving and effort when going round corners…

16 …but that's nothing compared to the difficulty you'd have in inserting the spreader strip without using a special tool. It's not exactly impossible, but it's at least ten times more difficult without it. Going round the bend is the trickiest bit, and if you find that the spreader strip hasn't gone in don't just carry on and hope you can come back to it later – ease back the section that went wrong and do it again before proceeding.

17 That's not to say that very small areas of rubber won't get pushed down as the spreader strip goes in, and it's then permissible to go back with yet more lubricant and a very small screwdriver to ease the lips on the rubber back out again.

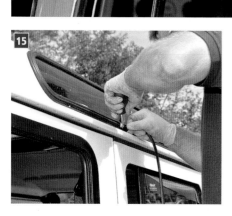

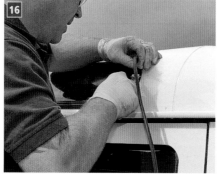

18 When cutting off the spreader strip to length, follow the same procedure described in picture 7, cutting the strip slightly overlength…

19 …then pushing both ends down together and easing the strip back into the rubber.

20 You'll always find there are a lot of marks left on the glass from hands, tools and rubbers, so finish off with another squirt of washing-up liquid lubricant, both inside and out…

21 …before having a careful clean and a wipe off, to leave both glass and rubber looking fresh and new.

We were assured that there was no need to use any kind of sealant additive and that the rubber would do its job of sealing properly, provided that both the body and the glass were thoroughly cleaned before starting work to remove any traces of dirt or old adhesive. If you're reusing a rubber, it must be even more carefully cleaned out, making sure there's nothing trapped in any of the channels.

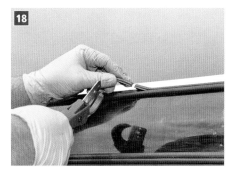

Truck cab removal

The cab is held to the cab mounting rail at the rear body with more nuts, bolts and washers. (If you want to replace any of the individual components of the cab, they also bolt together.)

The cab can now be lifted away; but note, when replacing it, that it's best to replace the sealing rubbers on the backrest panel capping and the front edge of the roof, because they go hard over time and will allow the elements in.

1 Remove the nuts, bolts and washers holding the cab to the windscreen and those fitting it to the rear panel. *(Illustration © Lindsay Porter)*

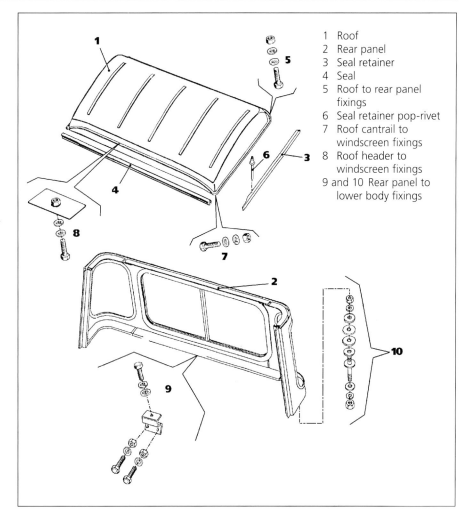

1 Roof
2 Rear panel
3 Seal retainer
4 Seal
5 Roof to rear panel fixings
6 Seal retainer pop-rivet
7 Roof cantrail to windscreen fixings
8 Roof header to windscreen fixings
9 and 10 Rear panel to lower body fixings

Hood and hood sticks

One of the many charms of the 90, 110 and Defender range is its strong connection with the earliest Land Rovers. The hood and hood stick arrangement (sometimes known as the tilt cover) is a very similar carry-over from the earlier models. Hood arrangements vary from model to model but are essentially as shown.

Before you attempt to fit a hood, make sure the cleats are in place on the rear side panels – they're sometimes missing, especially if panels have been replaced.

On all models, the hood sticks are held to the body and to each other with a series of clamps and clamp bolts. A combination of straps and draw strings is used to hold the hood taut and in shape.

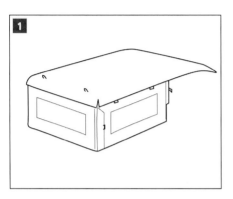

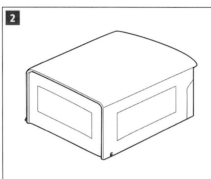

1 Note that there's one type of hood that's a full-length affair, covering the cab... *(Illustration courtesy PWB)*

2 ...while a different type fits the pickup-type body with a fully enclosed cab. *(Illustration courtesy PWB)*

Front floor removal

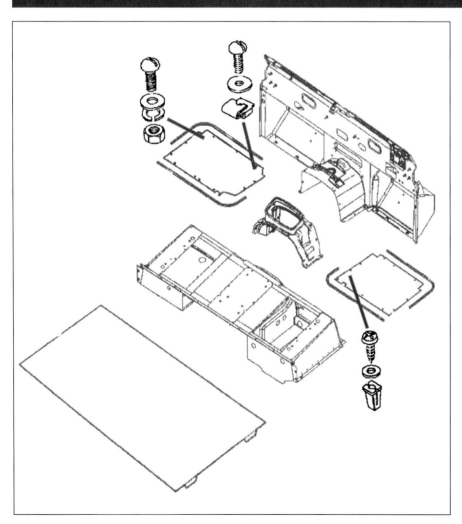

There are two separate sections of front floor, one on each side. When the vehicle is new, removal is straightforward, but after the passage of time corrosion can make things more difficult.

The screws with Phillips heads are self-tapping screws and are screwed into plastic inserts. Removal should be no problem, provided that the screw heads are properly cleaned out first. Other (machine) screws screw into spring clips, while a third type has a nut and spring washer beneath, where it's exposed to the elements. Soak liberally with releasing fluid before starting work, and be prepared, if necessary, to drill through the screw heads if totally seized or rounded off. *(Illustration © Lindsay Porter)*

Always refit (or replace) the seals around the perimeters of the floors before replacing them.

You can find further relevant information and illustrations in the section on body removal and chassis change.

Side and rear body replacement

Apart from disconnecting wiring and fuel tank filler connections, where applicable, the business of fitting new side and rear body panels is one of drilling out rivets and spot welds and replacing with pop-rivets. Be sure to remove the fuel tank or tanks before using power tools in the vicinity.

1 Use a sharp, new drill and drill the heads off all of the pop-rivets.

2 Treat all spot welds in the same way.

3 It'll take quite a while to separate the panels to be removed from their flanges. You'll also have to remove the remnants of pop-rivets and welds from flanges...

4 ...and true-up the surface of each flange with a hammer and a block of wood or other suitable dolly.

5 This is a PWB replacement rear panel for the 90 model – all versions are available.

6 It was used to repair this vehicle, after being carefully offered up into place, pop-rivet positions drilled and new pop-rivets fitted.

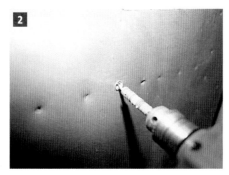

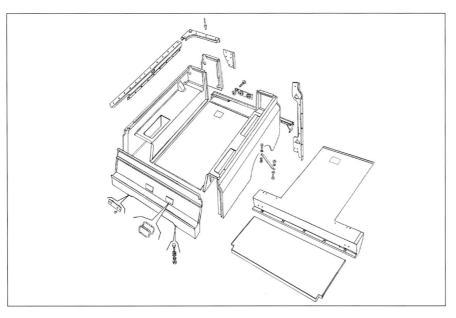

These are the rear body components. On the left of this illustration can be seen the type of body fitted to 90s and non-Station Wagon 110s, while on the right can be seen the floor arrangements for 110 Station Wagons, with the lower front section for the forward-facing rear seats.

Either the entire section can be unbolted from the chassis as a unit, or each individual part can be disconnected by means of its combination of screws, spot welds and rivets.

Defender 90 rear tub floor

This work was carried out by Ronnie Maughan Jr of YRM Metal Solutions Ltd, and the information was supplied by him. The pictures are also © YRM Metal Solutions Ltd. Parts used are:

Number required	YRM part no	Name
3	061	Underfloor support strut
3	087	Rear floor support top hat
1	091	Rear door threshold plate
1	092	Rear door rubber seal
1	103	Rear tub floor
1	116	Rear floor support

The 4.8mm diameter rivets (Aluminium/A2 Stainless with domed head) require 4.9mm holes to be drilled.

1 The spot welds have been located by using a wire brush and removing the paint, including those around the perimeter. If you aren't bothered about keeping the floor, they could be ground away using an angle grinder with an aluminium disc or, if you're keeping it, you could centre-punch the rivets and drill them out.

2 With the floor panel lifted away, you can better assess what needs replacing.

3 For example, this shows where the top hat section has corroded through – and wasn't even fixed down!

4 The top hat sections…

5 …and underfloor supports were removed by drilling out the rivets, as described earlier. To avoid drilling into the fuel tank, Ronnie used a bolster

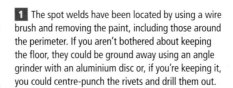
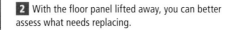

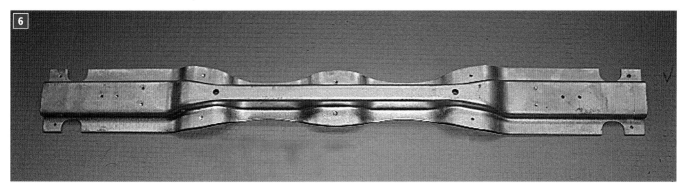

chisel to cut through the rivets in that area. The rear floor support can also be removed by drilling out its spot welds.

SAFETY: You are strongly advised to remove the fuel tank before starting work, and must ALWAYS do so on petrol models.

IMPORTANT: Before drilling, take plenty of measurements so that everything can be reassembled in their correct places.

6 This is one of the new underfloor supports.

7 The underfloor supports are shown having been placed in position loosely. They've had PVC tape put on their ends to act as a barrier between the mild steel underfloor support and the aluminium side-panels, to prevent corrosion (electrolytic reaction) from taking place.

8 Ronnie used a straight edge to line the holes up to make it easier for fitting the top hats.

9 Here, the top hats have been loosely put in place along with the rear floor support to be marked up for the rivets, ensuring that there's no clash with door threshold plate fixing or with previously drilled holes.

10 The rear floor support has now been pre-drilled and offered into place, ensuring it goes back in its correct position. When riveting back in place, ensure you don't use mild steel rivets, otherwise you'll get electrolytic reaction in future.

11 Ronnie positioned the centre top hat section in place, with the joggle to the rear. He marked where it contacted the underfloor supports...

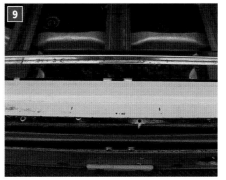

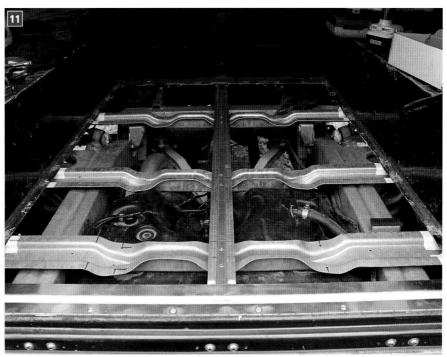

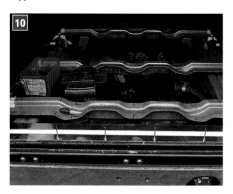

12 …and then marked up the other two top hat sections, not forgetting to apply PVC tape where contact is made with aluminium.

13 If you don't have a rear-mounted tank, you can match-drill from the underside. But if your tank is in the rear, put a piece of plate under the underfloor support to prevent the risk of drilling through the tank.

14 This view from underneath shows the top hat section having been match-drilled and riveted to the underfloor support.

15 Offer up the reused floor (or new one, as shown) and use a straight edge to help mark, drill and rivet in place. Insert two fixings to start off with then drill the rest. This will ensure positioning is correct and prevent the floor from moving, so the holes will line up correctly.

16 This is an alternative, chequer plate floor, fixed in place along with a new, rubber rear door seal and a YRM stainless steel rear door threshold.

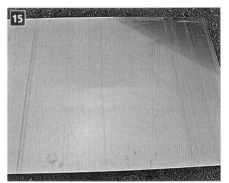

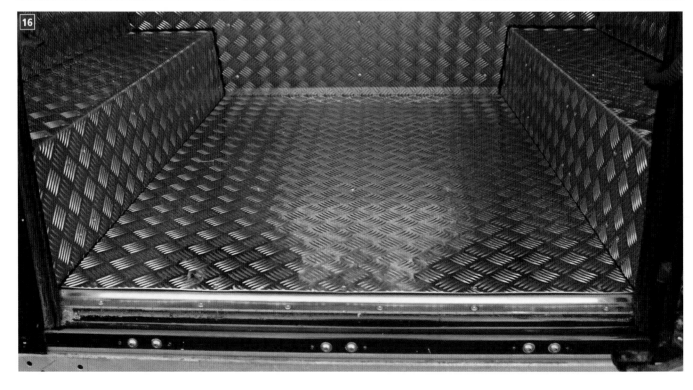

The work being shown here was carried out on a 'Series' Land Rover, but 90s, 110s and Defenders are remarkably similar. Britpart's Adrian Longstaff carried out the work.

1 The body tub is the bodywork section that's common to all conventional Land Rovers. It's the lower body section from the waist-rail down and from the doors back, and it's both sufficiently strong and versatile to allow the use of a pickup or enclosed rear body which is simply bolted on top of it. These are the rear body tub components for most models. Only parts that aren't obvious have been annotated:

a   rubber pad;
b   rope cleat (when fitted);
c   cover plate;
d   gasket;
e   nut plate and retaining rivets;
f   tailgate models;
g   mounting plate.

2 Here you can see the rear tub, having been unbolted from the chassis brackets, being lifted off over the back axle. Its almost all-aluminium construction makes it simple for two men to lift.

3 This is the Defender Station Wagon's rear tub.

4 Removing the rear threshold plate can be tricky! There are two layers of galvanised steel and one of rubber sealing strip. Unfortunately, the screws often can't be removed because of corrosion. You could try using the edge of the angle grinder blade to cut a screwdriver slot into each screw, allowing them to be removed.

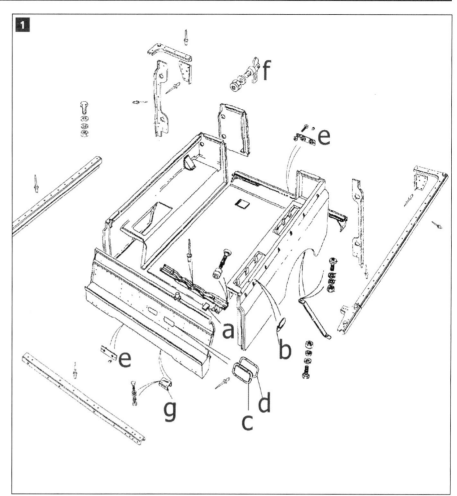

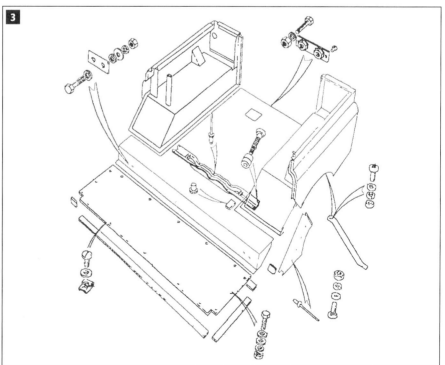

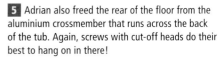

5 Adrian also freed the rear of the floor from the aluminium crossmember that runs across the back of the tub. Again, screws with cut-off heads do their best to hang on in there!

6 Adrian next turned the angle grinder on the fixings holding the strengthening crossmembers. All of these are currently available as repair panels, including for the special one used under the footwell on Station Wagons.

7 All of the shorter reinforcing members are common to all other rear tubs. Adrian used a strong lever to remove each one after grinding off the heads of all the fixings.

8 We decided to replace the rear floor, and Adrian used a 9in angle grinder to cut down the floor, just inboard of the seam with the wheel box. This would be highly dangerous for someone unskilled, because of the risk of the wheel jamming in the slot. A jigsaw or nibbler would be safer alternatives.

9 He did the same on the other side of the body tub...

10 ...and then cut across the rear end of the floor, just inboard of the aluminium crossmember.

11 The last fiddly cuts were made with a 4.5in angle grinder. Note that you'll need an aluminium cutting wheel in place of one made for steel. Steel cutting wheels will overheat and can explode when cutting aluminium.

12 Adrian next separated the old floor from the bodywork sides.

13 After drilling out the rivets...

14 ...he removed each of these two body panels, one on each side. They're only fitted to Station Wagons.

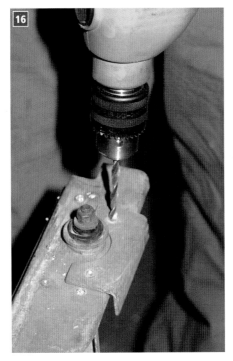

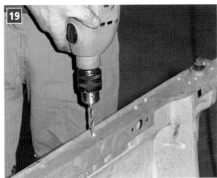

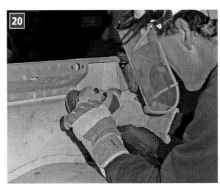

15 He also removed the remnants of the Station Wagon's steel door frame. There's usually a lot more of it than this, but it had rotted through at its front end at the point arrowed.

16 Adrian now turned his attention to the cappings that run around the perimeter of the body tub. First off were these reinforcing plates. He drilled through the rivet heads…

17 …punched out the rivets…

18 …and removed the plates.

19 The main cappings came in for similar treatment.

20 In some locations, traditional rivets were used with a round head on each side. These are extremely difficult to drill because of the dome, and Adrian carefully ground through one.

21 Again, this type of rivet has to be driven out with a punch.

22 Once the remaining pop-rivets are removed…

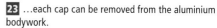
…each cap can be removed from the aluminium bodywork.

24 The rear section received similar treatment. It's a good idea to have access to the parts book or take more photographs so that you can see where everything will go.

25 Rivets removed, Adrian lifted off the rearmost capping.

26 Before any further dismantling could take place, Adrian found that the rubber seal for the rear door had to be taken off. This one was rotten and could be levered away, but you might need to drill out more of those rivets.

27 This reinforcing plate is held on with more of those domed rivets. It really is tricky to remove them without damaging the plate, bearing in mind that any damage will show through if you have them galvanised again.

28 After more drifting with the punch each of the plates can be lifted off.

29 Slightly more fiddly are the plates held with nuts and bolts on the inside of the body.

30 The lower sections are held with screws and the plates are slotted so that you can theoretically slide them out of the way without having to fully remove screws or bolts.

31 If you're reusing the wiring it'll pay to take care not to damage it as connectors are separated.

32 After removing each light unit, Adrian took out the rivets and removed the rear vertical capping – a different shape to this on Defenders.

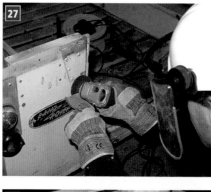

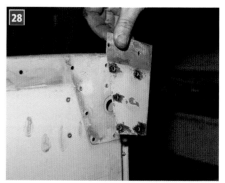

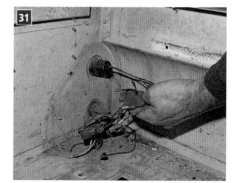

33 Earlier, we removed the rear floor in one piece. This left aluminium strips still fitted to the wheel boxes. After drilling through each of the rivets, the redundant strips of aluminium were removed.

34 Some surface corrosion had set in here and there, so the 4.5in angle grinder with a sanding disc was used to clean back to bright aluminium.

35 Immediately, the aluminium was primed with Würth zinc primer, which will bond to aluminium – not true of all body primer.

36 The heel board and toe board were both removed separately, but there were some steel plates on them that needed to be detached. From the inside of this toe board you can see the seat belt reinforcing section held in place with more domed-head rivets.

37 They were drilled out from the inside, where it doesn't matter so much if your drill slips off the dome. I started by drilling a pilot hole with a smaller drill and used Würth's Cutting & Drilling Oil to prevent the drill from overheating and losing its sharpness.

38 The two brackets, each of two separate pieces, were removed ready to be cleaned up and sent off for galvanising.

39 Now that the rear body tub was stripped, we checked it over carefully to decide what we would rebuild and what would be replaced with new. This is the inside of the seat box/wheel arch and shows one of the several strengthening ribs along the inner face. They're open at the top and sealed at the bottom, and you can see how these have filled up with mud over the years. Even aluminium will corrode given this much provocation, so it's a good idea to try to clean them out while you can.

40 This is a bit out of sequence, but it's when I did it. These steel reinforcing plates are a source of corrosion in the aluminium crossmember. Each one was removed after drilling out the rivets.

41 Adrian held up this new rear panel to help work out which welds and rivets needed to be removed and which ones were, in fact, part of the rear panel itself.

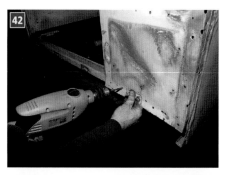

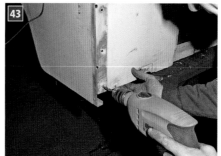

42 Adrian drilled out the welds holding the bottom of the rear panel to the crossmember referred to earlier.

43 He repeated the operation on the other side, and you can see that the remnants of the rivet holding the galvanised capping in place also had to be removed.

44 More welds hold the rear panel to the seat bases…

45 …on both sides of the vehicle.

46 Adrian found that these rivets held the sides of the seat base to the rear panel.

47 After drilling off their heads, he tapped out each one with a drift.

48 It was also necessary to drill more welds inside the channel into which the seal is fitted.

49 It can be quite tricky to determine just how deep to drill when removing a weld. Adrian used this old wood chisel to put a small amount of pressure on the seam as he was drilling it, so that it would ease itself apart as the drill cut through one half of the welded pair.

50 The same 'Pound Shop' wood chisel was used for easing apart the remnants of the welds where necessary. This is a tool I particularly recommend when working on this type of bodywork, especially when constructed of aluminium.

51 It seemed at times that the number of rivets and welds was endless, and Adrian found another rich seam deposited in the corner where the rear outer wing was held on.

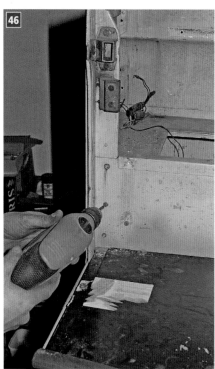

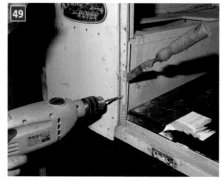

52 After drilling through each of the rivets…

53 …he repeated the trick with the punch, drifting out the remnants of each rivet.

54 Then, out came the chisel again…

55 …and with some careful levering, the welded joint was broken.

56 Next came the realisation that there were yet more pesky welds partway up from the base of the rear panel.

57 Then there was the strut strengthening the rear corner between the crossmember and the outer wing.

58 This needed both grinding and levering before the crossmember, strut and rear panel could start to come free.

59 With more work from the wood chisel…

60 …the rear panel on the right-hand side was lifted free.

61 The left-hand panel proved to be a little more awkward to shift.

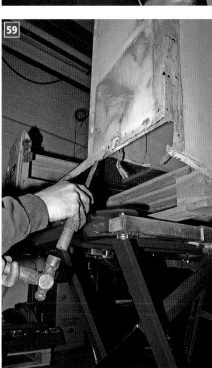

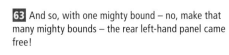

62 Adrian discovered these semi-concealed rivets were accessible through a friendly hole in the floor of the storage area inside the left-hand seat box.

63 And so, with one mighty bound – no, make that many mighty bounds – the rear left-hand panel came free!

64 Adrian found yet more rivets securing the crossmember to this self-same floor section. No room for a drill, so he ground off the heads with the angle grinder.

65 Here you can see the locations of the rivets on this particular vehicle, but, these being Land Rovers, they could vary from vehicle to vehicle.

66 More welds held the crossmember in place but Adrian discovered them all and drilled them out…

67 …before removing the crossmember.

68 Now, with the rear crossmember removed, each side panel could be taken away as a completely separate entity.

69 I noted that the reinforcing straps located between the rear panel and the wing were looking pretty ratty.

70 Before we disposed of anything, I carefully made a cardboard template so that replacements could be fabricated later.

RECONSTRUCTION

71 The first job was to construct an assembly table on which the new rear floor and both side panels could be placed. Adrian clamped the panels together where he could and used wire tourniquets to hold the tops of the side panels roughly in position.

72 Confirming that the floor was in the correct position relative to each side panel was crucial, so Adrian offered up one of the newly galvanised side frames.

73 This was fitted to the embryonic body tub along with this Station Wagon body panel, just to make sure that everything was in the correct place. The side frame and body panel were then removed again.

74 Adrian drilled the first tentative holes in the edge of the floor and through the flange on the left-hand side panel.

75 Before he could drill the other side, he found it necessary to add an extra timber support so that the flange and floor were tight against each other.

76 On the right-hand side of the tub, Adrian drilled another two or three holes.

77 The wires and clamps were then removed and each side panel carefully lifted away.

78 Adrian then used a Screwfix flap wheel to remove all the paint from the underside of the floor where it would touch the body panel flange. The bare aluminium was then treated with more Würth metal primer.

79 The side panel flanges had already been treated with etch primer, so Adrian put a bead of Würth Bond & Seal on to the seat box flange…

80 …then lifted each of the seat boxes back into position against the floor.

81 He next used a small number of bolts and nuts to hold the floor to the side panels in the correct location, then...

82 …tightened them all temporarily.

83 This large Würth pop-rivet gun was a godsend when it came to using some of the large rivets necessary for riveting the floors to the side panels all the way along the flange. This is just how it was built originally, except that we added Würth Bond & Seal to strengthen each joint and prevent water ingress.

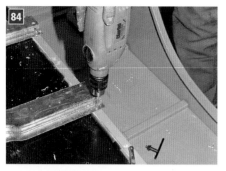

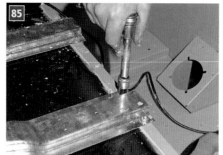

84 Strengthening ribs run across the floor and beneath it. We had had ours galvanised – they do tend to rot out quite rapidly – and Adrian now established their correct locations and drilled through the ribs, side panel flanges and floor.

85 This enabled him to bolt right through, adding extra strength.

86 To fit the longer strengthening rib at the front of the tub on the Station Wagon only, Adrian tipped the tub up on its end so that he could get at the bolts more easily. This larger Series 3 rib was not then available, so I had one fabricated.

87 Where these galvanised ribs cross the smaller aluminium ribs pre-welded to the base of the floor, they have to be drilled and riveted in place. We didn't want the end of the drill to mark the floor, so Adrian used a pre-drilled block of wood to act as a depth stop.

88 After adding Würth Bond & Seal to each joint, Adrian pop-riveted the ribs together.

89 This aluminium crossmember was in perfect condition and had been previously cleaned up and painted ready for fitting to the rear of the tub. In fact, we left it off at this stage, to be fitted later on when the tub was on the chassis.

90 It was now time to lift the rear tub on to the chassis.

91 There's quite a bit of latitude in locating the tub on the chassis and it was necessary to fit that side-frame again and clamp the front end of the tub to the C-post. You'd fit it to the B-post on three-door Land Rovers, of course.

92 The bracket on the side frame sits flat on the floor, so Adrian drilled through the aluminium and bolted it in place.

This stage marks the end of quite a significant phase in putting together a fully rebuilt Land Rover. It's as if you rebuild them in two halves, front and rear. The trick seems to be to make them fit back together again!

TD5 90 fuel tank carrier

The most common failings are lock-nuts that seize, and shearing bolts as the tank undertray is removed. With the tank out of the way, use an angle grinder to remove all traces of the old lock-nut, bolt on a plain nut as shown and weld the nut on to the fuel-tank carrier.

Bulkhead footwell repair

The *only* way to do this job properly is by cutting out all the corroded steel first. Having to make your own repair section for this area would be tricky for all but the very skilled. But it can be economical to start with a ready-made repair panel and cut away the part you need.

1 This hole in the lower end of the bulkhead is where the bracket used to be to which the inner wing is attached. To work out the full extent of the corrosion in this area, mechanic Dave used the angle grinder. Where no pitting or other form of corrosion is found underneath the paint and underseal, that's where you stop cutting the old metal away.

2 If possible, cut around any fixtures and fittings on the bulkhead, but if there's any corrosion there they'll just have to be removed first. Note that the bulkhead in this area is a double skin. Where pieces of metal touch each other, corrosion is far more likely to set in.

3 We started by cutting a replacement from a suitably thick piece of steel. The positions for the folds were carefully marked…

4 …and the angle required was measured with a protractor.

5 Here you can see how a folding machine makes light work of producing a perfectly folded repair section.

6 The repair panel was double-checked against the bulkhead footwell area…

7 …then tack-welded the repair in position.

8 We used the bracket that still remained in place on the passenger side of the vehicle to create a cardboard copy that could be folded to make a card replica of the original. A multi-angled bracket like this is trickier to fabricate than it looks! The card was then used to transfer the shape to a flat piece of steel. Note the 'tick-marks' at the top and bottom of each fold line. They were put there when the card

was in position on the steel so that the fold lines could then be transferred on to the steel after the card had been taken away, allowing the folds to be made accurately after the steel was cut out.

9 After making the bracket, We located its position precisely on the repair panel…

10 …before welding it into position.

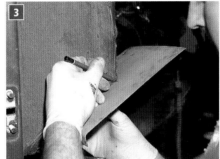

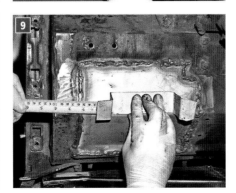

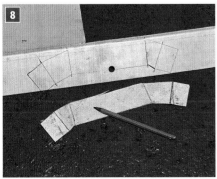

Bulkhead upper repair

In practice, rust in this area is often more extensive than that shown here. Remember that in this case, even this degree of corrosion couldn't be seen until we started probing...

1 Bubbles of corrosion could be seen around the top door hinge mountings on the bulkhead. To do this job properly you need to remove the front wing, because corrosion often spreads into the area behind it, and some of the welding will have to be carried out adjacent to the wing top anyway. The door hinge also has to be removed. In theory, you simply take out the two screws holding each hinge to the captive nut plates in the bulkhead. In practice, and especially if the bulkhead is so rusty as to need repair, the bolts will almost certainly be rusted solidly in place.

2 You could drill the heads off the bolts, but a quicker solution where hinges themselves are going to be replaced is to follow mechanic Stuart's lead

and cut into the hinge, right through the shank of the bolt. This Defender's door hinges had worn and were in need of replacement in any case. New hinges are relatively inexpensive; so much so that no one bothers repairing worn hinges – they're just replaced with new when worn.

3 This should have been done first, but all three of us forgot. The door stay had to be disconnected, but with the hinges free Dave had to support the door while Stuart removed the split pin and clevis pin holding the door stay in place.

4 Whenever repairing a panel, you always have to investigate the full extent of the damage first. Dave used a wire wheel on the angle grinder to remove all traces of old paint and filler from previously carried out 'repairs'.

5 This is the full repair panel for this area. As is usually the case, not all of the panel was required,

and we spent some time comparing the new metal with the old and working out what had to be cut away.

6 A square and straight edge were used when marking out the areas to be cut. It's very difficult to cut precisely to these markings when using an angle grinder, but doing it this way is far better than just hacking off a chunk and hoping for the best.

7 You can buy really thin cutting discs specifically for this sort of job and you can cut just inside each of the marks using one of these discs.

8 Some of the steel to be removed had been spot-welded in place. We lifted the area around each spot weld so that it could clearly be identified...

9 ...then used the angle grinder again to remove the plug of steel at each spot-weld position.

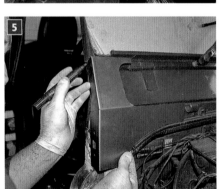

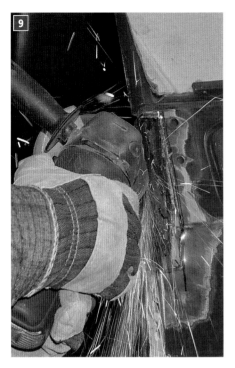

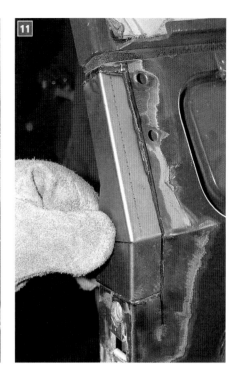

10 A corresponding repair section was then cut out of the repair panel, again using the thin-bladed cutting disc.

11 It's best to cut it slightly oversize and then to trim it down bit by bit until it makes exactly the fit you're looking for. You don't want an overlap here because the extra thickness of steel will be impossible to 'lose' completely with body filler.

12 Mechanic Dave started by tack-welding the repair panel in place.

13 Once he was satisfied that the panel fitted perfectly, he then went around it again, this time making stronger, more extensive welds.

IMPORTANT: Even though MIG welders don't create nearly as much heat (or panel distortion) as oxy-acetylene welders, the heat they create is still enough to damage adjacent trim or to crack glass if you're welding near it. It will also distort steel quite extensively. We used a water-soaked rag between the trim and the panel to prevent heat transferring into the plastic trim. If you do this, you need to stop and re-soak the rag every couple of minutes. The last thing you want is for it to dry out and catch fire. Wear gloves – don't get scalded!

In this instance, a third hand was needed to hold the wet rag in place, keeping the heat from the welder away from the vent flap and windscreen rubbers. Also note the bolts that have been loosely screwed into the captive nuts. In this instance Dave could always have removed them from the vehicle, but it's a good point in principle. You should always keep internal threaded holes plugged with a suitable bolt to prevent weld spatter from contaminating the threads.

14 Dave used the angle grinder to take off the highest areas of weld. The windscreen and mirror glasses MUST be covered so that hot sparks cannot land on them. These will be impossible to remove because they melt themselves into the glass.

15 Now, this is a cracking tool, and well worth recommending! From Screwfix Direct I purchased a few Flexidiscs. These are great for removing smaller amounts of excess weld but are far less harsh than a conventional angle grinder disc and leave a soft, smooth finish ready for filling and painting.

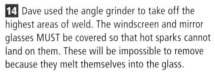

BULKHEAD REMOVAL

Lindsay's 2006-built Defender started life as a left-hand drive. Converting it 'properly' to RHD required a new bulkhead; and since replacing the bulkhead is most of the job, here's what's involved in replacing any rusty Defender's bulkhead, apart from the added frustration of rusty bolts.

WHAT'S IN A NAME?

If you look in the Land Rover parts catalogue for a bulkhead, you won't find one. That's because, while everyone else calls it the bulkhead, Land Rover still calls it the 'Dash Assembly'.

So, you might well ask, what do they call the dashboard? How does 'fascia' sound to you?

1 Once in the workshop, Nene Overland's impressive workshop foreman Michael Wright took off the bonnet then set about removing the doors, on the principle that you might as well improve access right from the start. If you're also stripping the door, the only tricky bit for novices will be the winder handles, which are held on with the spring clips that have to be hooked out from behind.

2 On all later models, hinge screws have TORX heads.

3 The bonnet and doors were stored leaning against a wall, protected by sheets of cardboard.

4 Michael removed the indicator shroud and the instrument panel.

5 The battery had already been removed and he next unscrewed and detached the stalk assembly.

6 Bearing in mind that this was a left-hand drive vehicle, the heater control and covering trim were detached from the fascia.

7 Meanwhile, inside the engine bay, Kurt was starting to make disconnections. Modern Land Rovers have electrical plugs and sockets that are detached by pressing on the relevant tabs and pulling on the connections – but not on the wires, obviously!

8 Mechanic Kurt also turned his attention to starting to detach the front wings.

The next job is to remove the dash panel – see 'Dash panel removal and refit' in Chapter 8.

9 Kurt next removed the grille and front panel. He'd disconnected all the wing wiring and connections and Michael was needed to help him lift away the remaining wing.

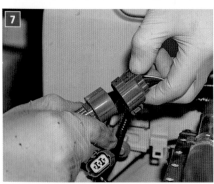
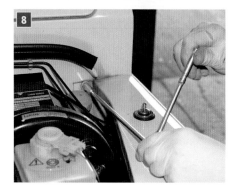
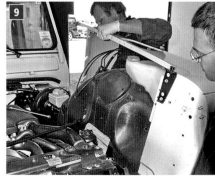

10 With engine bay access now immeasurably improved, the top steering joint was disconnected...

11 ...followed by the connection to the steering box.

12 With bulkhead mounting bolts removed, the steering column was taken away from the vehicle for reuse later.

13 Michael removed the transmission tunnel and the floors.

14 The base of the bulkhead is attached to the chassis with these two brackets, one on each side.

15 When you unbolt and remove the main bulkhead to outrigger mounting bolts, take careful note of where any packing washers are situated. With the new bulkhead on the horizon, you may not need them in exactly the same locations, but they will give you a good starting point when it comes to realigning the body.

16 To avoid having to remove the hardtop and front screen, Michael had a cunning plan! He removed the two bolts (found behind trim on the Station Wagon) holding the B-post to the roof.

17 This allowed him to ease the front of the roof and the windscreen surround upwards sufficiently to clear the locating pegs fitted to the top of the bulkhead.

18 With everything clear, the bulkhead was tipped back...

19 ...and away it went!

While all this was going on, the new Bearmach bulkhead was away at Nene Overland's spray shop being painted. Obviously, it would be ridiculous to paint it *in situ*, but the dilemma I faced was whether or not to inject it with rust-proofing fluid before fitting it. I decided against, on the basis that (1) it would make fitting-up an extremely messy business, and (2) because, should any holes need to be drilled or filed out, rust-proofer applied later would have more effect. (Also, swarf would stick to rustproofed surfaces.)

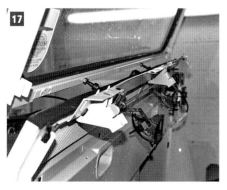

BULKHEAD REPLACEMENT

20 We needed a huge pile of parts from Bearmach because of that conversion from left-hand drive to right-hand drive. Most owners changing the bulkhead will reuse the great majority of parts from their old bulkhead.

21 Nene Overland's Michael knew from experience that these plastic 'lock-nuts' would be easier to fit before the bulkhead went on the vehicle.

22 Having seen earlier how the old bulkhead was removed while leaving the windscreen in place, here a three-man team reversed the process...

23 ...and positioned the new bulkhead in its correct location.

24 Do you remember those two long bolts, one holding each outer edge of the bulkhead to the outriggers?

25 But did you also remember the spacer washers? You can try reusing the old ones, but you might need more or fewer if the new bulkhead's alignment needs to be changed.

26 On this later Defender there's a fixed bracket, a leftover from where the windscreen hinge used to go on the earliest vehicles.

27 Michael pulled the windscreen down against the rubbers and aligned it correctly while Kurt tightened the fixings.

28 Note the packing piece behind the lower two bolts and the strap linking all three.

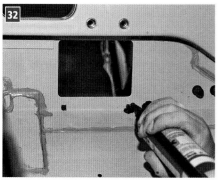

29 In addition to the locating spikes on the base of the windscreen…

30 …the bulkhead is also attached with this pair of brackets, one on each side of the chassis rails.

31 Michael prepared for fitting the steering by inserting two rivnuts into the holes provided. They appear to be a special size and only available as Land Rover parts.

32 More rivnuts on the other side, and Michael added Würth Bond & Seal to the long lines of joint sealer I'd already applied to the bare bulkhead.

33 On the inside, this self-adhesive strip was fitted to form a seal when the inner panels were in place.

34 On went the push-on spire nuts and the plastic inserts for the screws, and down went the floor panels.

35 Michael offered up the throttle pedal assembly, pushed the bolts through the bulkhead...

36 ...and added nuts and washers from the outside.

37 The steering column was offered up next. You can see that the seals for brake and clutch boxes have already been fitted.

38 Screwing into captive nuts and the rivnuts he fitted earlier, Michael fitted then tightened the retaining bolts.

39 On went the clutch pedal box, while feeding the pedal through the hole in the bulkhead...

40 ...followed by the brake pedal box and servo assembly...

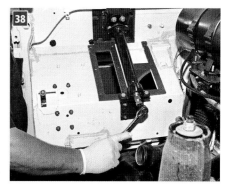

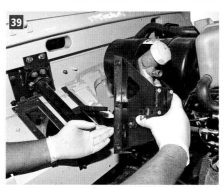

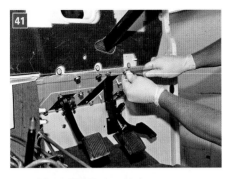

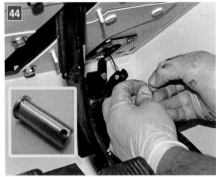

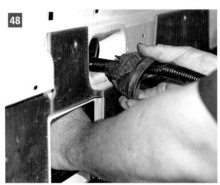

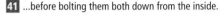

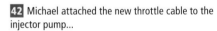

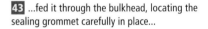

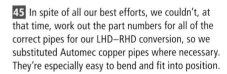

41 ...before bolting them both down from the inside.

42 Michael attached the new throttle cable to the injector pump...

43 ...fed it through the bulkhead, locating the sealing grommet carefully in place...

44 ...then fitted the looped end to the clevis pin (inset) on the throttle pedal, in turn holding that in place with a new split pin.

45 In spite of all our best efforts, we couldn't, at that time, work out the part numbers for all of the correct pipes for our LHD–RHD conversion, so we substituted Automec copper pipes where necessary. They're especially easy to bend and fit into position.

46 Michael must have taken half an hour disentangling the wiring loom and working out which bits would go where before attempting to fit it to the bulkhead. Even for someone as experienced as he is, it was time well spent. Getting the loom and its ready-fitted grommets into position takes a lot of pushing...

47 ...and pulling.

48 But it mustn't be forced. Indeed, you might want to make sure all parts of the loom are lying in their correct positions before fitting any of the grommets.

49 'What's this little devil for?' Michael wondered, before realising it needed to be fed into the A-post for the interior light switch.

50 Michael fitted the self-adhesive seal to the hole where the heater box would go...

51 ...and then offered up the complete heater-blower box assembly.

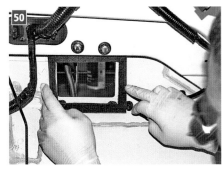

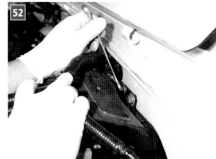

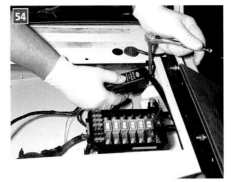

52 He loosely bolted the top of the heater box into position...

53 ...added the bolts that are fitted from the inside then carefully tightened the unit so that it sealed evenly against the bulkhead.

54 Some jobs don't necessarily have to be done in any particular order, and here's a case in point. The LHD–RHD conversion meant that the glow plug timer had to be fitted in a new location inside the seat box, so over it went.

55 Back to the bulkhead on the vehicle, you can see the wiring loom has been draped in position. Michael fitted the fuse box support from the old bulkhead.

56 Our transmission tunnel had NoiseKiller soundproofing on it by now.

57 The wiper box was fitted.

58 The usual seal and fixing bolt were replaced on the outside.

59 The wiper motor, once fitted, was plugged into the loom.

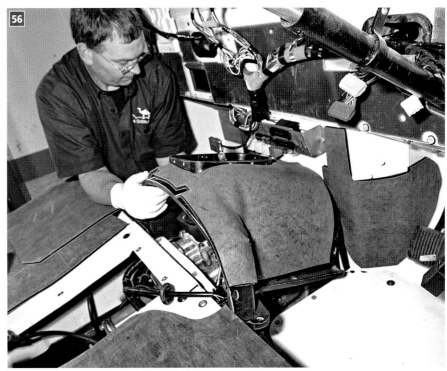

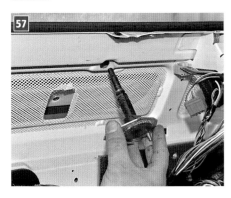

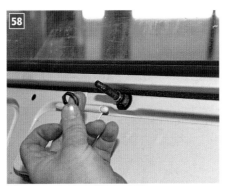

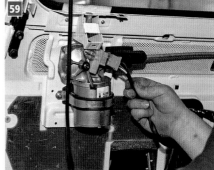

60 Meanwhile, on the outside of the vehicle, Kurt was carrying out some of his own reassembly.

61 This might look a bit veterinary but some of those more awkward-to-get-out wing bolts are easier to reach with the intake vent missing.

62 Kurt went to a lot of trouble to ensure that the wing shape matched that of the A-pillar before tightening the bolts.

63 Wiring for lighting is a doddle to reconnect when all you have to do is match the correct plugs and sockets. Refitting the fascia is shown in 'Dash panel removal and refit' in Chapter 8.

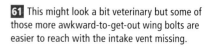
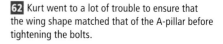

64 Confident that nothing will have to go over it later, Michael screwed the knob on to the blower adjustment lever using the tiny grub screw that has to be carefully inserted into the side of the knob.

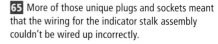
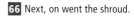
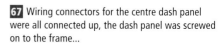

65 More of those unique plugs and sockets meant that the wiring for the indicator stalk assembly couldn't be wired up incorrectly.

66 Next, on went the shroud.

67 Wiring connectors for the centre dash panel were all connected up, the dash panel was screwed on to the frame...

68 ...with three screws in the positions shown here (plus two more visible ones at the bottom of the dash panel), and Michael then fitted the top rail...

69 ...and screwed it into place.

70 End caps went on next...

71 ...and some of the visible screws were covered with embossed trim.

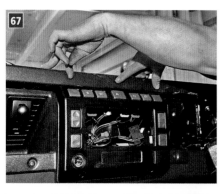

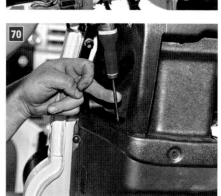

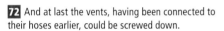

72 And at last the vents, having been connected to their hoses earlier, could be screwed down.

73 Back in the outside world, the other front wing was fitted, and you can see that I had wing-top protectors added while the wings were off.

74 Meanwhile, Michael's twin was still working on the inside of the vehicle, fitting the gearchange gaiter...

75 ...then bolting down the gearchange itself.

76 There's also a good deal of other wiring on vehicles that have been modified, and you might as well tidy it up by using existing grommets wherever possible.

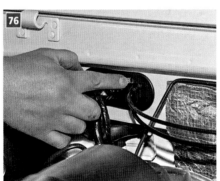

77 With the fuse box in place, in went the correct fuses.

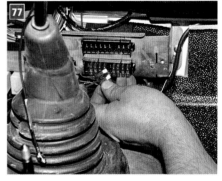

78 On went the main instrument panel, final connections were made and the steering wheel fitted.

79 With that, the final stage in replacing the bulkhead was complete and Michael professed himself well pleased.

Just to reiterate, this bulkhead was changed because of converting from RHD to LHD, but in essence the work described here will be much the same even if yours was a well-corroded bulkhead.

Under-seat tool and battery box replacement

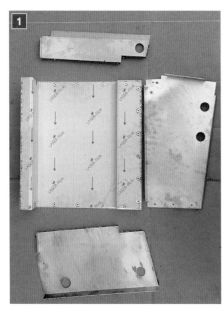

YRM's Defender under-seat boxes are made from 2mm thick aluminium and are CNC pressed and laser-cut for accuracy.

1 The battery box is supplied in four pieces for ease of fitting, pre-drilled to aid fitting and supplied with 50 aluminium/stainless steel rivets. It's 25mm deeper than standard, so at the shallow end of the battery box it measures 230mm deep. The flat base measures 480 x 312mm.

The rivets are 4.8mm diameter and require 4.9mm holes to be drilled.

The usual rot spot on a Defender's seat box is at the end panel. They can be purchased separately if required and installed while the seat box is still in place.

2 The spot-welds for the end plate have been drilled out and these holes can later be used to rivet the new toolbox in place.

3 Now the seat box has been removed, after removing the sill rail.

4 YRM advise to construct each box before fitting them to the original frame.

5 This is a fully constructed seat box clamped into position prior to riveting.

6 Clamp the seat box and end panel in position and match-drill where the spot welds were drilled out for the new rivets. Apply PVC tape where dissimilar metals touch, to prevent electrolytic reaction.

NOTE: On early models a little trimming will be required in the area of the handbrake mechanism, unless you opt for YRM's smaller seat box.

7 After riveting the seat box and seat-box end in place, the sill rail has to be refitted. The end plate needs to be match-drilled to suit the seat-box end, so that it can be bolted to the sill rail.

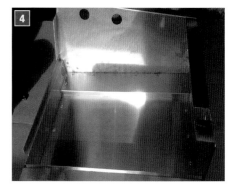

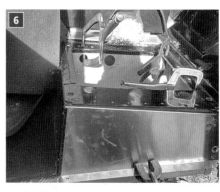

B-post lower repair

The lower B-posts on 90, 110 and 130 hardtops and pickups often corrode. YRM's repair sections are made from 2mm thick aluminium. The aluminium/A2 stainless steel, domed head, 4.8mm rivets required are also available from YRM. You'll need some in the 1.6–6.2mm grip range and some in the longer 4.8–11mm grip range.

This work was carried out and the information supplied by Ronnie Maughan Jr of YRM Metal Solutions Ltd. The pictures are also © YRM Metal Solutions Ltd.

1 This rear tub (separated from a vehicle) shows rear tub corrosion caused by the electrolytic reaction between the two different metals in the B-post and seat-belt mounting bracket areas.

2 You'll need to drill out spot welds well above the top of where the repair section is going to finish, in order to be able to cut the outer skin. Here, the spot welds have been drilled and the two skins on the B-post have been separated using a chisel.

3 The outer skin was then cut to remove the redundant metal. It was straightened out using a metal block and hammer, and you can then measure

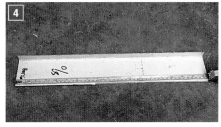

the length of repair section you'll need for your particular repair.

4 The YRM repair section happens to be 470mm long, and here one has been measured and marked and is ready to cut to length. It's made from 2mm thick aluminium and is CNC cut and bent for accuracy.

5 You'll need to clamp the repair section in place, then, using the spot-weld holes you earlier drilled out, you can either match-drill to those holes or mark and drill again using a 4.9mm drill.

6 This is the repair section drilled and ready to fit…

7 …and here it is fitted, using the Aluminium/A2 Stainless, domed-head rivets supplied by YRM.

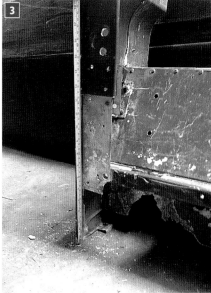

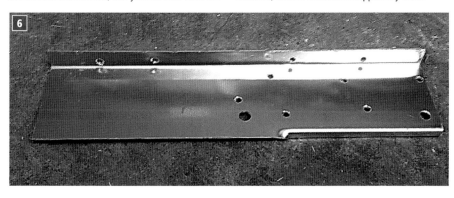

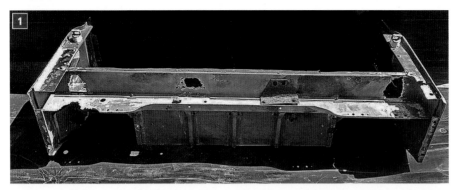

This work was carried out and the information supplied by Ronnie Maughan Jr of YRM Metal Solutions Ltd. The pictures are again © YRM Metal Solutions Ltd.

Parts used are:

Number required	YRM part number	Name
1	122	Defender 90 Seat Box/ Bulkhead Repair Panel
1	175	Defender Galvanised Front Seat Belt Mount Bracket

The 4.8mm diameter rivets (Aluminium/A2 Stainless with domed head) require 4.9mm holes to be drilled.

1 This, for demonstration purposes, is a cut-off section of rear tub lying on its back with the door shut (B-posts) facing upwards. The corrosion is – unfortunately – typical!

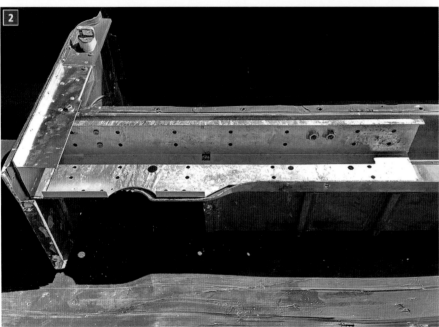

2 Here, the Front Seat Belt Mount Bracket (part 175) has been offered in place. Remember that you're viewing from what's normally beneath the vehicle. When the positioning is spot on, it must be clamped in place…

3 …before match-drilling (from the other side), ensuring you're drilling only into un-corroded metal. The repair panel can now be bolted (arrowed) in place against the upstand section. You only need to hand-tighten the bolts, to check for hole alignment, as you'll need to remove the panel again in order to fit YRM product ref 122.
IMPORTANT: Before going any further, cut away all corroded metal before treating the remainder with suitable primer. Any metal left bare will rapidly cause yet more corrosion.

4 Viewed now from above, this is the YRM Seat Box/ Bulkhead Repair Panel (part 122), having been cut in half because it isn't possible to fit it in one piece. It must be marked to be drilled with reference to the Front Seat Belt Mount Bracket's stainless steel studs for the seat-belt inertia reel and the bolts attached to it.

5 Here, the Seat Box/Bulkhead Repair Panel has been clamped and riveted (arrowed) in place.

6 Next, YRM 175 has been refitted and bolted up again…

7 … ready to match-drill along the top of the repair.

8 Viewed from beneath, this is the finished repair.

9 And here again, viewed from above and ready to repeat the process for the other side…

10 …after which, on an actual vehicle, the repairs would be sealed off with seam sealer to prevent water ingress.

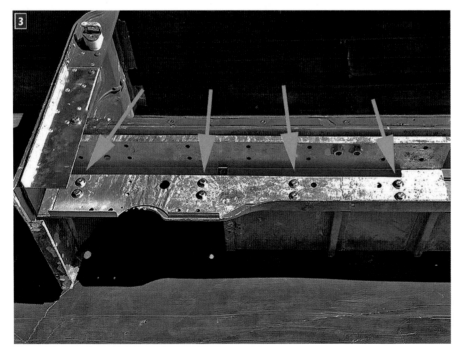

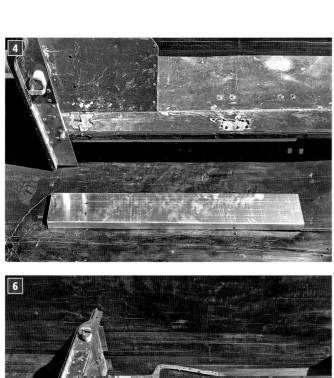

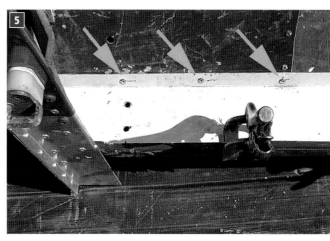

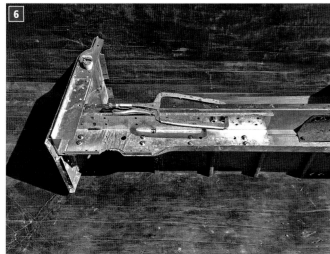

This work was carried out by Specialist 4x4 and the information was supplied by Ronnie Maughan Jr of YRM Metal Solutions Ltd. The pictures are again © YRM Metal Solutions Ltd.

Parts used are:

Number required	YRM part number	Name
1	108	Floor End Caps (next to C post)
1	114B	2nd Row Footwell to Rear Floor Upstand
1	117A	Underfloor Support (Aluminium)
1	1292	2nd Row Floor

The 4.8mm diameter rivets (Aluminium/A2 Stainless with domed heads) require 4.9mm holes to be drilled.

1 To remove the rear floor, mark a line between the front of the two rear wheel arches and cut along the line with a jigsaw. These pictures…

2 …show the second row floor and upstand already removed.

3 If you wish to replace the full rear floor, you'll require the panel YRM 114B, shown here, which is shorter than the standard floor, allowing you to fit the upstand.

4 The underfloor support has been cut away…

5 …so that when it's in position it'll fit around the rear underfloor ribs. The underfloor support panel can be seen, waiting its turn, on the right of the picture.

6 You can now clamp the underfloor support in place…

7 …ensuring that, on both sides, the holes on the underfloor support align with those on the angled C-post. Then drill and rivet between the wheel arches to hold underfloor support in place. Apply PVC tape between dissimilar metals to prevent electrolytic corrosion.

8 This is the new second-row floor, correctly braced on the underside.

9 The floor fits simply into place, only requiring drilling and riveting. In addition, the floor end caps are fitted…

10 …along the top of the upstand and underneath the angled C-post angle, and will need to be match-drilled and riveted.

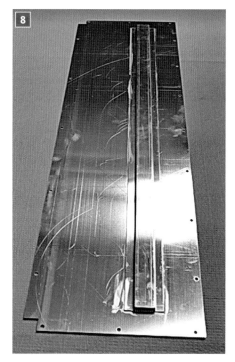

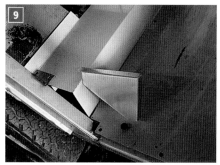

Chassis repairs

There's an almost infinite number of ways in which a Defender chassis can rust over time. This section covers some of the most usual ones. But the common denominators in carrying out chassis repairs are:

■ Only carry out the work if your welding is good enough. If not, leave it to the experts. The chassis is the most important part of a Defender's structure.
■ There will always be more rust present than you expect before you start cutting rust away. And if it's rusted, you must replace it. You can't weld to rust!
■ Dimensional accuracy is vital. You can often use the body to establish precisely where replacement parts must be fitted, but you'll need to measure, check and check again before final welding.

OUTRIGGER REPLACEMENT
It's perfectly OK to replace an outrigger with everything in place, provided you make sure the job is done thoroughly and that you follow the right approach.

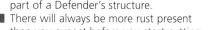

1 You can use either a Land Rover original outrigger or an aftermarket-pattern replacement part, though some of these are very poorly made and should be avoided. However, if the area of the chassis surrounding the outrigger is also corroded (it usually is), you'd probably be better off using a good quality aftermarket outrigger, one with a large plate on its inner end to enable you to fix it more easily to the chassis. In this case we chose a Land Rover part, because only the outrigger itself was corroded and not the chassis.

2 Mechanic Dave started by undoing the bolt holding the outrigger to the body and hammering the bolt out of its sleeve with a drift.

3 As you can imagine, this is often difficult to remove and there's frequently more rust than can be seen on our bolt. It pays to soak the bolt in releasing fluid a couple of days before starting the job.

4 Dave also removed this body-mounting bracket from the chassis, just ahead of the outrigger.

5 Even the Land Rover outrigger contained a little more metal than we needed, so this top section was cut away with the angle grinder.

6 This is where you need to get methodical! Dave used the large angle grinder to make a vertical cut at the front of the outrigger inner end…

7 …and then another at the outer end.

8 He then transferred to the smaller angle grinder to cut along the bottom…

9 …and the top, until the section shown here was removed.

10 The idea was to provide access to the back end of the outrigger, reaching in from the front. You'll see in a moment why you can't get at it from the back.

11 We almost forgot – OK we did initially forget! – the two washers, one on each side of the outrigger mounting, which came free from all the vibration and banging.

12 Dave had to cut through the support plate that attaches to the outrigger at an angle from behind (the one he's pointing at here), and then the old outrigger was removed in one chunk – or what was left of it.

13 Dave had to spend more time with the small angle grinder trimming back the metal left from the old outrigger and frequently offering up the new one to make sure that it would fit, but without removing more metal than was necessary.

14 Once it would slot into place, Dave held it there by temporarily fitting the body-mounting bolt…

15 …and drawing with a scriber down the edges of the new outrigger.

16 Dave's next job was to clean up the surface of the steel on the chassis where the new outrigger would be welded in place. It's hopeless trying to weld against old underseal, paint or rust. The surface must be scrupulously clean.

17 Dave then had to cut another section out of the flange on the outrigger…

18 …so that the supplementary body-mounting bracket could still be bolted to the chassis once the new outrigger was in place.

19 Dave cleaned up the bolt and smeared it heavily in copper grease – making sure that the washers were also cleaned up and correctly fitted in position this time!

20 The new outrigger was finally fitted into position…

21 …and tack-welded into place.

22 It's highly unlikely that fitting a new outrigger will cause severe body movement because the bulkhead itself is very strong. But it makes sense to check door apertures just to be on the safe side before finally welding anything into place.

23 This view is from the rear of the outrigger and shows the brace that we referred to earlier being welded on to the new outrigger. In our case the brace was very sound and completely undamaged by rust, but if yours is rusted away you'd have to build this up separately.

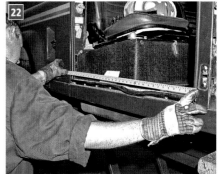

24 Dave went all around the outrigger MIG-welding the panel in place with continuous seam welds.

25 This view is from inside the vehicle, looking down past where the floor would be if it hadn't been removed. It just shows that you can access all the important parts in order to weld the new outrigger successfully in place.

26 Dave cleaned off all the high spots on the MIG welds…

27 …and finished off by fully tightening the mounting bolts and supporting bracket before rust-proofing the new outrigger and painting the outer surface to preserve it.

NOTE: You may have noticed that the base of the bulkhead went from being rusty to repaired during the course of the outrigger replacement. This was because the outrigger wasn't replaced all in one go. Instead, the old outrigger was cut away, the base of the bulkhead was repaired while access was improved, and then the new outrigger was fitted later. Restoration work is rarely straightforward!

28 This is one of three more chassis repair sections available from IRB. This later-type tubular body mount has a spigot on its inner end, so that after the old mount (arrowed) has been cut off flush with the chassis, the spigot is inserted into the chassis and the mount precisely aligned by attaching it to the body before welding it to the chassis.

29 Here's a rear outrigger. Note that you can't safely (not that you should have to) weld to galvanised steel. The gases give off are toxic.

FRONT CHASSIS RAILS

By starting with a mainly sound vehicle it was possible to properly repair the chassis and to give it a new lease of life without having to leave any suspect areas sitting there festering. But if you do find more extensive corrosion than this in the front end of a Defender chassis, you can buy a more extensive chassis front-end section. Obviously, the more you cut away, the more difficult it becomes to make sure everything lines up as it should, but, if you can weld, the principle won't be so different from that shown here.

30 We decided that the quickest and easiest route would be to remove the front body in one piece. My mate Dave Bradley-Scrivener came over to lend Britpart mechanic Stuart a hand. You can't remove this section single-handedly because of the amount of flexing that takes place. If you're working on your own, you'll just have to remove panels separately.

31 We also removed the radiator.

32 Both chassis rail front ends had corroded through quite badly. Now, the interesting thing is that this corrosion couldn't be fully appreciated until after the bodywork was removed. Remember: rust is always worse than you expect!

33 These replacements are nicely made and dimensionally correct – which isn't true of every chassis replacement you'll come across.

34 In order to align the replacement parts precisely, this plastic strip was drilled to take bolts that would drop into the bumper mountings (so it would be positioned in exactly the same place each time), and then front-to-back measurements were meticulously taken.

35 You rarely cut away the whole of a rusty area in one go. In any case, the chassis number lives on this part of the chassis. Fortunately, it wasn't corroded and we were able to repair around it. If it had been, it could have been dispensed with (they usually are) or new numbers stamped into the repair panel, which would be less worrying for anyone who might want to buy the vehicle in the future.

36 This is the front part of the rusty steel coming away and you can see the blobby welding of a poor quality repair carried out in the past. When new steel is welded over rust it won't only break through the new steel, it'll also leave a bigger problem than existed before.

37 Just look behind that disgraceful 'repair'! You can also just see that there's another, normally hidden, horizontal platform in there. This has rusted through completely and can't be replaced because it's entirely self-contained – well, not without rebuilding the rails in the same way they were manufactured in the first place. Instead, Dave decided to reinforce the outside of the box-section.

38 Dave thought he'd cut all the corrosion away, but you can never be certain until you get right back to bright metal. This power wire brush on the angle grinder is the best way I know of doing so.

39 We found a bit more corrosion behind the Panhard rod mountings. So, nothing for it but to unbolt the top bolt from the chassis...

40 ...followed by the bottom bolt. This bracket, by the way, also has another bracket bolted through it that supports the bottom of the steering box.

41 Then we decided to remove the Panhard rod from the mounting bracket altogether by removing the through-bolt.

42 Stuart released one from t'other.

43 It was at this point that we discovered that the rot continued into the area where the steering box was bolted. This was completely unforeseen! After knocking back the tab washers, Stuart unscrewed the bolts that pass through the chassis rail...

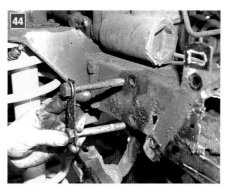

44 ...and removed them, complete with tab washers, for reuse later.

45 Meanwhile, Dave drained the power steering fluid from the box, disconnected the pipework and lifted the steering box away.

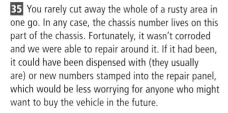

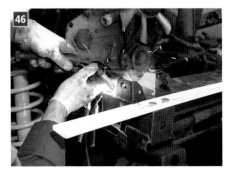

46 Dave fitted the right-side replacement after trimming it exactly to shape (see later) and used the guide we'd made earlier to ensure that it was correctly located.

47 After tack-welding, all the dimensions were very carefully rechecked, including the up-down location as well as the front-back one. The guide took care of the side-to-side position, which is why you only cut away one of these at a time. If you cut them both away you'll lose your reference points.

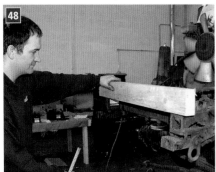

48 Stuart used a block of wood to provide an extra means of measuring height. The heights of the ends were compared with the front crossmember, which had not, of course, been touched.

49 Finally, Stuart temporarily refitted the old front bumper just to make even more certain that all was well. Measure lots of times but weld only once!

50 The other side was easier, both because one side had been 'explored' and because there's no chassis number on that side. You can't see it here but a felt pen has been used to draw cut lines. Without them, you can go quite badly off course!

51 Dave cut away a somewhat larger chunk this time, but you can see that the full extent of the rust hasn't yet been removed.

52 All cutting has to be done with reference to the repair section. Sure, you can add steel where the repair panel doesn't cover the full extent of the corrosion, and we had to in a few places. But you do want to be able to correctly position the repair section up against existing, rust-free steel so that you can make a good weld.

53 There'll always be some trimming and it can take quite a time to align the new panel precisely, but it's well worth spending as long as it takes.

54 This was deemed to be a satisfactory fit. There's a small parallel gap in one place, as you can see, but this can easily be filled with a strip of fresh steel.

55 More importantly, there were enough places where the fit was good enough to be able to weld the repair strongly into position.

56 Here you can see the welding completed on the right-hand side. There's an extra vertical plate to give extra strength, and although the bottom run

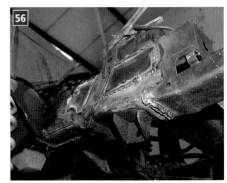

has sagged a bit that's not at all important, because the weld has penetrated to provide strength, and the excess can easily be ground off.

57 Although the repairs around the steering box didn't need replicating on the left-hand side, you can see that another vertical strengthening plate has been added, though taller this time because there's no chassis number to preserve.

58 An extra plate was also welded on the top of each repair to put back more of the strength left out by removing the internal platform.

59 Freshly welded steel will rust quickly, so Stuart sprayed primer over the outside and used aerosol cavity wax to protect the insides of the box sections.

REAR CROSSMEMBER REPLACEMENT

Don't take that Defender rear crossmember for granted! One with visible corrosion – or one that's been badly repaired – could turn out to be literally a death-trap when towing or winching. Here's how IRB carried out a 'proper' replacement, on this hard-working, hard-towing Defender, using one of their own crossmember repair sections.

The chassis to which you're planning to weld your replacement crossmember must also be sound, otherwise all you'll be doing is moving the weak point further along the vehicle. If chassis rails are too corroded to take a new crossmember it might be time for a replacement chassis, as described elsewhere in this manual.

60 Depending on what's there, you'll have to remove the tow bracket and wiring, anti-roll bar and any other accessories that may have been fitted to the crossmember.

61 Replacements can have different chassis leg lengths. The nearer to the bottom of the sweep you cut the chassis, the easier it'll be to weld all the way round.

62 On TD5 90s the rear fuel tank has to be removed along with its protective undertray. If bolts shear off, it's easy to weld on replacement captive nuts later.

63 Similarly, some of the anti-roll bar mounts share the same problem of seized bolts, and again, it's quicker to let them shear off and renew later.

64 Two of the fuel tank support mounting nuts are accessed through holes in the crossmember. Though easy to tighten when new, threads seize and bolt heads corrode badly...

65 ...meaning that the 'correct' socket won't fit. James, IRB's welder/fabricator, used a special socket with tapered flutes inside but had to cut part of the scrap crossmember away in order to gain access. There'll still be a problem with the length of the studs being greater than the depth of the socket, unless you can obtain a long-reach version of one of these special sockets, or you could make up your own tool by welding on your own extension.

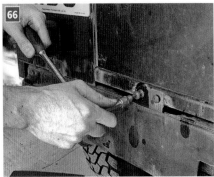

66 The screws holding the lower body in place will benefit from a preparatory soaking with releasing fluid. Some are captive; those at the ends have nuts on them.

67 IMPORTANT NOTE! You must remember to run the tank almost empty before starting work. If you don't, you'll have to pump the fuel out where there's no drain tap.

68 Running slightly out-of-synch – the protective undertray has been removed before the tank can be worked free from between the sides of its mounting frame.

69 The method favoured by Ian Baughan is to leave the filler hose on the vehicle; other disconnections were made, as shown here. Electrical and fuel supply connections have been unplugged.

70 Welder James decided that removing the rear section from the exhaust would significantly improve access.

71 We saw the body mounting bolts being removed earlier, but now they were temporarily refitted to the two brackets shown here to support the crossmember after cutting it free.

72 It's very easy to overlook the wiring loom. Disconnect it, cut where necessary and pull through with fish wire attached so that you can pull the loom back through when finished.

73 Bearing in mind that this particular repair section has the shorter chassis legs, James had

to cut away this reinforcing gusset with the angle grinder in order to gain access…

74 …to the chassis leg, where he needed to cut through. You must carry out careful measurements and checks first.

75 James made a point of cutting off insufficient of the old chassis leg to start with, in the knowledge that more could always be cut back later.

76 This chassis was also attached to the crossmember at the top on each side. James used a power saw, protecting the paintwork with masking tape to prevent 'chatter' damage.

77 Here it looks as if the crossmember simply lifted away, but it didn't! There'll almost inevitably be a lot of small areas of steel still attached...

78 ... and you have to patiently find them, working the crossmember up and down when loose to identify the culprits, before carefully cutting through them and removing the crossmember.

79 It is, of course, essential that you cut back to sound steel. Ian checked to see how much cleaning up would be required, and the repair section was offered up as a trial fit.

80 At this stage all it will tell you is how much tidying up you need to do; it won't tell you how much further back you need to cut the chassis.

81 The chassis rail stubs on this repair section were the same dimensions as the original chassis rail so needed to be tapped outwards, enabling them to slide over the chassis.

82 In order to line things up correctly, it's important to check carefully and methodically as you proceed.

83 It's OK to tap the crossmember with wood placed right across the height, but it's not OK to hammer on the metal of the crossmember itself or you'll dent it.

84 Part of the process of making the crossmember fit accurately might be the removal of small areas of metal from it. That's fine provided you leave enough meat in the sandwich.

85 You'll need to look for whatever clues you can find to line up the crossmember accurately. This chassis hole (left) conveniently matched one on the repair section (right).

86 However, as predicted, too little rather than too much metal had been removed, so James marked it out accurately and used the angle grinder cutting disc to remove the surplus.

87 Earlier we mentioned sheared fixing bolts. James ground off redundant captive nuts and welded on new ones while access was good. Note the bolt temporarily holding the nut in position.

88 Finally, after the single most time-consuming part of the job – ensuring a correct fit – Ian was satisfied that the new IRB crossmember could be located perfectly in position.

89 The bracket assembly for attaching the crossmember to the body is bolted on separately to provide adjustment, allowing for the Defender's famous – or should that be infamous? – bodywork variations.

90 You need to spend as long as necessary in correctly aligning the repair section. Clamp in place, apply a couple of spot welds, then check again!

91 Once spot welds were in place on one side, James transferred his attention to the other, checked alignment again and spot-welded in place once more.

92 If necessary, spot welds can easily be ground off for readjustment, before running complete, unbroken, strong welds all the way around the joints on the chassis rails.

93 James used a soft pad on the grinder to clean off weld spatter and any high spots – it can be tricky welding in such an awkward location.

94 The finished job – a treat to behold.

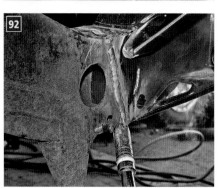

Body removal and chassis change

In reality, no two re-chassising jobs will be exactly the same because no two Land Rovers will require exactly the same amount of work carrying out on components associated with the chassis. They all rust and wear in different ways.

We chose a chassis from Richards Chassis because of their fine reputation for top-quality work and attention to detail so that the replacements you fit will be exactly right for the vehicle intended. The work was carried out with impressive speed and care by MJA Land Rovers, who have huge experience in fitting new chassis to Land Rovers. Even though this Defender didn't need a new chassis, we wanted to demonstrate how the job is done.

Before starting, disconnect or drain the following:

- The battery.
- Coolant.
- Brake lines and possibly the master cylinder if you can't clamp it off.
- Fuel tank (out of doors, for safety's sake).

1 Back at the workshop, MJA owner, Mark, and mechanic Bob started by lifting off the bonnet...

2 ...followed by the doors. The Defender had always been kept under cover during her 49,000-mile life, and all the door screws came undone easily.

3 The transmission tunnel has to come out, and so does the handbrake lever.

4 Floor bolts all came out smoothly as well. It's normal to have to turn to the angle grinder when bolts are rusted solid – why on earth did Land Rover use several different types and sizes on this one small panel, though?

5 Next, Mark turned his attention to the oily stuff. This is the top intercooler pipe being disconnected and removed...

6 ...and this the lower one, from turbo to intercooler.

7 'Time to remove the radiator hoses,' says Mark. What a serpent the bottom hose is on a 300 Tdi engine!

8 The radiator fan shroud is easily unscrewed before being wiggled out...

9 ...followed by the fan itself. To disconnect the fan from the viscous coupling you need a special cranked spanner, and a heavy hammer to crack the nut undone.

10 The radiator is removed after unbolting and removing the two top brackets, one on each side of the rad (along with whatever else is bolted on there, such as the horn).

11 This is the power steering pump. Rather than disconnect the hoses, Mark unbolted the pump from the engine and tied it to one side, inside the engine bay.

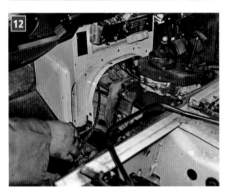

12 It's easy to overlook items such as the speedometer cable (on the transmission), the reversing light cable (shown here) and earth wiring. The only answer is to check and double-check, as you'll see Mark doing later.

13 Mark attached his engine-lifting chains to the engine...

14 ...and out popped the engine, like shelling a pea from a pod.

15 Next, Mark turned his attention to the transmission and removed the propshafts.

16 The gearbox crossmember is bolted to the chassis side rails and can be tapped down and out after removing the fixing bolts – but ONLY after the gearbox has been supported from beneath, of course!

17 After securing the gearbox to the gearbox hoist, Mark used it to lower then roll the gearbox from beneath the vehicle's nether regions.

18 With the major lumps out of the way, Mark removed the pinch bolt and drifted the steering column UJ off its splines.

19 He also strapped the power-steering reservoir out of the way, against the inner wing.

20 Next, it was time to start on all those body-to-chassis fixings. There's no particular order for removing them since the body will just 'sit' there on the chassis anyway. This is one of the front inner wing-to-chassis mounts, accessed from inside the engine bay.

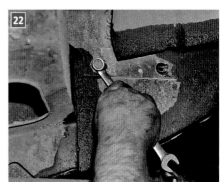

21 Mark then switched his attention to the underside and removed each of the bolts (both sides) to the bulkhead support brackets, seen here from inside the chassis.

22 This is the same bolt seen from outside the chassis.

23 The long bulkhead outrigger bolts pass through tubes in bulkhead and chassis and can be pretty well rusted in. Ours came out like good'uns.

24 Underneath the rear end, these are the fronts of the rear tub outriggers.

25 Floor support and wing stay to the front of the rear wheel arch.

26 This is the floor support from the chassis. (On the Station Wagon the bracket is shorter.)

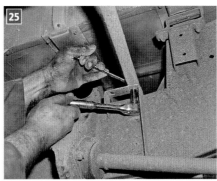

27 The mudflap brackets also have to be disconnected from the chassis...

28 ...and from the rear wing and its reinforcing support.

29 Mark used his rechargeable impact driver to whiz out the line of body mounting bolts above the rear crossmember.

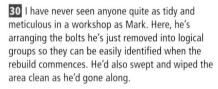

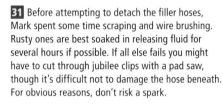

30 I have never seen anyone quite as tidy and meticulous in a workshop as Mark. Here, he's arranging the bolts he's just removed into logical groups so they can be easily identified when the rebuild commences. He'd also swept and wiped the area clean as he'd gone along.

31 Before attempting to detach the filler hoses, Mark spent some time scraping and wire brushing. Rusty ones are best soaked in releasing fluid for several hours if possible. If all else fails you might have to cut through jubilee clips with a pad saw, though it's difficult not to damage the hose beneath. For obvious reasons, don't risk a spark.

32 It's really difficult to remember to disconnect all of the wiring but it has to be done! These are the connections to the rear-light units found beneath those protective aluminium panels in the rear corners of the load area.

33 Now we're coming to the reason why Mark removed the engine and gearbox before removing the body when carrying out a Defender rechassis job. This is one of two poles Mark fits across the vehicle. This one requires a couple of holes to be drilled in the sill so it can be bolted in place. It passes through where the transmission once sat.

34 The one beneath the rear of the chassis pushed right through with obstructions.

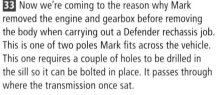

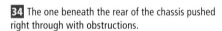

35 As you can see, Mark fitted a stand under each end of the poles and then he carefully and slowly lowered the rolling chassis from beneath the body, easing it down slowly to ensure that everything came free and that there were no hidden, still-connected pipes or cables trying to make life difficult.

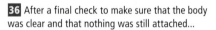

36 After a final check to make sure that the body was clear and that nothing was still attached...

37 ...Mark and Bob wheeled the rolling chassis out from under the body.

38 Now, in the foreground, you can see the new chassis from Richards Chassis, all gleaming and galvanised and ready to take the running gear.

39 Here we're looking at a common (though normally hidden) rot-spot, set up by interaction between the crossmember, which bolts in place at this point, and the chassis side member. It was the only area of corrosion we found on the 'old' chassis – not bad for a then 11-year-old, and testament to the strength of the Defender chassis.

40 Even this chassis had lumps of mud sitting on top of the outriggers, which is the primary reason why all conventional Land Rovers' outriggers are favourite areas for corrosion.

41 In the previous shot was the bulkhead outrigger, and here the body-mounting outrigger with its attendant brackets is another reason why a Defender chassis might need replacing.

42 Reinforcing gussets also tend to rot out, but what I forgot to photograph was the rear crossmember, the rear ends of the chassis rails and the front ends of the chassis rails, which are all heavily prone to corrosion. Bolts that have come apart relatively easily on this vehicle may be a good deal more difficult to separate on a rusty chassis, and you're more than likely going to have to use the services of a cutting disc on an angle grinder.

43 MJA's Mark had, out of habit, capped-off all the disconnected brake hoses whether they were going to be reused or not. If you're planning to reuse brake connections, it's essential that no dirt is allowed to get into them.

44 One item that was perfectly OK to reuse was the fuel tank. This version can't be lowered between the chassis rails unless the sender unit is removed first. The retaining ring, held here in Mark's left hand, has to be tapped anticlockwise to release it. Use a wooden drift to avoid the risk of sparks.

45 Even though the tank had been drained there's still a fair amount of weight, so Bob came over to help support the tank while Mark released it from the chassis.

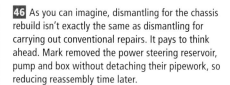

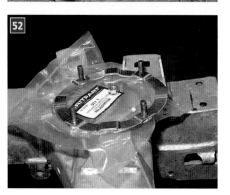

46 As you can imagine, dismantling for the chassis rebuild isn't exactly the same as dismantling for carrying out conventional repairs. It pays to think ahead. Mark removed the power steering reservoir, pump and box without detaching their pipework, so reducing reassembly time later.

47 Mark also made the point that cleaning off exposed threads with a wire brush (as well as applying releasing fluid) paid dividends in helping rusted threads to come undone. He also used one of those rechargeable impact drivers to speed the job along. If any conventional bolts had sheared off, too bad – they could always be replaced with new!

48 After detaching both axles from the chassis, Mark used an engine hoist to lift first one end of the chassis…

49 …and then the other, wheeling each axle out from under the chassis in turn.

50 Before starting to build up the new chassis, Mark laid out all of the new parts ready for fitting. We'd decided to replace all of the obvious wearing components such as springs and shock absorbers, plus those that deteriorate over time such as rubber mountings and brake lines. We'd also planned to replace all the bushes with Polybushes, but in the end the original ones were in such good condition that we didn't do so.

51 Getting the axles under the new chassis was essentially the reverse of the removal procedure.

52 Fortunately, we'd remembered to order new suspension turrets and shock absorber tower mounting plates…

53 …and these were fitted in conjunction with the new springs.

54 Once again, the engine hoist was used to lower the chassis a bit at a time while correctly locating the new springs.

55 Everything on the Richards chassis lined up, all holes were clear, and as a result fitting the suspension components back into place was a doddle. As you can see, the old body mountings were reused, the plan being to rustproof them later once the body was back in place.

56 Future generations of mechanics will bless Mark for using copious quantities of copper grease on bolts and threads.

57 Several steering and suspension location bolts pass right through the front end of the chassis and, like the bulkhead mounting bolts to be fitted later, they'll remain corrosion-free provided copper grease has been walloped on at this stage.

58 The only threaded captive nuts that don't come ready fitted to the chassis are those for holding the power steering pipework in place. Mark used a rivnut gun to fit threaded rivnuts into the holes provided in the chassis.

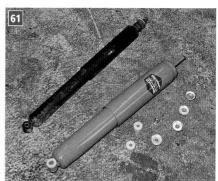

59 After bolting the steering box back on to the chassis...

60 ...Mark bolted the pipes into the rivnuts, leaving the still-attached pump resting on the top of the chassis.

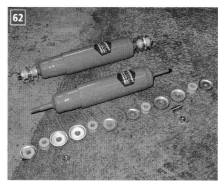

61 It's interesting to compare the size of this replacement steering damper with that of the original black one. It's sure to reduce the amount of steering shimmy compared with the original.

62 These are the new front shock absorbers with the fittings and bushes shown in the correct order.

63 Because the shock absorbers and thus the threads are new, you can use the workshop manual method of preventing the shock absorber from turning as the bottom nut is tightened.

64 And here it is! You use the open end of an 8mm spanner on the flats you'll find on the shaft of the shock absorber to prevent it from turning. Of course, when removing the fixing nut on an old shocker the 8mm spanner won't provide enough grip and you invariably end up having to grab hold of the body of the shock absorber.

65 Mark pushed the top of each shock absorber down far enough...

66 ...to enable him to bolt each tower to the mounting plates we saw earlier.

67 Here's a useful tip. Because, of course, there was no weight on the chassis, there was nothing to pull the springs down sufficiently. Mark therefore used a ratchet strap around chassis and axle to pull the two closer together.

68 Mark removed the fuel tank retaining bolts from the old chassis and screwed them into the threaded captive nuts in the new one.

69 Some of the brake lines had to be replaced, although others were literally as good as new. The beauty of using an Automec copper brake pipe kit is that all of the pipes are cut to length and marked to show where they go, and the copper is soft enough to bend by hand without requiring the use of a pipe-bending tool.

70 We did foresee that a number of pipe clips would be needed. These were identified by spending several hours poring over the Land Rover parts book.

71 Here's another useful little tip: Mark fitted the rear crossmember grab handles before the body went on. They're soooo much easier to get at without any bodywork in the way!

72 The same applied to the bump stops, which were also replaced now while access was good.

73 MJA prefer to leave as much of the body intact as possible, which means splitting the

engine and transmission. Alternatively, you'd remove the front body, separating it from the rear. There's a lot of dismantling whatever you do, but this is probably the lesser of two evils.

74 It was essential that the chassis was lined up perfectly with the body above it – quite a bit of fiddling about is always involved.

75 As much as possible of the power-steering pipework had been left connected. The reservoir and pump were now placed safely out of the way.

76 The front body mountings have to skim the insides of the chassis rails.

77 The bodywork was lowered millimetre by millimetre while Mark watched carefully to ensure the alignment was correct.

78 There's no argument about the back because the rear crossmember body mountings are visible for all to see.

79 Mark fitted all of the body mountings in turn; this is one of the bulkhead mounts. It's always good engineering practice to fit fixings loosely and then to tighten them up when they're all in place.

80 These body mountings are held with nuts, bolts and washers, so you need to use two spanners to prevent bolts from turning.

81 Do remember this front-most body mount. Access is easy without the radiator in place.

82 This mounting incorporates the mudflap bracket.

83 Some of the brake lines had been renewed. Those that clip against the body need bending into position. Automec's copper brake pipes make this easy.

84 Rigid brake lines on the body reconnected to flexible hoses; or, as in this case, new stainless steel braided hoses, again from Automec, were fitted.

85 One of the delights of all but the earlier Defenders is the way in which wiring connections are foolproof and easy to make – provided that no one's been messing with them!

86 Mark's next task was to use the transmission hoist to hold the gearbox up in the air, in the position where it'll be mounted. There's nothing to fix it to at present.

87 The gearbox crossmember was slid into position next. Note the coating of copper grease on the outer flanges. This helps the crossmember slide into place and, more importantly, discourages corrosion in future. It's a common rot-spot on the chassis.

88 This is the left-hand transmission (transfer box) mounting. The right-hand mounting looks different but the principle is exactly the same:
a   Four nuts and bolts – crossmember to chassis.
b   Transfer box mounting to crossmember nut.
c   Mounting bracket to transfer box – four bolts.

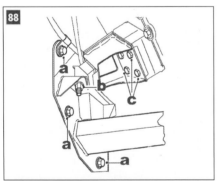

89 Some adjustment of the weight of the transmission was necessary before all of the boltholes would line up correctly. This is perfectly normal and to be expected.

90 With transmission secured, Mark connected the relevant propshafts.

91 Anything that was prone to wear was renewed. This included the engine mountings, and Mark fitted the new ones while the engine was still out of the vehicle.

92 The new Britpart shock absorbers came with their own polyurethane bushes.

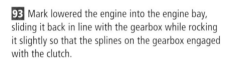

93 Mark lowered the engine into the engine bay, sliding it back in line with the gearbox while rocking it slightly so that the splines on the gearbox engaged with the clutch.

94 From underneath, engine to gearbox fixings were screwed on finger-tight...

95 ...followed by those accessed from above. All the fixings – 14 in all – were then tightened until the two units were flush and then, finally, they were fully tightened.

96 Mark fitted the power-steering pump, drive pulley and drive belt to the front of the engine.

97 In went the radiator, and after the brackets had been fitted...

98 ...the oil cooler pipes were connected.

99 One of the last jobs is to fit the cooling fan and its shroud, which have to be introduced into position at the same time.

100 A great tip from Mark is to fit exhaust-pipe brackets to the exhaust while it's off the vehicle. It's easier to bolt the bracket to the body than to push the mounting rubber over its pin while working above your head.

101 In cases where the bracket has to be fitted first, you won't stand a chance unless you apply plenty of lubricant. Don't use oil, because it rots rubber. Silicone lubricant is best but releasing fluid is OK because it evaporates away before it can do the rubber any serious harm.

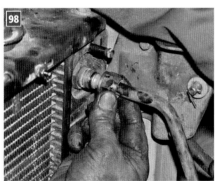

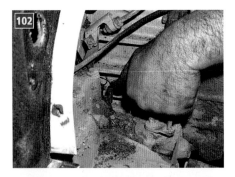

102 There are many connections you can easily forget about, such as reversing-light switch connections and earth cables. You just have to be meticulous in checking that there aren't any loose cables or connections flapping around after you've finished.

103 'Well, I don't know!' said Mark (or words to that effect) after he fitted the transmission tunnel cover – and then wished he hadn't.

104 Rather than take it out again, he wangled the floor panels into place beneath it. A large centre punch was used to move the floor around so that it lined up with the threads beneath.

105 Transmission trim and gearstick covers were fitted later.

106 You have to remember that, on this version, the ECU is beneath the seat base.

107 Mark refitted the doors and adjusted them for height, refitted the bonnet, and was done.

108 Be prepared! When you go disturbing major mechanical components, you mustn't be surprised if some of them – especially those that were on the point of failure anyway – decide to let go. There's an (in)famous coolant gasket on the engine, and ours sprang a leak.

109 Then later, lo and behold, so did the radiator. We fitted a new radiator at chez Porter to save Mark the bother of trekking over once again, although he did offer.

It's worth emphasising that you really can't be surprised when something like this happens after a major strip and rebuild. It could be a clutch slave cylinder, a brake caliper that starts to seep, or the water pump – which 'went' later on this vehicle. You just never know, and you do need to be prepared for some ancillary repairs to be carried out later.

Painting

Fewer enthusiasts paint their own Land Rovers than ever before. There are health and safety problems, noxious fumes for yourself and neighbours to worry about, an increasing difficulty in getting hold of materials (H&S again) and the high degree of skill required in getting it right.

For those who want to carry out their own painting, it's strongly recommended that a copy of the author's *Classic Car Bodywork Repair Manual* is purchased and studied, as was recommended at the start of this chapter.

Lettering and decals

Here's how you get badges and logos to stay in place.

Removing old, stuck-on logos isn't difficult, but you do have to take great care not to damage the paintwork beneath. You'll need a hair dryer, or (if you're feeling brave) a hot-air gun, to soften the adhesive, and a wooden or plastic spatula to gently lever the sticker or logo away from the adhesive beneath. There's always some adhesive left behind, even after you've carefully scraped away as much as possible. Use panel wipe or methylated spirit (though not paint thinners, for obvious reasons) on a rag to wipe away any remaining residue.

Ian Bourne at IRB Developments lent a pair of hands to stick a Defender logo in place on a new grille panel.

1 It'll be essential to remove all traces of traffic film, wax or even oil from fingers using the same panel wipe or spirit.

2 Before attaching a sticker such as a Defender logo it's best to measure and mark the panel (use something easily removable!) so that it'll be fitted symmetrically. What you do next is counter-intuitive – you get some soapy water and wet the surface to which the logo will be attached.

3 You peel the backing paper off the logo…

4 …and, using the marks you made earlier as a guide, place the logo in position. You'll be able to position it easily because of the soapy water beneath, which temporarily prevents the adhesive from sticking.

5 It's best to use one hand to hold the logo in position while the other, starting from the centre of the logo, pushes out surplus soapy water from beneath.

6 Ian then used my library card as a spatula to ensure every last drop of water and – most importantly – every air bubble was squeezed out.

7 The new logo will be partly stuck down but not properly fixed in place until all the last traces of water have evaporated from beneath. So, you need to hold it in place…

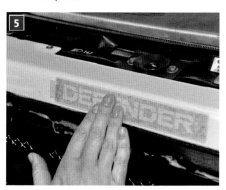

8 …while carefully peeling off the top cover tape without lifting the logo off the panel.

9 If the logo should lift up, carefully push it down again with your fingers and/or the spatula, ensuring there are no air bubbles left behind.

10 Post-TD5 Land Rovers have their eponymous logo on the front of the bonnet while the top of the grille is left mysteriously blank. The 'Land Rover' lettering is raised, giving it a 3D appearance.

11 The owner of this vehicle has done something similar but with flat, vinyl lettering.

12 These are genuine Defender decals attached to the templates with which they're supplied.

13 The front of the bonnet is carefully cleaned and then wiped with panel wipe or, as in this case, Würth Silicone Remover.

14 I then used masking tape, both to provide a level edge against which the lettering could be fitted…

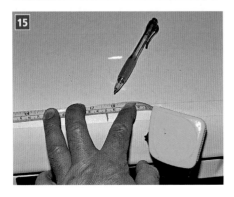

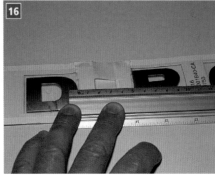

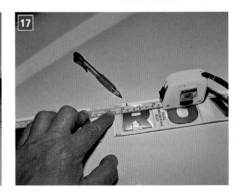

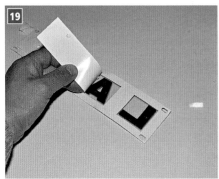

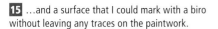

15 ...and a surface that I could mark with a biro without leaving any traces on the paintwork.

16 I 'guesstimated' the distance between the two words at 50mm, but I think it should have been a touch wider. It pays to check with an original vehicle beforehand.

17 You also need to measure and mark out the starting point for each word...

18 ...so that the whole appearance will be symmetrical on the front of the bonnet. Double-check by temporarily fixing the words in place with masking tape before you start.

19 Just as with vinyl lettering, you start by peeling off the backing paper.

20 Because I was working with a template, I decided against using soapy water and stuck the decals straight on to the paintwork.

21 Fortunately I got it right, but in retrospect it might have been best to use soapy water to reduce the risk of errors. It was just as important to press down each letter, ensuring a complete absence of air bubbles beneath...

22 ...and when all of the letters are firmly in place you can peel off the top covering complete with the template panels.

23 This Defender does not, of course, have the later vehicles' bonnet bulge that normally goes with these later decals. But it's a free country!

When planning rust control, it's important to remember that more than 75% of vehicle rust takes place from the inside outwards. A really effective protection must therefore strike at the root of the problem: inside cavities, double

skinning and welds. It's worth remembering that even mechanical rust removal, such as sand blasting, can fail because only loose rust is removed.

Over the years I've tried just about every rust treatment you could think of, and much of it is little more than quackery. However, I first tested Fertan by trying it out on rusty steel and leaving it unprotected over a period of six winter months, and the results were amazingly good – even though I deliberately left the surface unprotected to see what would happen. Fertan is a water-based product that penetrates the rust, converts it chemically and leaves 'bronzed' metal on the surface. It's important to note that Fertan doesn't cover the rust, like other products, but dissolves it. The resulting black powder can simply be washed off and the layer which lies underneath is extremely well protected by a new bond to the metal. It's also really effective in cavities, joints etc because of its viscosity.

Fertan also forces its way into overlaps and seams, double-skinning, welds and joints and even blistered paint, and then reacts. It can be used on both dry and damp metal. It isn't damaging to rubber, chrome, plastic, glass and undamaged paintwork, though it can mark paler surfaces, so you should cover the surrounding areas.

Fertan only becomes active when it encounters metal or rust. It can be removed

from all other surfaces simply by washing it off with water. It isn't damaging to health, either by inhalation or by contact. In addition it's non-flammable and minimises the environmental damage of rust removal. As long as the surface treated is also treated with a protective coating, the effectiveness of Fertan lasts for years. Fertan shouldn't be applied at temperatures lower than 5°C.

PREPARATION

1 I was lucky enough to meet Alan Thomas, the highly technical yet practically minded man behind Fertan UK. He took out his endoscope and examined the insides of the Defender's chassis rails. He found that the manufacturer's rust treatment (there was none on earlier models!) had managed to keep internal rust at bay, but a typically rusty surface might look like the inset picture. So, though we knew there wasn't a great deal of interior rust to deal with, the treatment was carried out just the same.

In spite of Fertan's ability to work well in damp conditions, it seems wise to carry out this work only on dry bodywork. Because the work was to be done after a prolonged period of wet weather, I parked my Defender in the garage and left a dehumidifier on for a full week to make sure the underside was as dry as possible.

2 Because it's water-based, Fertan can't effectively react with rust in the presence of dirt, oil, grease or silicone, so first you need to clean the surface, removing loose rust at the same time.

3 After using a simple scraper, mechanic Dave blew any loose dust off with the airline…

4 …then washed the surface with a wet rag. Obviously, more heavily corroded surfaces than this, or one covered in oil and grease, would require a lot more cleaning off.

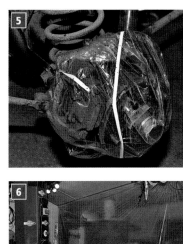

5 I once heard of someone who injected wax-based rust treatment into his Land Rover's chassis only to find that, first time out, the brakes were non-existent. Cover the darned things up with plastic bags so you don't get any slippery rust treatment on them!

6 Another useful tip is to grab some old carpets from someone who's throwing them away to cover the floor. I also bought some plastic decorating protection sheets from the pound shop. Atomised rustproofing stuff can get everywhere and make a terrible mess in your workshop, floors and walls and all. These precautions solved the problem completely.

PROTECTION

7 Further treatment is particularly important to protect sound areas on the vehicle. Dave found a few areas of surface rust, such as on welded seams, and these he treated with Fertan rust killer before overpainting with the inelegantly named but fantastically effective Ferpox, which is one-pack epoxy paint.

MATERIALS AND EQUIPMENT

8 There are some items of equipment that you simply can't do without if you want to properly rustproof your Land Rover. You need a compressor to run an inexpensive Schutz gun…

9 …and a rather more expensive injection gun. I bought this SATA set-up donkey's years ago and it's still going strong.

10 Of course, you also need the materials. Slightly confusingly, the company is called Fertan and so is its main rust-killing product. Fedox has a slightly different role and we'll come to that later. A litre of Fertan is sufficient for an area of about 15m². In a closed container Fertan will keep practically indefinitely.

11 There are also Fertan's own versions of Shutz and cavity protection, both of which have different qualities and appear to me to work much better than run-of-the-mill versions.

12 There are even aerosol applications available.

With a pressure gun the pressure must be kept at 7–9 bar and with a cavity gun it should be 3–4 bar.

Use of a hand spray-gun is only recommended for doors, bonnets etc, because this can only be used with a maximum pressure of approx. 1.2–1.5 bar, and that isn't sufficient for complete atomisation of the Fertan product in normal box sections.

Note that the product must penetrate into all cavities, seams and double-skinned areas in order to work effectively.

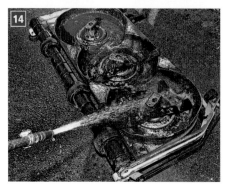

APPLICATION PRINCIPLES

Now, the eagle-eyed among you will already have spotted that the next few pictures don't look much like Land Rover parts! But my rusty mower deck was in a much worse state than my Defender, so I thought it would be ideal to demonstrate how Fertan works.

13 First, after scraping off loose rust and paint, I applied Fedox and allowed it to work for 24 hours.

14 I used the garden hose to wash off rust loosened by the Fedox treatment. Unlike other rust removal treatments I've used, Fedox isn't a highly corrosive acid but a rust remover that's biodegradable and can safely be washed away down the drain.

15 Next, I applied the famous Fertan itself. Treated metal surfaces can be left from a few days to a maximum of six months before applying finish coats. Before doing so, the black dust created by the rust conversion process should be rinsed from the surface with water, or wiped off with a rag.

16 Fertan should be left on for at least 24 hours (or 48 hours in temperatures of less than 12°C). I gave it two days. As you can see, the surface was now a lovely rich, almost purple colour where the rust had been. Interestingly I found a few more areas of flaking paint and, after scraping them off, I discovered that the Fertan had got beneath them successfully and rustproofed the metal found there.

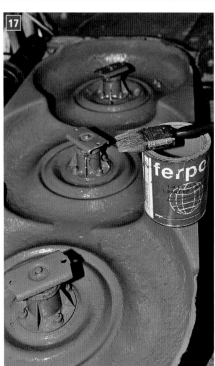

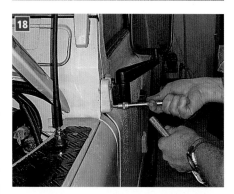

17 The final step was to paint the whole deck with two coats of Ferpox epoxy paint, which should, I hope, resist the extreme abrasion experienced inside a mower deck and, therefore, easily cope with the underside of my Land Rover.

18 Access to the outer-top of the bulkhead can be gained by selectively removing hinge screws…

19 …and in other places you should look for existing access holes.

20 Dave poured the Fertan neat into the injection gun container…

21 …and injected the Fertan by pushing in the tube, with its 360° spray head, as far as it would go before holding in the trigger on the injection gun while slowly withdrawing the tube.

FOLDS AND SEAMS

22 Before treating doors, removal of trim is usually recommended, partly to improve access and partly to avoid soiling trim parts.

23 Because of its viscosity, Fertan will partly penetrate into folds and some will drip out of its lower parts. To avoid marking, excess material should be washed off with water as quickly as possible.

Ideally, especially if dealing with a particularly rusty vehicle, you should allow Fertan to act for 24 hours and then liberally treat the fold with clean water. Water, as well as dirt and dust, will flow out through the water drain holes, and it's therefore vital that these remain open. Once the folds are absolutely rust-free, they're protected with wax. The outer areas of folds are finally treated with paint in the normal way.

CAVITIES

24 After Fertan treatment you should use only cavity wax in cavities. Remember never to use any product that hardens, such as paint.

25 Mechanic Dave removed the rear door trim.

26 When treating cavities in bonnets and doors the openings are often much smaller than usual, and can't be reached with a normal (8–10mm) attachment. If there's excessive wax leakage it can be cleaned off with white spirit or panel wipe.

27 In smaller openings, Fertan and cavity wax can be applied with an aerosol spray and a narrow probe.

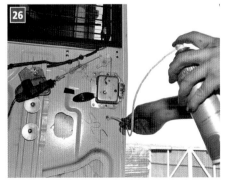

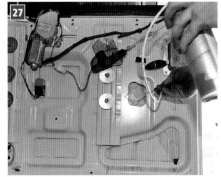

BOX SECTIONS

The rusting process in box sections begins largely as a consequence of condensation forming on inner surfaces. There, this dampness is enriched by salts, which combine to form an acid that aggressively attacks the metal, and any protective coatings which are present, and in the course of time causes massive damage. On Land Rovers, because of the design of the chassis, particles of dirt are thrown up, get lodged and baked hard, and then cause heavy corrosion when they get wet again. Research has shown that large quantities of water and very high humidity levels are generally found in box sections and cavities.

Daytime temperatures inside box sections can reach nearly 90°C in summer, but when the temperature drops in the night there will be a noticeable increase in atmospheric humidity. This means that box sections and cavities are usually damp or even wet all of the time, day and night.

TREATING RUSTY INTERNAL CHASSIS MEMBERS

On vehicles with loose flakes of rust that peel off and lie on the base of the box sections, two applications of Fertan are recommended, because these flakes must first be sufficiently loosened that they can later be removed by rinsing with water. For this application you can mix Fertan with up to 50% water for the first treatment, spray it in, and allow it to react for at least 48 hours at 20°C. During this time the vehicle can be used normally. If the temperatures are lower than 20°C, for instance at night, the reaction time allowed should be at least doubled. Fertan shouldn't be applied at temperatures of less than 5°C.

RINSING

After the reaction time has elapsed rinse the box sections and cavities thoroughly with water. Use approx. 15 litres of water for every litre of Fertan used, and operate the pressure gun at a pressure of 6 bar and the cavity gun at 4 bar. For this important rinsing don't park the vehicle on a light-coloured surface such as concrete, tiles, paving stones etc, because the run-off water will stain it.

Now spray unthinned Fertan into the still-damp box sections as described previously, and allow to react again at 20°C for at least 24 hours. Again, the vehicle can be used normally, and the reaction time can be stretched to six months without any problem.

Before the final treatment of the box section with protective wax it's vital that the box section be rinsed out once more with clean water.

This treatment may seem involved, but it's the only way all rust and damaging

chemicals can be successfully removed from the box section.

Incidentally, rinsing water used in this process won't cause any new corrosion, because the layer which has been created on the surfaces of the box section is completely insoluble in water. Also, running water washes away rust-causing electrolytes, which noticeably slows the rate of corrosion. Be sure to dispose of rinsing water in an environmentally responsible way.

To ensure that no rinsing water remains in the seams and low points, raise one side of the vehicle and then the other with a jack and allow all water to run out. When the box section or cavity has been rinsed out completely, it's free of rust and damaging chemicals, and after the surface has been dried it can be coated with wax.

NOTE: Water drain holes must be opened up. If they're blocked, covered with underbody protection or aren't present, new holes should be made in areas which don't affect the appearance or integrity of the bodywork. Before doing so, obtain suitable sealing grommets and then drill holes of the correct diameter.

TIPS:

- DON'T drill holes first – chances are you won't find grommets to fit.
- Coat the drill bit with high melting-point grease in an attempt to gather swarf before it can enter the box section, as it could cause corrosion later.

WAX TREATMENT

Final protection of box sections and cavities should only be carried out at temperatures of over 20°C.

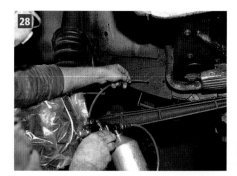

28 Protective wax should always be applied in several thin coats.

29 Allow each layer to dry before application of the next coat. If possible assist the process by blowing air through the cavity at low pressure. Work should be carried out at a temperature of at least 20°C, because at low temperatures the fluid has less 'creepability'. If the wax is being applied in an unheated workshop, the application should, if possible, take place only at a warm time of the year. This should be easy to achieve because of the long reaction time of the Fertan.

30 Fertan protective wax contains resin which prevents run-out from the cavities, or only in small quantities.

31 So, rather than a thick layer collecting at the base of the box section, the whole of the cavity wall is effectively protected by a thick and homogeneous layer for many years. It's advisable to supplement the wax layer every 5–7 years or so with a new, thin layer of wax, in order to slightly dissolve the surface of the old, pre-existing layer and stabilise it.

REMOVAL OF RUST AND CORROSION IN THE UNDERBODY

Finishes that are securely attached to the underbody may be allowed to remain, because in general no corrosion is present here. However, it should be carefully checked that there are no areas where the rust has lifted areas of the paint and penetrated under it.

SURFACES

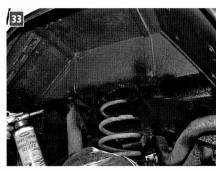

32 After cleaning off – and, where necessary, using Fertan treatment, we applied Fertan's own brand of Shutz.

33 The stickiness of this stuff was proved when Dave regretted that he hadn't covered his hands and arms. It stuck to him like something else beginning with sh.... But at least his arms won't go rusty!

34 Even though you try your hardest, you'll be amazed how many bits you miss when you go back to check later, so don't assume you've got it all the first time!

35 In a few nooks and crannies, where direct abrasion wasn't likely to be a problem, Dave added some of the more flexible cavity wax.

36 Fertan products aren't the cheapest so it's worth making the most of it.

37 The Shutz coat dries off quite quickly but is quite fumey, so you need to make sure there's plenty of ventilation in the workshop.

38 Again, there's an aerosol version available for touching up small areas.

The undersides of 'special' Land Rovers, used only in summer or primarily for shows, are sometimes painted in body colour. This paint coat can be very effectively protected by a transparent underbody wax or a glass-clear wax, such as Fertan Protewax BP527, a glass-clear protection for vehicle and machinery. BP527 is ideal protection for aluminium tanks, bumpers, and window and door frames and provides an excellent coating for cleaned aluminium and chromed wheels. BP527 is also suitable for painted suspension mountings, steering parts etc, though it isn't recommended for vehicles used all year round and exposed to road salt in the winter months, for which a more durable coating must be used.

On vehicles such as Land Rovers that are subjected to flexing or heavy duty as part of their construction and use, you could use a non-hardening coating such as UBS 220. This flexible coating will almost never crack.

39 With axles and most suspension components also given the Fertan treatment, I feel totally confident that my Defender now has a greatly extended life expectancy.

CHAPTER 5

Engine removal and refitting

The process of stripping and rebuilding an engine is the sort of task that you'll find described in your workshop manual. However, there are a number of matters that are common to engine restoration (rather than straight repair), as IRB Developments' Ian Baughan explains.

Engine overhaul

This section is very brief for the following reasons: any good workshop manual will tell you the correct order in which to dismantle and reassemble engine components and, in that sense, engine overhaul isn't necessarily part of 'restoration'. Moreover, it'll always be necessary to use an engine machinist to work on the cylinder block, cylinder head and crankshaft, and it isn't necessarily cost-effective to carry out the rest of the work yourself, though some owners may prefer to do so. If you do, it'll probably be best to purchase the components from your machinist so that you can be sure to buy the correct sizes of pistons and rings, bearings and so on, after they've been machined.

The following information has been gleaned from Land Rover specialist and engineer Ian Baughan of IRB Developments, and comprises additional information relevant to older and worn engines that may not be covered by a workshop manual.

ALL TURBOCHARGED TYPES
Check for turbocharger wear. Try to move the vanes. If there's any noticeable sideways free play the bearings are worn and you'll need a replacement turbo. Check there's no oil in the exhaust side. If there is, the turbo seals have probably gone.

2.5 LITRE NON-TURBO, TD AND 200 Tdi ENGINES
Check by removing the oil filler cap with the engine running. Oil mist appearing through the filler aperture suggests excessive bore wear. On all these engines, there's a frequent problem (worse on the earlier units) of the crank pulley chattering on the crank nose, which damages the crank, necessitating a new crankshaft. Some engineers have been known to machine the crank to take a longer keyway or a second Woodruff key to prevent the problem from recurring.

Ian says that turbo diesel cylinder heads tend to crack in the area of the hotspot; 200 Tdi heads crack between the injectors and glow plugs, while normally aspirated engines' heads don't tend to crack at all.

300 Tdi ENGINES
Always replace the earlier timing belt tensioner with the upgraded timing belt kit, part number STC4096L, which consists of belt, idler, tensioner, bolts and gaskets. This fixes the misalignment problem on early 300 Tdi models and contains a shouldered pulley to stop the cam belt wearing away on its edge and eventually shredding.

TD5 ENGINES
Ensure that a TD5 engine isn't fitted with a combination of early (10P) engine's and later (15P) engine's injectors and ECU. Green-top (early) and black-top (later) injectors shouldn't be mixed and must be used with the appropriate engine ECU for their colour coding. Engines with the wrong combination will run but won't run efficiently and, according to Ian Baughan, there's a major risk of engine damage taking place.

You're not 'supposed' to skim a TD5's cylinder head, but that's because – according to Ian – you'd harmfully change the compression ratio. Ian can recess the valve seats, restoring the correct 'squish' volume and thereby making cylinder head skimming a practical possibility.

Exhaust manifolds frequently warp, bowing out at the numbers 1 and 5 cylinder ends. Ian recommends skimming the existing manifold rather than renewing it because there's every likelihood that all the warping is done with, whereas a new one can warp all over again.

Crank dampers are two-piece, anti-vibration units and frequently degrade, requiring renewal.

Engine removal

Most of the illustrations for this section were taken with Ian Baughan at IRB Developments. You can find further relevant information and illustrations on removal and replacement of 300 Tdi engine and transmission as a unit in Chapter 4.

You'll need lots of strong boxes to hold all the parts that you remove. Be methodical and make note of what nuts and bolts go where. Start with a nice clean engine and take all the auxiliaries off.

1 Start by disconnecting the battery leads, removing the bonnet or tying it back to the windscreen, and draining the engine oil and coolant.

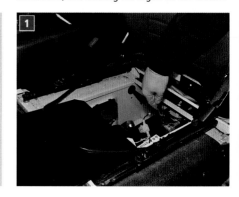

SAFETY NOTES
■ *Always* disconnect the battery first.
■ Diesel engines: disconnecting fuel injection pipes can be dangerous! Even after the engine hasn't been run for some time, high pressure can persist in the injection system. The jet of spray that can be emitted when the pipes are first undone could cause eye damage, or could be fatal if the jet of fuel should penetrate the skin and enter the blood stream – which it's capable of doing! So always follow the following precautions: (1) wear goggles and industrial work gloves; (2) wrap several layers of rag around the union as it's undone; (3) disconnect the union slowly and carefully, releasing the pressure safely under the rag, until the pressure has dispersed from the pipework.

FOUR-CYLINDER ENGINES

2 When it was time to disconnect the terminals from the back of the alternator, Ian Baughan found that one of the terminal pins screwed out of the back of the alternator because the nut was jammed-on solid, 'wasting' a quarter of an hour. It's the sort of unexpected thing that can happen, can't be foreseen, and you have to be prepared to deal with calmly and methodically.

3 Air cleaner removed, complete with trunking to save dismantling time.

4 Ian's preference is for the more conventional, out-of-the-front approach. Off came the grille and the grille surround. To remove the bottom fixing bolts, you have to lever out the plastic inserts for the bottom grille screws. Off came the surround...

5 ...and then Ian set about removing the threaded stud that's fitted to some Defenders. He used a proper stud-removal tool to avoid damaging the threads. If you don't own one, you could lock two nuts together on the outer thread using a pair of spanners, then turn the inner nut to wind out the stud.

6 This enabled Ian to lift off the bonnet-slam panel. The radiator top brackets were left attached to this panel because there was simply no need to remove them.

7 Ian's mate Matt lifted out the radiator assembly, complete with intercooler, and stored them safely out of the way at the back of Ian's workshop.

8 If your Defender has air conditioning, it must have its gas extracted by a specialist, for safety and environmental reasons. They'll be able to store it for you, ready to refill the system later.
a   The three a/c belt tensioner fixing bolts were slackened, the tensioner turned to release the tension on the belt and the belt lifted out of the way.
b   The air conditioning compressor was removed.
c   Then the compressor cradle was taken off.

9 The air filter bracketry will need to be removed if you're stripping or swapping the engine. It's unbolted from the cylinder head, the two head bolts having to be removed completely.

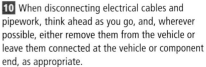

10 When disconnecting electrical cables and pipework, think ahead as you go, and, wherever possible, either remove them from the vehicle or leave them connected at the vehicle or component end, as appropriate.

11 The inlet manifold had to come off, and by removing it now access to items such as the exhaust pipe at the exhaust manifold was improved.

12 Later, another of Ian's mates, Kev – like Ian a factory-trained and highly qualified Land Rover engineer – came along to lend a hand. Kev disconnected the exhaust system at the front pipe.

NOTE: This vehicle has had a non-standard, automatic transmission conversion, but we're not covering that part of the work.

13 The engine mounting on the right-hand side of the engine is adjacent to the oil filter position...

14 ...while this is the location on the other side of the engine.

15 Some of the bell-housing bolts, in particular those on the bottom, are very easy to reach...

16 ...whereas others take a little bit more effort. You need to support engine and transmission where they join, otherwise you risk putting harmful strain on the transmission first motion shaft, the one that fits into a bush on the back of the engine crank.

17 This 300 Tdi engine was now ready to be lifted out.

18 Kev hooked up to the engine lifting eyes on the engine, while Ian Baughan stood by...

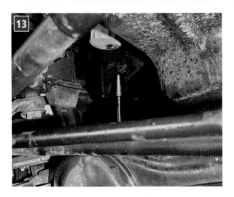

19 ...ready to lift and separate. As you can see from their concentration, it's important to check that nothing is damaged – the power steering reservoir, for instance, is a mere sliver away – and that nothing is still connected. When all is clear, get the engine back on the ground as soon as practicable – it's safer there!

TD5 ENGINES

1 Undo the three bolts and remove the plastic engine cover.
2 Remove the turbocharger:
   a Take off the airflow sensor from the engine cleaner cover, disconnecting the wiring plug as it's withdrawn.
   b Remove the air intake trunking from the turbocharger.
   c Remove the heat shield (three bolts) from above the exhaust manifold.
   d Disconnect the vacuum hose from the turbocharger wastegate control diaphragm.
   e Disconnect the turbocharger outlet hose.
   f Undo the oil feed pipe at the banjo connector.
   g Detach the exhaust front pipe (three bolts).
   h Remove the three nuts holding the turbocharger to the exhaust manifold.
   i Undo the union holding the turbo drain pipe to the engine block.
   j Remove the turbocharger.
3 Disconnect the coolant hoses from the fuel cooler and coolant rail.
4 Disconnect the fuel hoses from the fuel cooler. (Slide off the plastic collars; depress release button; plug openings to prevent dirt ingress.)
5 Remove the servo vacuum hose and then the fuel cooler (four bolts).
6 Without disconnecting the fluid hoses, remove the power steering pump pulley (three bolts) and then the four mounting bolts. Move the pump to one side, out of the way.

Refitting the engine

NOTE: Engine removal and refit is broadly the same in principle for all types.

1 Have all the new gaskets you will need to hand and check to see if any clips need replacing before starting work.
2 Engage a gear to prevent gear shaft rotation. Offer the engine to the gearbox – it may be necessary to rotate the engine sufficiently to align the gearbox primary pinion with the clutch plate splines. When aligned, push the engine fully to the rear and secure the bell housing to the flywheel housing, tightening the fixings evenly.
3 Lift the engine sufficient to remove the packing or jack from beneath the gearbox and insert the engine front mounting rubbers. Then lower the engine and fit the upper and lower fixings to the engine mountings.
4 Remove the sling supporting the engine. Secure the speedometer drive cable in the cable clip adjacent to the fuel pump.
5 Connect the engine electrical leads at the snap connectors at the right-hand rear side of the engine compartment. Also connect the following:
   a The fuel inlet pipe to the fuel pump, and secure the battery lead in the adjacent cable clip.
   b The alternator and starter motor leads at the dash panel.
   c The throttle cable.
   d The engine earth cable.
   e The distributor leads at the ignition coil.
   f The heater hoses in the engine compartment.
   g The front exhaust pipe to the exhaust manifold.
   h Diesel fuel pipe.
6 Once all this has been completed, the front floor, radiator, air cleaner and bonnet can be refitted.

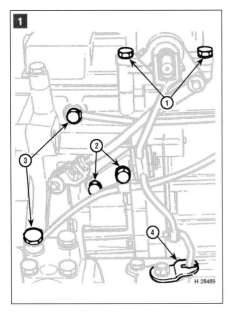

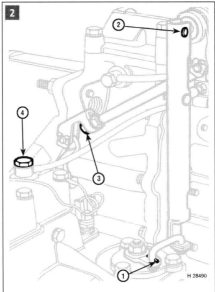

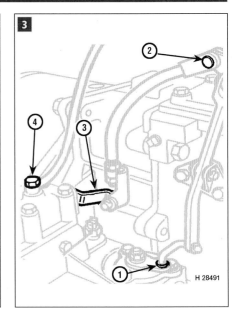

The gearbox and transfer box are best separated before removal to cut down on weight and to increase safety. You'd need to remove the complete seat base to remove the gearbox from inside the vehicle. Most specialists remove gearboxes and transfer boxes from underneath the vehicle, and always split the two units first.

SEPARATING LT230R TRANSFER BOX FROM MAIN GEARBOX

1 The following notes relate to this drawing and can be used when the two units have been removed from the vehicle in one piece. However, it's possible to remove the transfer box with the main gearbox still in place in the vehicle.
a   You can start by removing the transmission brake.
b   Take out the two bolts (2) holding the pivot to the casing.
c   Remove the breather pipe connectors (3) from the casing.
d   Disconnect the diff lock lever from the casing (4), removing the lock-nut, nut and split-pin or spring washer as applicable.
e   Remove the four bolts (1) holding the transfer gearchange housing to the main gearchange housing. The transfer box will now slide from the main gearbox casing.

SEPARATING LT230T TRANSFER BOX FROM MAIN GEARBOX

2 The following notes all relate to this drawing (early LT230T transfer boxes)…

3 …or this drawing (later LT230T transfer boxes), and all assume that the two units have been removed from the vehicle in one piece. It's possible

to remove the transfer box with the main gearbox still in place in the vehicle, however.
a   Disconnect the diff lock lever from the casing (1), removing the lock-nut, nut and split-pin or spring washer, as applicable.
b   Disconnect the selector shaft operating arm by removing the clevis pin (2). On later models you'll also have to disconnect the lower end of the selector shaft arm from the clamp on the gear selector lever (3).
c   Remove the breather pipe union and disconnect

the breather pipes (4).
d   The bolts holding the two units together can now be removed and the transfer box will now slide from the main gearbox casing. Note that on early models it'll be necessary to raise the transfer gear selector lever to gain access to the main gearbox to transfer box retaining nut.

4 Both front and rear propshafts have to be disconnected.

GEARBOX REMOVAL

5 The crossmember on 90s and 110s is unbolted from the chassis.

6 If the gearbox is to be removed from inside, the gearbox mountings should be removed completely from the chassis (obviously making sure the gearbox is supported on a hoist). This aids removal and refitting back to the engine.

7 If the gearbox is to be removed from underneath then just the floor and centre turret need to be removed from the inside. In both cases the gearstick should be removed…

8 …as well as its housing.

On all but the earliest vehicles, the handbrake cable is easier to remove from the operating handle rather than the transfer box end. The gearbox tunnels should always be removed when removing the transmission. The clutch slave cylinder shouldn't be left hanging attached to the flexible hose, as remaining hydraulic pressure can push the piston out.

9 Wiring plugs/sockets must be disconnected.

10 Disconnecting part of the exhaust improves access.

11 If the transmission is to be removed from underneath, a suitable gearbox stand should be in place before the bell-housing bolts are slackened and removed.

12 The gearbox is a very heavy unit and takes two people to move around.

REFITTING TRANSFER BOX TO MAIN GEARBOX – BOTH TYPES

Before refitting the transfer box to the main gearbox, make sure that 'low range' is selected in the transfer box.

Clean the mating surfaces of the two gearboxes, make sure that the upper locating dowel is in place on the main gearbox casing and fit the two units together, using the correct fixings in their original locations. Use a new lock-nut or split-pin, where applicable, on the nut holding the diff lock connecting rod to the lever on the transfer box. On LT230R models, note that the longest bolt fits at the rear, right-hand side of the housing. Also,

on later LT230T models the transfer gear selector rod has to be fitted into the clamp as the two units are brought together.

REFITTING TRANSMISSION TO VEHICLE

Refitting the transmission is the reverse of removal, with the following additional points:

a The clutch will need to be perfectly aligned before starting work.

b Some recommend that sealing compound should be applied to the mating surfaces of the flywheel housing and bell housing (after checking that they're completely clean) immediately before reassembly, although it isn't used at the factory.

c Put a large spanner and tommy bar on the crankshaft pulley nut and have a helper turn the engine (spark plugs/glow plugs removed) as the two units are brought together, helping to align the splines on the first motion shaft and in the clutch. ALWAYS ENSURE THE BATTERY IS DISCONNECTED BEFORE TURNING AN ENGINE OVER. (A PETROL ENGINE WILL FIRE UP IF THE IGNITION IS ON.)

d Use a combination of lifting hoist and a trolley jack to change the angle, to line up the two units while they're slid together. Draw them together with bell-housing bolts (or even special long bolts, used just for the job of pulling the units together before being removed) but DO NOT attempt to force the units together. If they absolutely refuse to get together, try realigning the clutch before trying again. Care should be taken not to damage the clutch diaphragm with the input shaft of the gearbox.

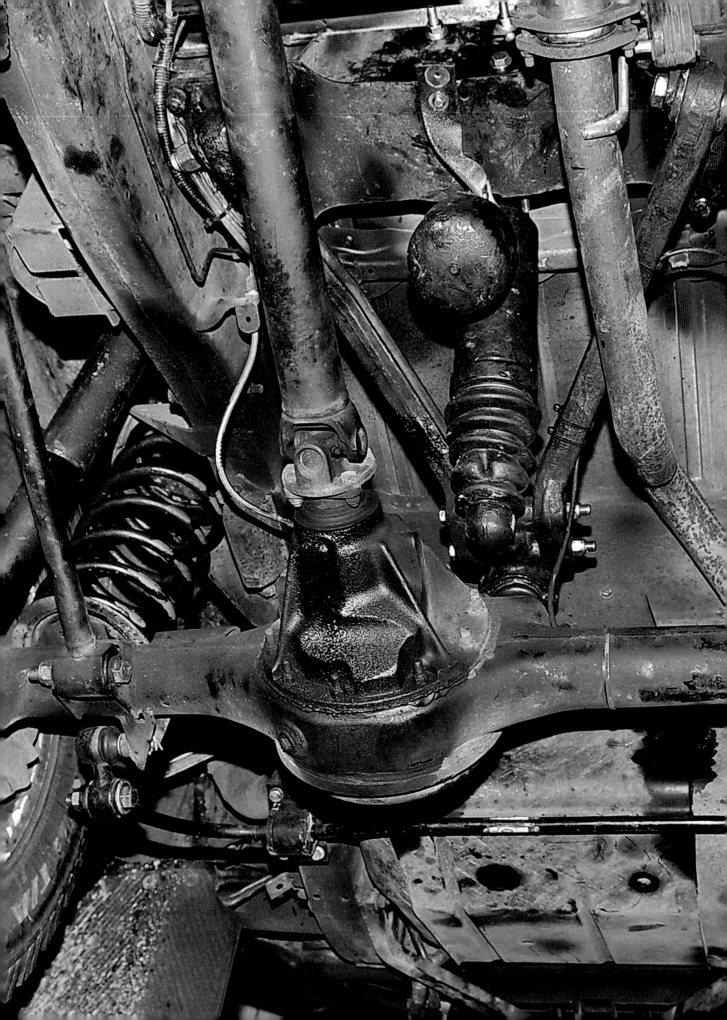

Running gear

Working on almost any part of the Land Rover's running gear involves raising the vehicle off the ground. Follow all the usual safety procedures when working beneath the vehicle, as outlined elsewhere in this book.

Also, note that if a halfshaft has to be removed the handbrake will be ineffective because of the fact that the handbrake operates on the transmission system only. Therefore, it's doubly important that the wheels remaining on the ground are carefully and adequately chocked to prevent movement.

Most work on the running gear can be carried out with the axle housings fitted to the vehicle if you need to remove the complete axle for any reason. Note that at least two people, and preferably three, will be needed in order to handle the axle unit safely.

SAFETY: BRAKING SYSTEM

Do not carry out any work on your Land Rover's braking system unless you're fully competent to do so. If you haven't been trained in this work, make sure that you have a garage or qualified mechanic check your vehicle's brakes before using the car on the road. Always replace disc pads and/ or shoes in sets of four – never replace them on one wheel only. If friction components are contaminated with oil or grease, replace them – there's no way of cleaning them off because the oil or grease will have soaked into the friction materials. If the rear brakes are contaminated with oil, you may need to replace the rear axle oil seal.

SAFETY: HYDRAULIC FLUID

There are several hazards associated with hydraulic fluid, so take careful note of the following:

a Hydraulic fluid is poisonous. Do not ingest, keep away from children, and seek immediate medical advice if swallowed.
b Wear gloves when handling hydraulic fluid, and if any gets on to your skin wash it off immediately with soap and water.
c Hydraulic fluid deteriorates when exposed to the air. Never reuse old hydraulic fluid and always top-up with fluid from a freshly opened container. Be sure always to use the correct, recommended type for your vehicle.
d Most hydraulic fluid is flammable. Keep away from sources of heat, sparks or ignition.
e Hydraulic fluid is a slow but effective paint stripper and will also attack plastics. Wipe up any spills immediately then wash off the residue with washing-up liquid and warm water.

General installation notes

Whenever you refit components held in place with a lock-nut, the old lock-nut must be discarded and a new one fitted.

Before replacing a bolt in a tapped thread, make sure that the female thread has been properly cleaned out. If you have access to a thread tap of the correct size and type, use it to clean out the threads; if you don't have a thread tap, make a hacksaw blade cut part of the way down a spare bolt (of the correct size and type, of course!) and run it through the thread to be cleaned out. This won't recut a thread, but it will clean out debris such as old thread sealer. You'll

have to remove the bolt and screw it in again every time the slot clogs up.

Most suspension components that aren't fitted with lock-nuts should have liquid threadlock applied to the thread before it's refitted. This is how to apply Würth threadlocker: make sure that both male and female threads are clean, dry and free of lubricant. Apply a few drops of threadlock to the bolt or machine screw being fitted immediately before fitting it into place, then tighten it to the recommended torque, using the specified number and positions of washers.

In several leak-prone locations, such as at the swivel hubs, it pays to use a non-setting gasket compound to help ensure that no leaks can occur. Make sure that both mating surfaces are clean, dry and free of lubricants. Wipe a thin but even coating of gasket compound on both sides of the gasket, taking care not to contaminate the compound with grit or dust. Fit and use the gasket in the normal way. Do not use a setting-type of compound because this will make future dismantling extremely difficult.

Front axle removal and refitting

1 These are the front axle and suspension components. The numbers and letters in the text in this section refer to this drawing.

Chock both rear wheels, fore and aft, raise the front of the vehicle and support it on axle stands placed beneath the chassis.

Disconnect the brake hose brackets from the swivel housings (A), then refit the bolts to the swivel housings to prevent oil leakage.

Remove the brake caliper as shown in a later section, and hang the caliper on a piece of wire to the front suspension coil spring, but take care not to place any strain on the hydraulic hose.

Disconnect the propshaft from the front differential and tie it out of the way.

Take the weight of the front axle on a trolley jack placed beneath the differential housing.

Disconnect the following items as described elsewhere in this book:
a Disconnect the track-rod end from the steering arm.
b Take the steering drag-link off the swivel pin housing.
c Disconnect the right radius arm (B) and left radius arm (9)…
d …and the Panhard rod (7).

2 Disconnect the anti-roll bar connecting links from where they're connected to the axle.
e Disconnect the bottom of the shock absorber from the axle.

Refit the wheels to the axle, lower the axle to the ground. You can now, relatively easily, roll the axle

from underneath the vehicle. Note that the front coil springs become unseated as the axle is lowered.

Refitting the front axle is essentially the reverse of its removal. Bear in mind the following points:
a When the axle is raised into position, both coil springs (2) will need to be correctly seated.
b The upper swivel-pin retaining bolts (A) should be cleaned and fitted with locking compound applied to each thread.
c None of the fixing bolts should be finally tightened up before the road wheels have been refitted to the axle, and the vehicle has been lowered to the ground and rocked vigorously to settle all of the components. All of the fixings should then be tightened to the correct torque. This doesn't apply to the brake components, of course. These should have been tightened to the correct torque when reassembled.

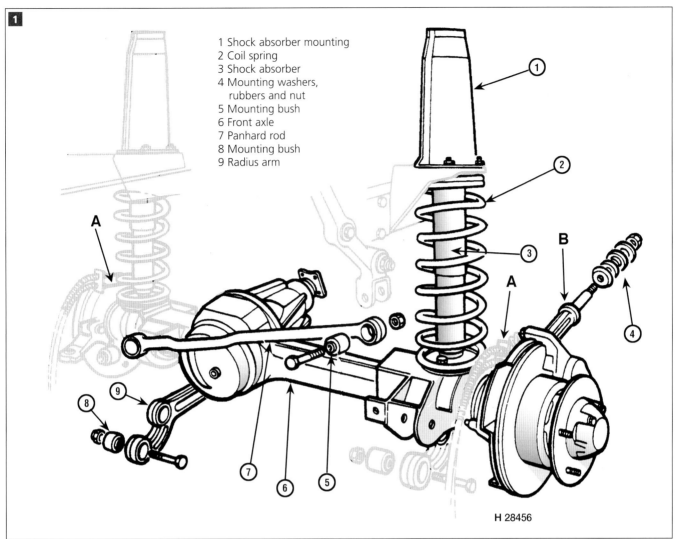

1
1 Shock absorber mounting
2 Coil spring
3 Shock absorber
4 Mounting washers,
  rubbers and nut
5 Mounting bush
6 Front axle
7 Panhard rod
8 Mounting bush
9 Radius arm

H 28456

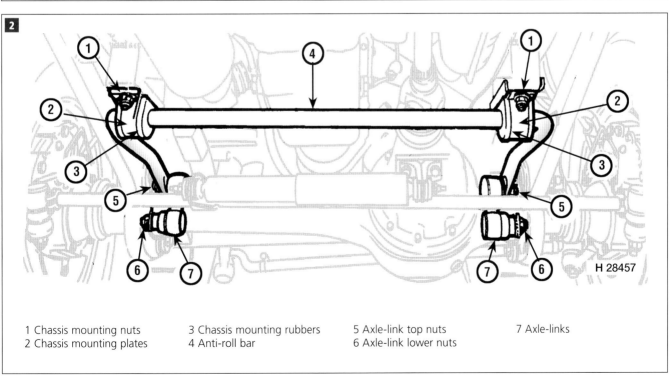

2

1 Chassis mounting nuts
2 Chassis mounting plates

3 Chassis mounting rubbers
4 Anti-roll bar

5 Axle-link top nuts
6 Axle-link lower nuts

7 Axle-links

H 28457

Front stub axle, halfshafts and CV joints

Also see Front brake caliper, disc and hose replacement for further information.
This section shows the fitting of Ashcroft Transmission's Heavy Duty halfshafts but the procedure is exactly the same with standard halfshafts.

1 Bill, the boss at Autoland, one of Ashcroft's fitting stations, started by removing the rubber cap, the circlip and the washer behind it…

2 …which, once the ring of bolts holding it in place had been removed, allowed the drive flange to be levered free.

3 He also had to remove the brake caliper, suspending it carefully out of the way.

4 On these later Defenders, the hub nut is a use-once fitting with a tab that needs opening up…

5 …before removing and discarding the nut.

6 At least, that was the theory! This nut couldn't be shifted, so Bill had to resort to careful use of the cut-off grinder…

7 …stopping before he reached the component beneath and springing the nut free with hammer and chisel.

8 Later, with the hub removed, you could see that the thread had picked up last time the nut was fitted, probably because old threadlock hadn't been thoroughly removed before refitting it.

9 Bill removed the six bolts retaining the stub axle to the swivel housing…

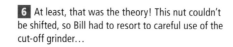

10 …removed and put down the swivel housing…

11 …and, while catching spilled oil…

12 …withdrew the halfshaft and universal joint.

13 He removed the mud shield…

14 …and disconnected the steering arm.

15 Next, the swivel pin housing was unbolted from the end of the axle and removed.

16 Rather than reusing the old seal, Bill levered it out…

17 …offered up a new one…

18 …and drifted it in evenly and with meticulous care.

For oil seal and bearing replacement, see the section entitled 'Rear hub and bearing overhaul' for more detailed information.

19 Remembering what had happened earlier when old threadlock hadn't been removed by a previous mechanic, Bill ran a tap down each female thread.

20 A thin wipe of non-setting gasket sealant helps to hold the new gasket in place when refitting.

21 All the bolt threads were cleaned, removing all traces of threadlock so that fresh threadlock could be used before reusing the bolts.

22 You should always fit gaskets and fully tighten bolts with threadlock immediately after applying sealant or threadlock. It's important that this is carried out before the sealant can dry, or the

threadlock can harden inside the thread, which it will do as soon as air is excluded. If you wait, there's a risk of causing a leak or of hardened threadlock causing problems before the thread is properly tightened to the correct torque.

We also fitted stronger, Ashcroft Heavy Duty CV joints. They look different to standard but, once again, the fitting procedure is identical.

23 The halfshaft splines must be greased and the circlip placed in position.

24 This has to be inserted into the end of the new Ashcroft CV joint.

25 It can be a tricky business and is best carried out with an extra pair of hands and at least one screwdriver to spring the circlip and help it on its way into the CV joint.

26 Insert the axle shaft, and when the differential splines are engaged, push assembly in fully. CAUTION: Take care not to damage axle shaft oil seals.

27 You have to fit the stub axle with its flat side at the 12 o'clock position. The stub axle also received a new gasket.

28 Bill coated the threads of the stub axle bolts with threadlock. IMPORTANT: Ensure that the constant velocity joint bearing journal is butted against the thrust ring on the stub axle before the stub axle is tightened.

29 Back on went the hub and brake disc assembly…

30 …followed by a new lock-nut.

31 After tightening to the correct torque, the nut was staked into position.

32 These are the components of the earlier type of hub with lock-washers that have tabs to be opened up for removal; then, using new washers on reassembly, the tabs on lock-washer (h) are knocked inward to lock the adjuster nut (i), and outward to lock the lock-nut (g).

a   Dust cap.
b   Driveshaft circlip.
c   Driveshaft shims.
d   Drive member.
e   Drive member joint washer.
f   Drive member retaining bolt (five off).
g   Lock-nut.
h   Lock-washer.
i   Hub adjusting nut.
j   Keyed washer.
k   Outer bearing.
l   Hub.
m   Inner bearing.
n   Grease seal.
o   Brake disc.

33 Here's how to adjust the earlier type of hub:
a   Fit the hub adjusting nut. Tighten by hand while turning the hub until all end-play is taken up.
b   Mount a dial gauge and slacken off the adjusting nut until there's end-play of 0.1270 to 0.1016mm.
c   Fit a new keyed lock tab washer.
d   Fit and tighten the hub adjusting nut and recheck the end-play before bending the lock tab over.

HALFSHAFT
To check the driveshaft end-play use a dial gauge.

Fit a suitable bolt to the threaded end of the driveshaft and use pliers to move the driveshaft in and out. The end-play (dial gauge reading) should be between 0.127 and 0.254 mm.

DRIVE FLANGES

34 This section shows the fitting procedure for Ashcroft Transmission's heavy duty drive flanges, which are dimensionally larger than standard ones though the procedure is the same. For illustrations showing standard drive flanges, see the 'Differential removal and overhaul' section.

35 Note that Bill temporarily inserted a bolt into the threaded hole in the end of the halfshaft so that he could adjust its position before fitting the new circlip.

36 Here, Bill has stripped and removed the old rear halfshafts and begun to insert the new Ashcroft shaft. He applied a good coating of grease to the spline…

37 …before fitting the new heavy-duty drive flange to the end of the halfshaft before fully pushing it home. Bill finished off by tightening the drive flange bolts with the torque wrench.

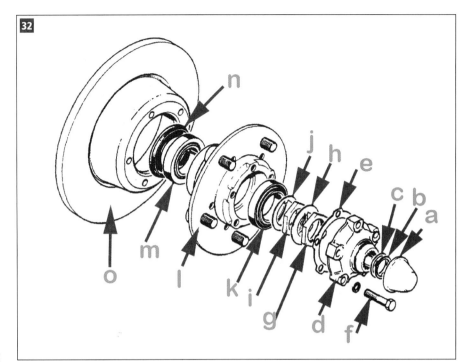

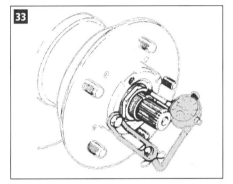

Here's how to replace a worn swivel hub ball (or 'swivel bearing housing') on earlier Defenders. They do wear, and, when worn, the oil seals follow close behind – followed by the oil from inside the housings.

SAFETY FIRST!
- Make sure the end of the axle is supported on an axle stand (NOT a jack) positioned on firm, level ground.
- Push the spare wheel under the axle too, as an extra safety measure.

The first job is to remove the front hub assembly. See 'Front stub axle, halfshafts and CV joints'.

- You have to remove the brake disc shield bracket.
- Ideally, you should drain the swivel-pin housing and refit the plug. However, many mechanics just catch the oil later.
- On later vehicles the swivel-pin housing is filled with grease for life; there are no level and drain plugs fitted.
- You could also remove the six bolts holding the stub axle to the swivel housing, then remove the stub axle and joint washer, or leave them until later.

1 These are the swivel assembly components:

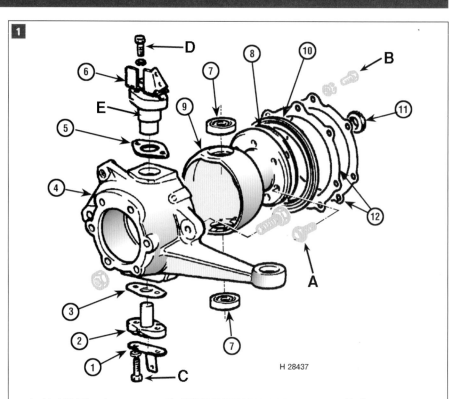

H 28437

1. Mudshield bracket
2. Lower swivel pin
3. Gasket
4. Swivel pin housing
5. Gasket
6. Upper swivel pin and brake hose bracket
7. MODELS WITH REAR DISC BRAKES.
   Swivel pin bearing and race
7. EARLIER MODELS.
   A bush and thrust washer
8. Shim
9. Swivel ball
10. Oil seal
11. Oil seal
12. Retaining plate and gasket
A, B, C, D. Fixing screws
E. Top swivel pin

SWIVEL PIN AND HOUSING

2 First, Britpart's Stuart Harrison – who was carrying out the work shown here – removed the two bolts retaining the brake hose bracket and the top swivel pin.

3 Next, he removed the two bolts retaining the lower swivel pin.

4 You have to tap the lug, rotating it a little...

5 ...to remove the lower swivel pin and joint washer.

6 Next, Stuart removed the brake hose bracket and the top swivel pin.

7 His next job was to remove the bolts and loosen the oil seal retaining plate and joint washer. They can't be removed yet!

8 He pulled away the swivel-pin housing assembly...

9 ...and the halfshaft. Note the container on the floor, catching the swivel-pin housing oil.

10 OK, perhaps draining the oil first would have been best. It'll still be messy, though! Here, Stuart slides the halfshaft out of the swivel-pin housing.

SWIVEL-BEARING HOUSING

11 The bolts holding the swivel-bearing housing in place will be caked with mud and corrosion. Spend time cleaning the heads...

12 ...so that you can get a ring spanner on each bolt.

13 The swivel bearing housing is frequently stuck in place and will need a sharp rap or two to remove it.

14 The result of all that sticking will be a glued-on gasket. A power wire brush is ideal for returning to shiny metal without causing scratch damage.

FIT SWIVEL-BEARING HOUSING

15 Here's a new swivel-bearing housing, gaskets and oil seal for the back of the ball. This is a Teflon-coated ball with greater life expectancy than the original chromed ball. Note also the new retaining bolts complete with integral thread-lock compound.

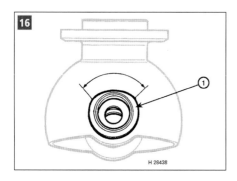

16 IMPORTANT NOTE: On early models, make sure the cut-away area on the lip of the upper swivel bush (1) is facing the inner side of the housing.

17 Wisely, Stuart decided to fit the lower bush to the bearing housing (the 'ball') before it was fitted to the axle. It's imperative that it goes in square, and that can be tricky when working beneath the ball.

18 You MUST remember to hang the swivel-housing inner oil seal (with the seal lips trailing), gasket and retaining plate on to the rear of the housing. You can't get them on later!

19 Coat both sides of the gasket with a sealing compound. Fit the bolts holding the swivel-bearing housing to the axle flange (seven bolts) and tighten to 73Nm (54lb/ft).

20 It's fairly easy to fit the top bush now because you've got the weight of the axle to hammer against, but it must still go in square, and you must NOT cause damage to the upper faces of the bush when hammering.

21 This is the thrust pad that fits in the top bush only. Stuart lubricated the insides of the bearings with swivel grease.

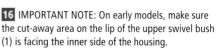

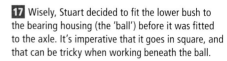

FIT SWIVEL-PIN HOUSING

22 The housing has to be thoroughly cleaned and the wire brush came in handy once more.

23 Stuart prepared to grease and fit the upper and lower swivel-pin taper-roller bearings. See picture 1.

24 This time the halfshaft has been reinserted first, followed by the swivel-pin housing.

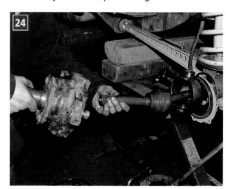

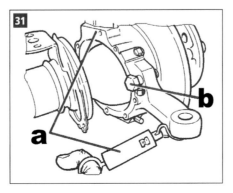

25 Stuart's tip is to insert the bottom bearing with one hand while sliding the housing into place with the other.

26 Reading from left to right: one of the new pins; shims for adjusting preload; thrust pad; swivel-pin bush. Beneath: bearing.

27 Coat both sides of the joint washer with sealing compound and position on lower swivel pin. Loosely fit the brake shield bracket plus the lower swivel pin (with lug outboard) to the swivel-pin housing. The bottom swivel pin can be fitted and the bolts fitted finger-tight to hold everything in position.

28 To start off with, you take a guess as to how many shims you might need. There's no way of knowing.

29 Don't use gasket sealant on the top pivot gaskets.

30 The bottom bolts must be treated with threadlock and tightened to 78Nm (58lb/ft) before bending over the lock tabs.

31 Before fitting the oil seal, in the words of the Land Rover manual you should 'Attach a spring balance to ball joint bore (a) and pull balance to determine effort required to turn swivel-pin housing. Resistance, once initial inertia has been overcome, should be 1.16 to 1.46kg. Adjust by removing or adding shims to top swivel pin.' Note that the (b) is the steering lock stop – frequently neglected! When the tension is correct:

- ■ Remove the top swivel bolts.
- ■ Apply threadlock and gasket seal to the gasket if required.
- ■ Refit the bolts, tighten to 78Nm (58lb/ft) and bend over the lock tabs.
- ■ Fill the swivel assembly with 0.33 litres of Molytex grease (or Britpart Swivel Pin Lubricant) rather than the traditional oil, which is far more likely to leak away.

32 After greasing the oil seal lips, fit the oil seal with retaining plate and securing bolts. Tighten to 11Nm (8lbf/ft).

The remainder of the front hub assembly can now be completed and you'll have a swivel assembly that's good for tens of thousands of miles to come.

Rear axle removal and refitting

Much of the information relating to removal of the front axle also applies to the rear axle, where applicable. The components referred to are shown here and the part numbers are mentioned in the text. Follow the instructions for front axle removal, but note the following main differences:

1 Remove the brake master cylinder cap. Refit it with a piece of plastic bag between cap and reservoir. This seals the cap and minimises the amount of brake fluid lost when you carry out the next step.

2 Disconnect the brake pipe flexible hose, at the point where the pipe that runs under the bodywork is connected to the axle.

3 Disconnect the lower links from the axle, the anti-roll bar (when fitted)...

4 ...and the lower shock absorber connection.

5 Disconnect the upper link ball joint where it connects to the top of the axle. You have to remove the split-pin before removing the nut at the bottom of the ball joint.

The axle can now be removed as described for the front axle. After refitting, bleed the brakes – see the relevant section of the workshop manual.

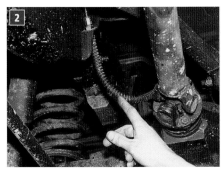

Rear hub, bearing and halfshaft overhaul

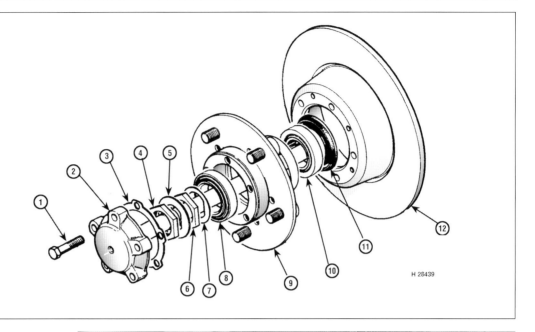

1. Retaining bolt
2. Halfshaft
3. Gasket
4. Lock-nut
5. Lock-washer
6. Adjusting nut
7. Spacer
8. Outer bearing and race
9. Hub
10. Inner bearing and race
11. Seal
12. Brake disc

H 28439

COMBINED DRIVEN MEMBER WITH HALFSHAFT

1 Models with driven member (2) integral with halfshaft: Remove the bolts (1) and withdraw the halfshaft.

ALL OTHER VERSIONS

2 Take the dust cap from the end of the shaft, remove the circlip and separate the driving member from the halfshaft (arrowed).

SPLINED HALFSHAFT MODELS

3 Remove the (separate) driven shaft…

4 …remove the circlip (a), screw a bolt into the end of the halfshaft (b) and withdraw the halfshaft.

REMOVING A BROKEN HALFSHAFT

5 The X-Shaft from X-Engineering has a 'super-strong', rare-earth magnet which will grip an irregular object incredibly well. By inserting the X-Shaft into the axle and pulling out the broken-off end of a sheared halfshaft, you can change a shaft without having to lie in the mud and be rolling again in no time at all.

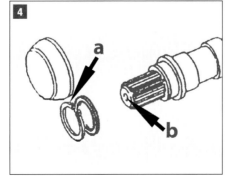

a   Halfshaft/integral 'driven member'
b   Bolts and washer – to hub
c   Gasket
d   Hub
e   Brake disc
f   Gasket
g   Stub axle
h   Bolts and washer –
    to axle case
i   Seal
j   Inner bearing
k   Outer bearing
l   Seal track spacer
m   Hub nut
n   Tab washer
o   Lock-nut

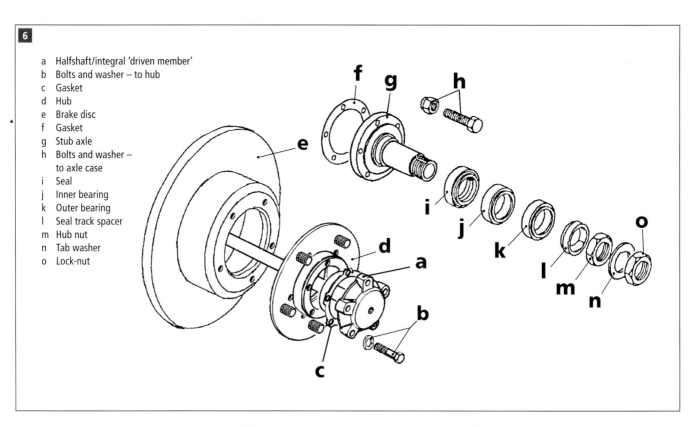

REAR HUB AND BEARING OVERHAUL

6 This is another view of the earlier halfshaft with integral driven members including the stub axle.

7 This is the later system wiht halfshaft separate from the driven member.

a   Halfshaft
b   Stub axle
c   Gasket
d   Stub axle to axle
    casing, bolt
e   Inner bearing
f   Hub
g   Inner oil seal
h   Oilcatcher (110 only)
i   Stub axle to axle
    casing, lock-nut
j   Outer bearing
k   Seal track spacer
l   Lock-washer (only one
    – between nuts, some
    models)

m   Gasket
n   Hub driven member
o   Spring washer
p   Hub driven member
    bolts
q   Dust cap
r   Circlip
s   Brake drum retaining
    screws
t   Lock-nut
u   End-float adjusting
    nut
v   Outer oil seal
w   Axle casing
x   Keyway

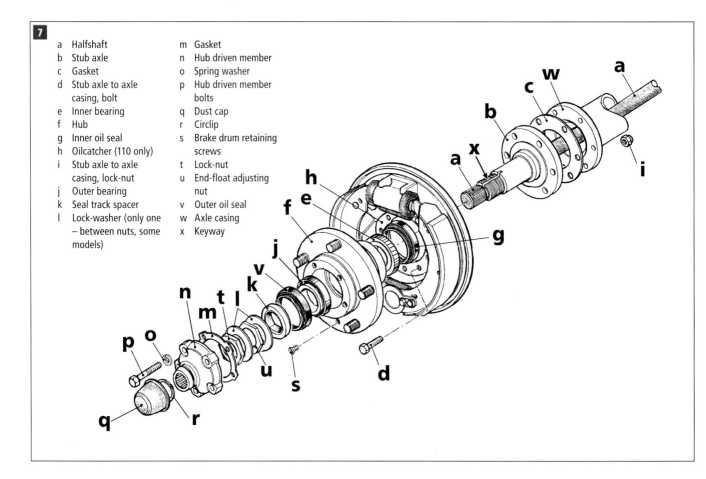

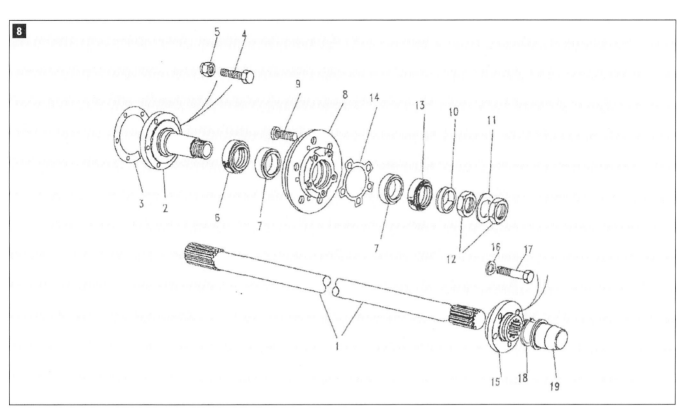

Drawing number	Name	Quantity
1	Halfshaft, rear RH	1
2	Hub bearing sleeve	2
3	Joint washer	2
4	Bolt	12
5	Nyloc nut	12
6	Oil seal	2
7	Bearing	4
8	Hub assembly	2
9	Stud	10
10	Spacer	2
11	Lock plate (washer)	4
12	Nuts (adjustment/lock)	2
13	Oil seal	2
14	Gasket	2
15	Driving member	2
16	Spring washer	5
17	Bolt	10
18	Circlip	2
19	Dust cap	2

8 Remove the brake drum or caliper, as appropriate. TIP: You need to prevent the hub from turning. It's a good idea to place a long lever between two of the wheel studs. The following text refers to the annotations in this illustration (© Lindsay Porter)

1 The two large locking nuts retaining the hub bearings are now exposed. There's a lock plate which is bent over both of the nuts – this must be straightened before you can undo them. The inner nut shouldn't be too tight on its thread, so a tommy bar probably won't be needed. Behind the inner

nut is a thrust washer or spacer washer. Unscrew the hub-nut and slide off the seal track spacer from beneath it, noting which way round it goes.

2 The whole hub can now start to be removed. The trick is to pull it away without dropping the inner bearing on the floor or in any dirt!

3 Before taking out the oil seals, make a note of which way round they go. Use a screwdriver to lever out both seals.

4 Take out both seals and inner bearing inner races.

5 Both races must be minutely examined for the smallest trace of scoring, shiny stripes, swarf and pitting, assuming that you've stripped the hub for a purpose other than replacing the bearings...

6 ...and if damaged, they can be drifted out, working around with the drift so that they don't jam as they come out. Also, look closely at the oil seal housings in the hub, and if there are any burrs that could damage the seal, remove them.

7 Tap or press the new bearings into place, taking VERY GREAT CARE to only bear on the outer races and to ensure that the bearings go in completely square.

8 Make sure that the inner bearing is packed with high-melting-point grease...

9 ...and put a liberal smear (in other words, don't pack!) in the cavity between the seal lips.

10 Each seal – whether there's just an inner, or an inner and an outer seal – must be fitted perfectly square into its housing, and for that reason once it's been started it must be pushed in with a large tube that bears on the four pads in the channel around the seal.

11 Both the inner and outer seals are fitted with lip side facing the outside of the vehicle. Both seals must be square and recessed between 4.8 and 5.3mm (0.19 to 0.21in) from the outer faces of the hub.

12 The lips of both seals must be smeared with high-melting-point grease, otherwise the new seal will be destroyed within a few seconds of use.

When refitting the hub, take care not to allow the weight of the hub to rest, even momentarily, on the seals, otherwise damage could well occur.

With the hub in place and the seal held clear of the stub axle, fit a new seal track spacer, with the seal lip leading.

WITH ALL NEW SEALS FITTED
Refit the hub-nut and tighten it while slowly turning the hub until all end-float has been removed. Back off the nut by half a turn and then retighten the nut to give the correct hub end-float of 0.05 to 0.1mm (0.002 to 0.004in), compressing the rubber on the new seal track spacer by the correct amount.

NOT USING NEW RUBBERS
Check and set the end-float with a dial gauge as described in section 'Front stub axle, halfshafts and CV joints', earlier in this chapter.

ALL VEHICLES
Fit a new lock-washer and refit the lock-nut. Drift one section of the lock-washer over a flat of the hub-nut and then, gripping the hub-nut so that it can't turn, tighten the outer lock-nut to 95 to 108Nm (70 to 80lb/ft). Rotate the hub several times to settle the bearings and recheck the end-float. Now a section of the lock-washer opposite the one that has already been bent over the hub-nut can be bent forwards and over a flat of the lock-nut.

Use a new gasket with non-setting gasket compound thinly spread over each side of it and...

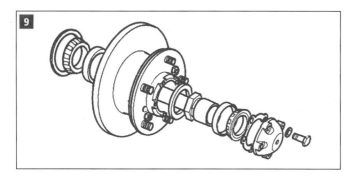

SEPARATE DRIVING FLANGE MODELS

...refit the halfshaft, driving member and circlip and five or six bolts, as appropriate.

INTEGRAL DRIVING FLANGE MODELS

...refit the halfshaft.

ALL VEHICLES

Use a drop of threadlock fluid on each bolt immediately before fitting.

REAR HUB AND BEARING OVERHAUL – LATER TYPE WITH REAR DISC BRAKES

9 There are two versions of this axle. The earlier-later type (as it were) had tab washers, similar to those in the previous section, while the latest type uses lock-nuts as shown here. See 'Differential removal and overhaul' section for the latest type.

10 Clamp the flexible brake hose. Release the rigid hose from the axle casing clips, remove the brake caliper and secure it carefully – don't kink the brake hose.

A   Remove the five bolts securing the axle shaft to the hub and withdraw the shaft either complete with the driven member or by removing the circlip and separating halfshaft and driven member. **11**

B   EARLIER MODELS
Bend back the lock tab and remove the outer nut using a box spanner and remove the lock washer and the inner nut.
LATER MODELS
Open the staking on the bearing nut and remove the nut.

C   Remove the seal track spacer.

D   Withdraw the hub complete with bearing oil seals and brake disc.

E   Remove the inner and outer oil seals.

F   Remove the inner and outer bearing cones (races).

G   Drive out the inner and outer bearing cups.

H   On ABS models, the ABS ring can be removed by unscrewing the five nuts. Often the studs come free and they can be removed after the disc has been detached. The disc is attached to the hub with five bolts. Mark the relationship of the hub to the disc if the original parts are to be reassembled.

I   Examine the stub axle and in particular check that the inner seal track is smooth and free from blemishes. **12**

J   If necessary remove the six retaining bolts and remove the stub axle complete with the mudshield and joint washer.

REASSEMBLY

A   Using a new joint washer, fit the stub axle and mud shield. Coat the threads of the retaining bolts with threadlock and tighten to the correct torque. **13**

B   Place the assembly inside a wheel to prevent it from turning while tightening. **14**

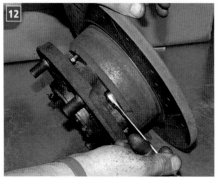

C   Refit the ABS reluctor ring, if applicable. **15**
D   Fit the new inner and outer bearing cups to the hub.
E   Fit the new inner bearing cone and pack with hub grease.

PACKING A BEARING

A   Place a small egg-sized amount of grease in the palm of your gloved hand.
B   Push the grease into the bearing while turning it…
C   …until all of the grease has entered the bearing.

INNER OIL SEAL

A   Clean the hub oil seal housing and ensure that the seal locating surface is smooth and the chamfer on the leading edge is also smooth and free from burrs.
B   Examine the new seal and ensure that it's clean and undamaged and that the garter spring is properly located. Even a small scratch on the seal lip could allow it to leak.
C   Apply bearing grease to the outside diameter of the seal before fitting. This is important, since a dry seal can be destroyed during the first few revolutions of the hub. **16**
D   Place the seal, lip side leading, squarely on the hub and, (ideally) using a seal replacer tool, push the seal into position… **17**
E   …until it's flush with the end face of the hub. **18**

OUTER OIL SEAL

Fit the new outer bearing cone and pack with hub grease. Carry out instructions shown above.

FIT HUB TO STUB AXLE

A   Select a new seal track spacer and check that the outer diameter is smooth and free from blemishes, and that there are no burrs on the chamfered leading edge.
B   Taking care not to damage the seal lips, fit the hub assembly to the stub axle. Do not allow the weight of the hub to rest even temporarily on the outer seal, otherwise damage and distortion could occur. Therefore hold the hub clear of the stub axle until the seal track spacer is fitted.
C   Carefully fit the seal track spacer, seal lip leading.
D   HUBS THAT HAVE BEEN FITTED WITH ALL-NEW COMPONENTS
    Fit the hub inner nut and tighten the adjusting nut while slowly revolving the hub until all end-float is removed, then back-off the nut approximately half a turn and retighten the nut to 13 to 15in/lb, which will automatically allow for compression of the rubber on the new seal track spacer while giving the required hub end-float of 0.013 to 0.10mm (0.0005 to 0.004in).
    IF ORIGINAL COMPONENTS ARE BEING REFITTED
    If the rubber on the seal track spacer has previously been compressed, the hub end-float can be checked by mounting a dial indicator and bracket on the hub so that the pin rests on the nut. Rotate the hub to settle the bearings and check the end-float by pushing and pulling the

hub. End-float must fall within the limits given in the previous instruction.
E   EARLIER TYPE
    Fit a new lock-washer and lock-nut. Making sure the inner adjustment nut doesn't move, tighten the outer lock-nut to 70 to 80ft/lb (95 to 108Nm).
    LATER TYPE
    Use a new 'one-shot' lock-nut, tighten until the hub won't rotate, back off and retighten to the recommended torque and stake the nut to lock it. **19**
F   EARLIER TYPE

If original components have been refitted, rotate the hub several times to settle the bearings then recheck the end-float.
G   EARLIER TYPE
    Bend one segment of the lock-washer inward over the adjusting nut, and another outward over the lock-nut, taking care not to damage the outer seal.
H   Using a new joint washer, fit the hub driving member and evenly tighten the retaining bolts to the correct torque.
I   Refit the brake caliper and the brake pipes to the axle casing.

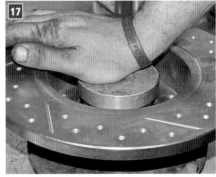

Here, Quaife limited-slip differentials are being fitted in place of the originals. They're a direct replacement for the standard, factory-fitted 'open' differentials, so the process is identical. The work was carried out at Autolands, near Luton, on behalf of well-known Land Rover transmission specialists Ashcroft Engineering.

For earlier types of rear hub, see 'Rear hub, bearing and halfshaft overhaul' section.

FRONT DIFFERENTIAL

1 Autolands' mechanic Danny decided that the best way of removing the front halfshafts was to detach each front hub complete. There's a bit of work involved, of course, including detaching steering arms.

After clamping off the brake hoses, he removed them from the calipers and took off each front hub complete with caliper assembly and halfshaft still fitted at the outer end. On reassembly, brake bleeding took a mere two pumps per side, but another approach would be to leave the hoses connected to the calipers, unbolt the calipers from the hubs and leave the calipers hanging in the wheel arches, taking care not to put any strain on the brake hoses.

2 After detaching the propshaft, the fixing nuts were removed and the front differential – very slightly reluctantly – was freed and lifted down to the ground.

REAR DIFFERENTIAL

3 At the back, the process is somewhat simpler. After removing the dust cap, the circlip is freed and removed...

4 ...the hub bolts extracted...

5 ...allowing Danny to remove each back axle halfshaft...

6 ...before taking out the back axle differential.

7 At Ashcroft Engineering, where the diffs were taken, engineer Craig made witness marks on the bearing caps with a centre punch so they could be refitted on their original sides and the right way round.

8 Next he drove out the locking pins in the bearing adjusters so that the adjusters can be turned when the diff is reassembled later. The pins are left in place – no need to remove them completely.

9 After unbolting the bearing cap bolts, Craig simply lifted them off...

10 ...and then removed the bearing side adjustment nuts.

11 The differential crownwheel assembly could now be lifted out of the differential casing.

12 Craig removed the bolts holding the differential to the crownwheel...

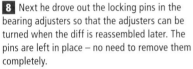

13 ...and used a mallet, tapping evenly around the perimeter of the crownwheel – which is a tight fit – until it was free of the flange...

14 ...and the 'old' open diff could be lifted away from the crownwheel. Note that Craig left the old bearings on the ends of the diff...

15 ...because he would be fitting new ones to the Quaife diff. It would be madness not to, in view of the amount of dismantling carried out and the cost of fitting the new diffs.

16 Each of the new bearings was pressed on using the hydraulic press and applying pressure only to the centre part of the bearing.

17 Now, with both new bearings fitted, the new Quaife diff (right) was ready to be built back up. Differentials that don't have any torque-sensing or lock-up mechanism are known as 'open' diffs and the standard diff (left) is quite literally open in the sense that you can see the gears inside – though

that's not what's meant by 'open' in this context, of course! It means that the diff will allow one wheel on an axle to sit stock, stone still if the other one is spinning freely.

18 Craig placed the crownwheel over the open jaws of the vice and lowered the differential into position.

19 He used all-new high tensile bolts and applied threadlock to them. It's not unheard of for bolts inside a differential to come loose, but it's horrible, expensive and would potentially be a very dangerous thing to happen if it caused the diff to lock solid. So Ashcroft always fit new bolts.

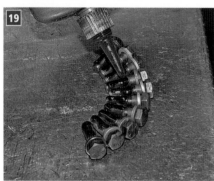

20 Holes and threads were perfectly aligned and each of the bolts was started off by hand before being tightened across opposite sides, first one side, then the other – though not fully tightened yet.

IMPORTANT NOTE: Don't leave the bolts between first tightening and torquing them down, because otherwise the threadlock will go off (which it does as soon as air is excluded) and all you'll do is break the threadlock joint, destroying its effectiveness.

21 Final tightening was carried out with the torque wrench. This has to be done according to the torque figures shown in the workshop manual for the particular differential fitted to your Land Rover.

22 On this differential, Craig knew that the height from the top of the pinion should be between 76.1 and 76.2mm. The reading he got was 76.22mm and this was deemed to be perfectly acceptable. If it had been outside the acceptable range, the pinion height would have to be adjusted by adding or removing shims from beneath the pinion, as necessary. Craig says that it's rare for a diff that hasn't been badly worn to need any adjustment in this area.

23 The assembled Quaife differential and crownwheel were lowered into position in the casing after first checking that they were going in the right way round. You can't get it wrong because the crownwheel matches the cut-away inside the casing.

24 Note that the adjustment nuts are threaded, and it's essential that the threads on the nuts bed fully into the threads in the casing...

25 ...as well as those in the caps. Craig checked carefully as each cap was properly bedded down into its thread before he fitted and carefully tightened each cap bolt. If you're not as experienced as Craig, it would be best to tighten each of the bolts with a spanner. Constantly check that the nut turns freely as each bolt is tightened up. The nut must turn freely even after the bearing cap is fully home.

26 The process to be followed here is quite critical, but it's logical when you think about it.

The bearing adjuster on the opposite side to the crownwheel is backed off quite a long way and then the adjuster on the same side as the crownwheel...

27 ...is tightened using the correct spanner, pushing the crownwheel against the pinion...

28 ...until you can JUST feel no backlash between the propshaft flange and the crownwheel when trying to turn one against the other. Then the adjustment nut on the opposite side is tightened up again, in effect pushing the crownwheel away from the pinion until you can just feel a little backlash.

29 Now, it has to be said that most of us, without Craig's experience, wouldn't feel confident in judging what is and isn't the right amount of backlash. In such cases it's best to follow the procedure described in the workshop manual as shown here, in brief.
a   Fit the differential unit and lever the unit away from the drive pinion until the opposite bearing cup is seated against the housing.
b   Place a dial gauge on the casing with its stylus resting on the back face of the crown wheel. Zero the gauge.
c   Lever the differential unit to engage the crownwheel teeth in full mesh with the drive pinion teeth.
d   Note the new reading obtained on the dial gauge. From this figure subtract 0.010in to obtain correct crownwheel backlash when fitted. This indicates the thickness of shimming to be fitted between the differential case and the bearing cone at the crownwheel side of the differential.

30 Another rather technical area is that of establishing that the crownwheel is in the correct position relative to the pinion. Craig applied engineers' blue to four of the teeth on the crownwheel...

31 ...and after turning the crownwheel so that the blued area was in contact with the pinion, he worked it backwards and forwards several times so that some of the blue was rubbed off the crownwheel, thus indicating the area that was in contact with the pinion.

32 These roughly oval patches are the areas of contact. Once again, it takes a certain degree of engineering experience to be able to ascertain with certainty the actual area of contact.

33 This picture has been taken from the actual workbook used by Ashcroft Transmissions to show acceptable patterns on the teeth of the crownwheel. The bottom four are typical faults where the crownwheel position would need adjustment.

34 Note that the area of contact on the 'backs' of the teeth, correctly described as the 'drive' side, have to be checked as well.

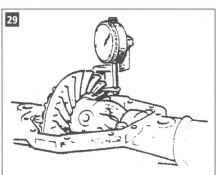

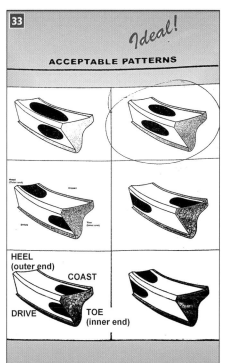

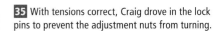

35 With tensions correct, Craig drove in the lock pins to prevent the adjustment nuts from turning.

36 Earlier, Craig had fitted the bearing bolts so that the adjustment nuts could be set. But it's crucially important that threadlock isn't applied until you're ready to torque each bolt down, as already explained. Now, one at a time, Craig removed each bearing bolt, cleaned off any old threadlock found in the threads, applied new threadlock, refitted the bolt and tightened it down to the recommended torque setting.

37 Ashcroft Transmissions' work was done and the differentials were returned to Autoland, where this time mechanic Andy was involved. He applied silicone gasket to the diff (no paper gaskets were used on this version)...

38 ...offered up the diff carefully, taking care not to disturb the liquid gasket...

39 ...and placed it on the studs on the axle casing before refitting the nuts that Danny had removed the previous day.

40 The halfshafts do have paper gaskets, and Andy fitted new ones...

41 ...before sliding each halfshaft into place. There's often a measure of jiggling required to persuade the splines on the halfshaft to enter those on the differential.

42 With front and rear axles fully reassembled, the last job was to top up with (in this case) semi-synthetic differential oil. Note that earlier vehicles, those whose oil seals weren't designed for use with synthetic oil, will almost certainly spring a leak if synthetic oil is used.

Removing a rusted-on drive flange

1 Sometimes, a drive flange (or member) refuses to come off the hub. There's a number of tricks you can work through. If you're replacing seals, apply strong heat to the localised area around the splines. Plan to fit a new drive member, because heat will probably weaken the structure of the old one.

2 This is a 'pound shop' wood chisel being sacrificed in trying to encourage the heated flange to come off. In this case, it didn't budge.

3 You might as well try a puller if you've got one. It may work – but probably won't!

4 When all else fails, use an angle grinder to cut down each side of the splines. Don't cut into the splines or the hub! Stop before you get to the bottom of the drive flange.

5 In this case, the cut grooves released the pressure on the splines and it became possible to drift off the scrap drive flange without damaging any other components.

When reassembling, ALWAYS use copper grease on the halfshaft splines.

Front brake caliper, disc and hose replacement

The work carried out here was part of a brake upgrade at MM 4x4, but the processes involved are exactly the same as for standard components.

You'll need new gaskets (or liquid gasket) for the drive members (flanges) and new nuts for later models with one-shot hub nuts (as shown here), as well as things like split pins. When you're ordering your parts, talk to your supplier, such as MM 4x4, who'll be able to advise you on whatever ancillaries you'll need, depending on the age and model of your Land Rover.

1 MM 4x4's mechanic Andy removed the dust cap, followed by the circlip, using circlip pliers. He made the point that you must retrieve, and retain for later reuse, all the shims found beneath.

2 Look at the rust already forming on the driveshaft splines. That explains why it was a minor struggle to get the driven member off the end of the shaft. Andy says he always does this part of the work first because (especially on earlier models) there's often an oil leak once the driven member has been removed, and he can now leave a tray beneath the hub to collect the oil while he carries on with the brakes.

3 After removing the split pins from the inner ends of the brake pad retaining pins, each pin can be slid out, making sure that you retrieve the spring fitted to each one.

4 You might need to lever the pistons back in, especially if the old discs have a wear ridge around the outer edge, before sliding out the brake pads.

5 In order to remove the two bolts holding the caliper in place, you'll need a long breaker bar and 12-point socket.

6 If you're removing the caliper but not replacing the flexible hose, you must hang the caliper so that it's not dangling on its hose, potentially causing it damage.

7 Inset you can see the hub nut we're dealing with here, while the annotated illustration shows the components of the earlier layout. The components shown in the diagram are:

1 Dust cap.
2 Driveshaft circlip.
3 Driveshaft shim.
4 Drive member.
5 Drive member joint washer.
6 Drive member retaining bolt (five off).
7 Lock-nut.
8 Lock-washer.
9 Hub adjusting nut.
10 Keyed washer.
11 Outer bearing.
12 Hub.
13 Inner bearing.
14 Grease seal.
15 Brake disc.

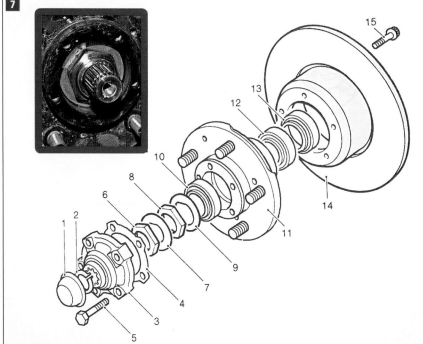

8 The large nut is quite difficult to start off because of the retaining system that you'll see later.

9 Unlike the earlier model, this one has a taper bearing assembly, and after removing it...

10 ...the hub and disc assembly can be lifted away.

11 Five bolts hold the disc to the hub...

12 ...and after ensuring that the mating surfaces are perfectly clean, Andy placed the new brake disc into position.

13 The retaining bolts must be either renewed or completely cleaned to remove all traces of threadlock before fresh threadlock is applied...

14 ...and the bolts fitted and immediately tightened to the correct torque.

15 Note that it's possible to fit grooved brake discs the wrong way round. The slots in the disc must be aligned so that they throw any water out as the disc rotates when the vehicle is travelling in a forward direction.

16 Andy refitted the bearing and washer and applied a new lock-nut. The lock-nut must, of course, be tightened to the recommended torque.

17 There's a flat against which the lip on the lock-nut has to be hammered, locking it in place.

18 Next, although he didn't need to do it at this stage, Andy refitted the caliper.

INSIDE INFORMATION

■ After threadlock has been applied, always fully tighten nuts or bolts as soon as possible.

■ Threadlock starts to go off (set) as soon as it's in an environment with no air.

■ If you leave fitted threads with threadlock on them, the threadlock will set, with the result that when you fully tighten the bolt later you'll break the threadlock, rendering it useless.

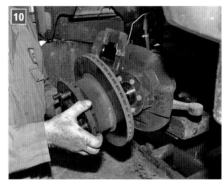

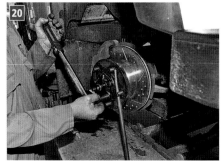

19 The old gasket was thoroughly cleaned off the drive member, any rust removed from the splines and a new gasket fitted.

20 Here's how Andy locks the hub to prevent it from turning while tightening the drive member bolts to the correct torque.

21 Invariably, the caliper pistons will need pushing back in before new pads can be fitted. The 'correct' way of doing it is with a special tool, but provided you're careful there's no reason why you shouldn't be able to do this with a screwdriver. If the pistons are too stiff to move easily there's probably some corrosion going on in there, and you should consider exchange calipers.

22 You'll help to reduce brake noise by applying a thin smear of copper grease or (better still) Würth Brake Paste to the outer edges of the metal plate. Note that these brakes have anti-squeal pads fitted to them, but if yours don't you could add an extra wipe of Brake Paste to the back of the metal backing plate – not the friction surface of the pad, of course.

23 Andy slid in the new pads...

24 ...followed by the retaining pins and springs, plus new split pins to hold the retaining pins in place. Don't bother trying to reuse the originals.

25 Next, he prepared to fit the flexible brake hose – stainless steel braided in this instance.

26 At the caliper, he cleaned off the hose connection as thoroughly as possible then disconnected the flexible hose...

27 ...before pulling out the retaining clip. On earlier models the hose is held on with a nut and washer. Hose fixings at the other end are similar, and it's a simple matter to replace the old hoses with new, being scrupulously careful not to get any dirt on the hose connections. However, Andy waited until later when he could fit all of the flexible hoses in one go, both front and rear.

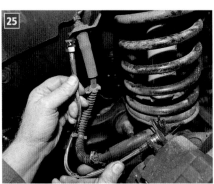

28 The rear brakes are very similar to those at the front except that they're single pot and there's a shim on the back of each brake pad. You may need to remove the old shims and reuse them on the new pads, if they're in sufficiently good condition.

29 Because there's no steering at the back, of course, the brake pipe is rigid. Andy is still happy to

leave the pipe connected to the caliper, but first, as he shows, it has to be detached from its fixing clips on the axle.

30 Andy removed the caliper, though this bolt required the use of a ring spanner, there being insufficient room for a socket.

31 He moved the caliper over as short a distance as possible so as not to strain the rigid pipe, and suspended it carefully out of the way.

32 The new MM 4x4 rear disc isn't vented, though it's thicker than some standard rear discs and is, of course, cross-drilled and grooved, as with the fronts.

33 The retrieved shims were fitted to the new pads before installing.

34 This is the top end of the front flexible hose being detached. Andy removed the clip before separating the hose joint.

35 However, when refitting the hoses he found it best to at least start the threads without the clip in place because it made it much easier to line up the threads, making sure that they aren't crossed.

36 You could then, if you wanted to, refit the clip before tightening the two halves of the hose...

37 ...or fully tighten the two halves before fitting the retaining clip – the choice is yours.

38 There are two different hoses for the rear axle so make sure you have the correct one.

39 Although it's slightly more fiddly because it's in a more restricted space, the process of swapping the rear axle flexible hose is essentially the same.

40 You'll need to bleed the brakes as described in the workshop manual. We used Automec silicone brake fluid, because it'll never cause corrosion inside the braking system, unlike conventional brake fluid, and it never needs replacing (except for topping-up, of course).

Be aware that new pads are notorious for being very noisy for the first couple of days of use until they bed in, when they quieten down.

WARNING: Brakes are one of the most important safety items on a vehicle and you should only work on them if you're fully competent to do so.

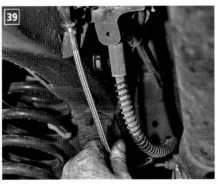

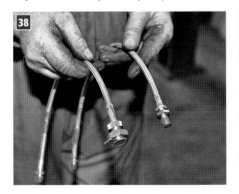

Rear drum brake overhaul

Right up to the early '90s Defenders had drum brakes at the rear. Here Britpart's spanner-man Stuart demonstrates how he sets about changing brake shoes, wheel cylinders, drums and those all-essential but oft-forgotten springs.

1 The first job is always to slacken off the brake adjusters. If you forget, and the brakes have been kept adjusted, the old drum will almost certainly bind on the shoes and you'll wonder why you can't remove it. 90 models have just one adjuster.

2 110 Land Rovers have two adjusters at the rear in the positions shown here (b). Don't be surprised if you need lots of releasing fluid and sometimes even heat to free off a stubborn adjuster. The correct brake spanner, with a square hole, will be a really big help, but if you haven't got one find a spanner that fits well, because the adjuster heads are easily rounded. The screws (a) hold the wheel cylinder in place.

3 The Defender has one screw holding the drum in place. If the screw is rusted in, try cleaning out the screw slot first and then try an impact screwdriver – it almost always works. In the worst case, you'll just have to drill the head off and replace the screw later.

4 If you need to, hammer with a soft-faced mallet – unless you're sending the old drum to the recycling skip, of course, when it won't matter if you crack it when using a regular hammer.

5 I think it makes sense to remove the brake shoe retaining (anchor) plate first. Some manuals tells you to disconnect the top spring first. You can obviously do whichever you prefer.

6 After tapping the tab washers flat, Stuart removed the two screws holding the plate in position.

7 On 89in and 90in models, the top spring goes from the leading shoe to a post on the backplate. Stuart found a spare backplate and fitted it with a brake shoe and spring to demonstrate what it is you're looking for.

8 The easiest way to remove the spring is to release some of the tension first. The leading shoe is being levered out of its seat on the wheel cylinder and eased to one side so that it sits nearer to the trailing shoe. It'll now be easier to pull the spring off with a screwdriver or self-grip wrench.

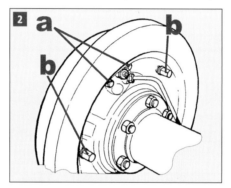

9 The trailing shoe is free at the top in any case, so Stuart pulled back on it and freed it from its seat on the pivot...

10 ...which enabled him to free the leading shoe and to remove both shoes together with spring still attached.

SAFETY FIRST!
- Brake dust can be very harmful, and dust from an older 'barn find' system can contain blue asbestos, which is a killer.
- Always wear an efficient breathing mask.
- Wash dust from the brakes with a proprietary brand of brake cleaner and gather up dust with a damp rag.
- Dispose of dust and wiping materials carefully and thoroughly in a sealed plastic bag, preferably one that won't rapidly biodegrade.

---

11 Wheel cylinders aren't all that expensive, but if an old one springs a leak you'll lose a single brake (really dangerous!), you'll scrap your contaminated brake shoes and you'll have to do all the work again.

12 After disconnecting the rigid pipe, Stu removed the two screws holding the wheel cylinder to the backplate.

13 Corrosion had welded the old wheel cylinder in place, so Stuart tapped it free with a hammer.

14 It's a simple job to fit the new wheel cylinder, but be sure to leave the protective bung in the pipe connector threaded hole...

15 ... until you're ready to reconnect the pipe. You'll need to bleed the brakes on both sides after the drums are back on and the job's finished.

16 The bases of the shoes must be linked together with their pull-off springs before attempting to fit the new shoes. Stuart used inexpensive new springs. Old springs weaken, corrode and work-harden, so that their ends often break off.

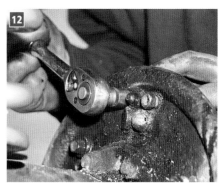

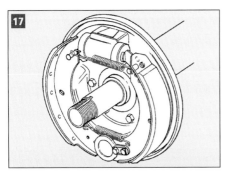

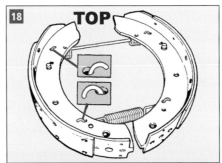

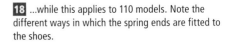

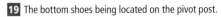

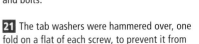

17 Note that the springs fit differently on short-wheelbase and long-wheelbase models. This is the 90 model's layout...

18 ...while this applies to 110 models. Note the different ways in which the spring ends are fitted to the shoes.

19 The bottom shoes being located on the pivot post.

20 The fixing kit should include new anchor plates and bolts.

21 The tab washers were hammered over, one fold on a flat of each screw, to prevent it from unscrewing.

22 The new top spring was taken from the kit and held so that its longest extremity was towards the shoe.

23 It was then hooked into its hole on the leading brake shoe, which was pulled to one side of the wheel cylinder...

24 ...while the other end of the spring was hooked on to its post. The leading shoe was then pulled into its seat on the wheel cylinder. It's important to note the different way in which the top spring works on 110 models. See picture 18.

25 The trailing shoe on the 90 has to be located in its slot on the other side of the wheel cylinder.

26 In order to get the new drum on, Stuart had to slacken the adjusters off even further than they were before (because of the extra 'meat' in the new shoes) and to work them up and down to make them as symmetrical as possible.

27 New drum, new fixing screw – and a touch of copper grease on the threads wouldn't be a bad idea, to prevent any seizing up in future.

After both drums are in place, the next job is to adjust the brakes and bleed them if wheel cylinders have been replaced.
1 The hydraulic system is bled at the rear, both sides, in accordance with the manual.
2 The brakes are 'worked' at the foot pedal and...
3 ...the adjuster(s) are tightened so that both shoes are fairly hard against the drums. Both of these help to centralise the shoes inside the drum.
4 The adjuster(s) are then backed off the minimum amount so that the wheel turns without the brakes binding.

Master cylinder, servo, pipes and hoses, ABS brakes

MASTER CYLINDER REMOVAL – EARLY MODELS

We strongly recommend that you don't attempt to overhaul the brake master cylinder yourself. It's such an important component of the braking system, and its replacement cost is so relatively low, that if the master cylinder is faulty you're strongly advised to replace it with a new one from a reputable company.

1 EITHER connect a piece of plastic tube to one of the brake bleeding screws, slacken the screw, place the other end of the tube in a container and gently pump the brake pedal until all of the brake fluid has been pumped out of the reservoir (tighten the brake bleeding screw); OR draw out as much brake fluid as you can with a syringe, bearing in mind that extra fluid will be left in the front chamber, so you'll have to manoeuvre the tube on the syringe through to the front of the reservoir.

2 Unscrew and remove the two brake pipes from the master cylinder body (a). Be sure to mop up any drips of brake fluid, and blank off the brake fluid openings so that no dirt can get in. Wash off spilled fluid with warm, soapy water to prevent paint damage. You can improve access by either removing the fluid reservoir (see below) or removing the vent on 300 Tdi models from the wing top. Take off the two nuts and washers (b) holding the master cylinder to the servo unit and pull off the master cylinder assembly.

3 Be sure to hold on to the O-ring from the end of the master cylinder. A good-quality replacement will come with a new seal – it fits on the shoulder (arrowed).

4 **90 models up to VIN HA701009 and 110 models up to HA901220**
On the early type of master cylinder, the reservoir (1) is held to the top of the master cylinder with two roll pins (5). Tap them out with a suitable drift and ease the reservoir out of the two seals (6) in the top of the master cylinder.

When purchasing the new master cylinder, make sure that the seals for mounting the reservoir are supplied with the replacement master cylinder unless supplied ready-assembled. Wipe a very small amount of brake fluid around the O-ring (11) before inserting the new master cylinder into the servo unit, and take great care not to damage the O-ring.

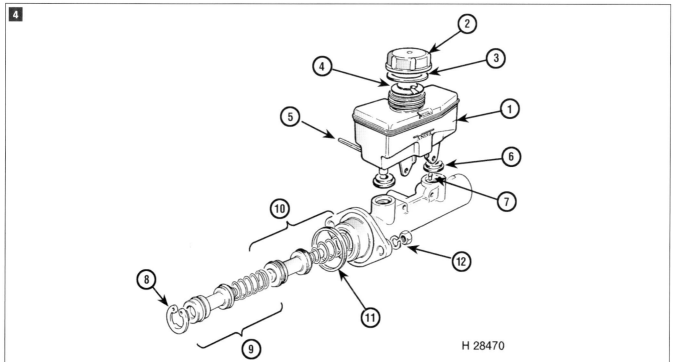

H 28470

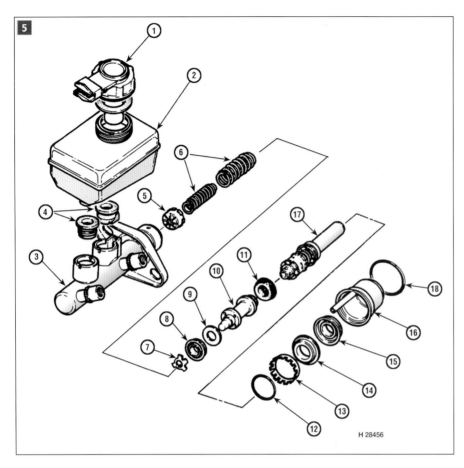

5

6

6 When inserting the master cylinder into the servo, ensure that the pushrod – the domed nut seen here – is centred into the recess in the master cylinder.

Bleed the system as described elsewhere in this chapter. Take this opportunity to eject all of the old brake fluid from each of the brake lines, replacing it with new.

BRAKE SERVO REPLACEMENT

7 It isn't recommended that you attempt to overhaul the brake servo unit yourself. If it fails, check first that the vacuum hose is connected properly and has no splits in it. Then remove and examine the check valve. See if there's any damage to the rubber sealing grommet and try both blowing and sucking through the check valve. Air should pass through it in one direction only. The check valve can be removed from the front of the servo unit by removing the vacuum hose then pulling and twisting the check valve until it comes free. If the servo unit is found to be faulty, replace it with a new unit, purchased from a good-quality source. (Illustration © Lindsay Porter)

A   Remove the retaining nuts and bolts (a) and take off the master cylinder (b), as shown in earlier section.

B   Disconnect the vacuum hose (c) from the check valve (d), taking off the spring clip (e) from later models.

C   Working from inside the vehicle, lever out the rubber sealing grommets from the brake pedal mounting box and, inside the aperture, take out the split pin, remove the washer and pull out the clevis pin holding the pedal to the servo unit pushrod (f).

D   Take off the four nuts and washers (g) holding the servo unit to the pedal mounting bracket...

E   ...and lift out the servo unit from inside the engine bay. Be sure to hang on to the rubber seal that's fitted between the servo and the bracket, but be prepared to replace it if it shows signs of deterioration.

F   Installation is the reverse of removal, but make sure that you grease the brake pedal lever where it connects to the fork on the back of the servo, and make sure that the fixing nuts have their spring washers under them and that they're tightened to the correct torque.

5 **90 models from VIN HA701010 and 110 models from HA901221**

With the later type of master cylinder, there are no roll pins holding the reservoir (2) into the master cylinder body (3), but the seals (4) are more substantial in size. Carefully ease the reservoir up and away from the master cylinder body – rolling it sideways is the best approach (see picture 2) – and note which seal goes where. When refitting the reservoir to the master cylinder body, wipe a very small amount of brake fluid around the seals to help everything to slip into place.

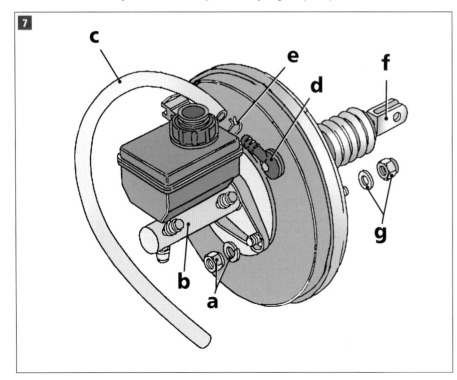

7

8 This is a slightly different way of removing the servo, complete with master cylinder. After disconnecting the hoses the pedal pushrod can be detached by removing the split pin and taking out the clevis pin through the hole in the pedal box (red arrow), while the yellow arrows show the positions of the fixing bolts.

ABS BRAKES

Interestingly, this system is described by Wabco, the system manufacturers, as 'Hydraulic ADD-ON ABS system' (their capitals) – so it's very much an addition to the existing braking system, though most parts aren't interchangeable. Note that it provides traction control as well as ABS braking.

9 This is the layout of ABS brake pipes, clips and brackets.

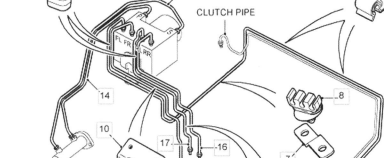

CLUTCH PIPE

10 Mechanic Dave removed nut, washer, outer bearing race and distance piece (later type), before...

11 ...drifting out of a top swivel bearing. NOTE: If you ever have a seized ABS sensor, you'll have to take off the complete hub in order to drift it out from inside the swivel housing, as shown here.

12 The top swivel has a bushed hole in it on ABS systems.

13 These are the reluctor teeth on the ABS-type constant velocity joint. These Ashcroft Heavy Duty ABS CVs look slightly different to standard but the principle is exactly the same. These reluctor teeth...

14 ...are what interact with the speed sensor, shown here with the new insert.

15 You push the sensor in until it just touches the CV joint, then ease it back 'just a bit' to provide minimal clearance.

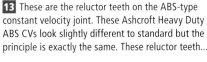

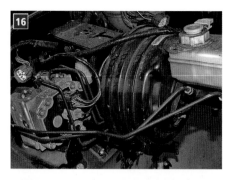

16 You can see the location of the ABS-type servo (it's larger) and master cylinder and, to their left, the modulator unit, normally partly hidden away.

17 If you need to change the modulator, you have to remove the right-hand wing…

18 …before it can be taken out. For speed's sake, you can loosen the nut holding the retainer at the bracket front, slip it on to the rubber foot, angle the modulator into position and retighten the front nut.

19 The modulator has two rubber 'feet' on the right-hand end in this picture and one on the left.

TESTING ABS WHEEL SENSORS

The logic of ABS brakes is that a locked, skidding wheel has (usually) less grip than one that's being 'pulsed'. An ABS pulses the brakes on a locking wheel (or wheels) far more effectively and rapidly than even the finest driver in the world could possibly manage by pumping the pedal.

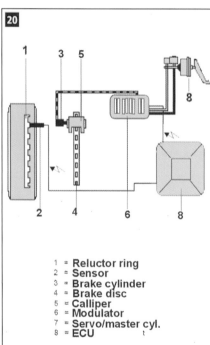

1 = Reluctor ring
2 = Sensor
3 = Brake cylinder
4 = Brake disc
5 = Calliper
6 = Modulator
7 = Servo/master cyl.
8 = ECU

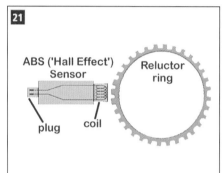

20 Wheel sensors are always on the 'look-out' for a skidding wheel. These sensors work on the Hall effect principle. Each wheel sensor 'points' at a reluctor ring – like a cog with square teeth – which spins with the road wheel. The end of the sensor contains a coil that produces a small magnetic field. Every time a 'tooth' in the reluctor ring passes through the magnetic field created by the coil, the field is altered, producing a change in voltage, which is fed back to the ABS' ECU (electronic control unit). The ECU therefore 'knows' the speed of all the road wheels. If one or more tyres skid and the wheels lock, the ECU directs the ABS system's modulator to pulse the brakes to each particular wheel – provided the driver is pressing down hard on the pedal, of course!

If a sensor stops working, you need to find the cause. It could be:
- A faulty sensor.
- Damaged wiring, a blown fuse or a blown warning light on the dash.
- A worn wheel bearing, allowing the sensor to move too far away from the reluctor ring.
- Corrosion around the sensor.

21 Here's how to test the sensor itself, using a regular multi-meter, even if you haven't got the correct diagnostic equipment as used by IRB Developments.

Set your multi-meter to ohms, connect the probes to the sensor connectors and rotate the wheel. You should see the resistance readings fluctuate as the reluctor ring passes through the sensor's magnetic field. If it does change, the sensor is probably OK; if it doesn't, it's new sensor time!

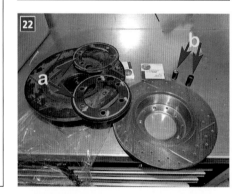

22 There are dirt excluders (a) and hardened steel sleeves (b) on ABS systems' rear axles.

23 If you need new reluctor rings (they can suffer from damaged teeth, which will show as an ABS fault), use a protective smear of Würth copper grease to prevent things from rusting solid in future.

24 When removing old reluctor rings, it's likely the

studs will screw out instead of nuts coming free. It's then a fiddle in the restricted space between disc and hub – but do-able!

25 The ABS sensors don't just push into the bare axle casing. There are steel bushes, interference-fitted into the holes in the axle – which means they're a tight friction-fit. The spacers have to be tapped in until they protrude 8mm through the back. An 8mm bolt and straight edge will ensure accuracy.

26 Not only is there an ABS twin brake line from front to back, but there are also various clips and fittings that are different from those used on the non-ABS Defender.

27 The T-piece fits to the same axle bracket mounting, via a single bolt, as the non-ABS type being held here separately. Note the flexible hose thread patterns.

28 You can buy all-new pipes, but they're very expensive! We used copper brake pipe from Automec and their neat and inexpensive little pipe bender to form new axle pipes.

29 The sensor and copper retaining clip are inserted separately from the inner side...

30 ...of the axle. The clip is pushed in, then the sensor. To improve electrical contact , I used electrically conductive ASG Ultimate Switch Grease (inset) – expensive, but it should help maintain electrical contact long-term.

31 Here's where the twin rigid and flexible hoses come together on the rear axle.

32 If you need to make-up pipe runs, Automec copper pipe is much easier to shape than steel pipe – and it won't corrode.

It's worth pointing out that ABS can be temperamental unless it's set up properly – and that means good connections all round and correctly located wheel sensors, as well as all components functioning correctly, of course, including the ABS' ECU that lives beneath the right-hand seat. Non-Land Rover wheel sensors are sometimes much cheaper but are also far more prone to giving trouble. A diagnostic tester won't lead you unerringly to any problem you may have, but it'll certainly point you in the right direction and, if obvious faults have been ruled out, you'll need one to delve deeper into Defender ABS problems.

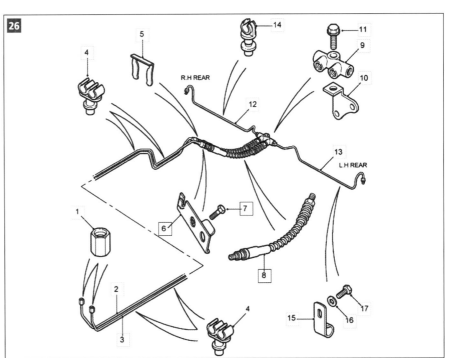

Diesel engine vacuum pump

Because there's no vacuum in their inlet manifold, diesel engines are fitted with a vacuum pump to supply the necessary vacuum for the servo unit.

1 On all engines up to TD5, the direct-drive vacuum pump is mounted on the right-hand side of the engine cylinder block. This is the pump fitted to all pre-300 Tdi engines, except for the very early and rare 2.25 diesel engine. (Illustration © Lindsay Porter)

2 This 200 Tdi-type vacuum pump can be rebuilt. The green arrows show the approximate positions of the screws holding it to the engine.

3 This is the pump repair kit, available from

Famous Four: new vanes, seal, gasket and a load of spring washers.

REMOVAL
Disconnect the battery, move any ancillary hoses or clips out of the way and remove the servo hose from the vacuum pump.

TD and 200 Tdi engines: remove the three screws holding the pump to the engine and lift the pump off its drive peg. Be very careful not to disturb the drive gear in the cylinder block.

4 300 Tdi engine: position No1 cylinder at top dead centre to release the tension from the pump-operating plunger. The bolt (arrowed) securing the air cleaner support's bracket strut must be

unscrewed. Take out the six bolts holding the vacuum pump to the engine.

5 TD5 engine: slacken and detach the drive belt then remove the four bolts (arrowed) holding the pump to the body of the alternator.

Unbolt and remove the pump, in the case of the 300 Tdi complete with the strut and harness bracket.

When you refit the pump to the cylinder block, always use a new gasket, and make sure that the driveshaft is correctly aligned. For 300 Tdi engines:
- Ensure No1 piston is still at TDC.
- Fit vacuum pump, fit and finger-tighten five of the six bolts in their original positions.
- Fit the sixth bolt when the air cleaner bracket is fitted.

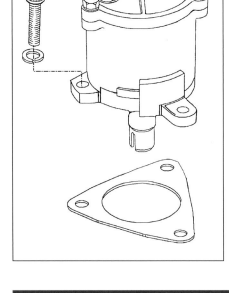

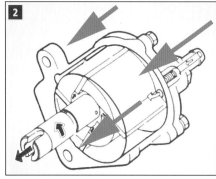

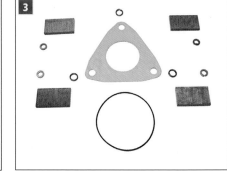

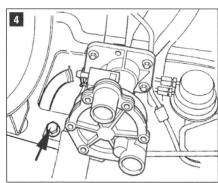

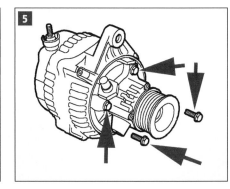

Brake bleeding

You can buy various gadgets to assist with the process of brake bleeding, but the basic procedure is the one described here. The idea is to push fresh fluid through each part of the system, expelling any trapped bubbles of air. Any air caught in the system will make the pedal feel spongy, and could even leave you with no brakes when you need them most. Don't reuse brake fluid and don't be afraid to 'waste' fresh fluid in the interests of expelling all the air. It's a lot cheaper than a life! If you aren't qualified in carrying out this work, have the vehicle checked before using it again.

You'll need the following items: lots of fresh brake fluid; a clean glass jar; a piece of clear plastic that fits tightly over the bleed screw and is long enough to reach the bottom of the jar when it's on the ground; a ring spanner to fit the bleed screw; a willing assistant.

1 Take the cap off the master cylinder reservoir and top it up. It's MOST IMPORTANT that the level in the reservoir doesn't drop below the minimum mark at any time. If you draw fresh air into the system, you'll have to start again from scratch.

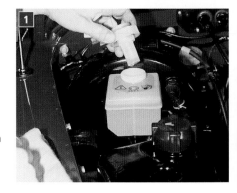

2 Take off the dust cap from the bleed screw that's furthest away from the master cylinder. This will be at one of the rear brakes, but it all depends on whether your vehicle is left-hand or right-hand drive. Fit the spanner to the screw, push one end of the tube over the end of the screw and place the other end in the jar. Pour in sufficient fluid to cover the end of the tube.

A   Unscrew the bleed screw about one turn while your assistant inside the car pushes down on the brake pedal. The push should be firm and steady but not too vigorous. When the pedal reaches the bottom of the stroke, the person in the car shouts out the word 'Down!' and holds the pedal down until the bleed screw has been retightened.

B   The person at the bleed screw shouts out the

instruction 'Up!' and the person in the car lets the brake pedal rise again.

C   The bleed screw is loosened once more, and the person in the car pushes on the brake pedal and shouts 'Down!', the process being repeated over and again until no more air can be seen coming down the plastic tube or out of the end of the pipe.

D   It's important that, after every few strokes, the level of the fluid in the master cylinder is checked, as described earlier.

E   The other rear bleed point is then bled, followed by the front wheel furthest away from the master cylinder and then the fourth wheel. If the pedal still feels spongy, or sinks too close to the floorboards when the brake is applied with the vehicle stationary and the engine running, you may have to repeat the entire sequence again.

Transmission brake overhaul

Over time, the transmission brake will be prone to seizing up. So if you're planning a brake shoe replacement, you might as well go the whole hog and make sure that the entire assembly is functioning properly.

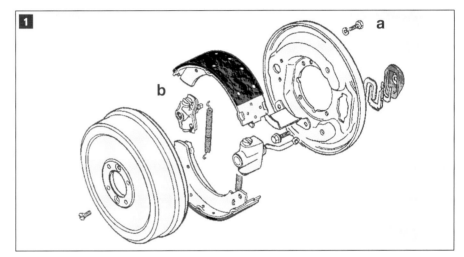

1 These are the components of the Borg-Warner transfer box's parking brake assembly. The adjuster (a) protrudes through the backplate while the operating mechanism (b) fits opposite the adjuster and is held in place by a relatively complex set of keys on the back of the backplate.

2 First job, as always with brakes, is to slacken off the adjuster screw by turning it anticlockwise until the brake shoes are as far away from the drum as they'll go.

3 The brake drum is held on with two screws and they can be tricky to remove. When mechanic Don used an impact screwdriver, both screws waved the white flag and surrendered meekly.

4 In this case, the brake drum simply slipped off. If yours sticks, tap it all the way around with a copper or wooden mallet – never use a hammer, because you can easily crack the drum.

5 These are the visible brake components, showing the operating lever at the top of the photograph and the adjuster at the bottom. Note that the springs are fitted on the backs of the shoes, but fortunately there's no choice of holes in which to fit the springs, so you can hardly get it wrong.

6 The operating mechanism is connected to a lever at the rear of the backplate. Remove the split pin, push out the clevis pin and make careful note of the correct positions of the flat washers. Note how the clevis pin that was removed from the outer end of the lever has been refilled temporarily with washers and an old split pin so that none of the parts are lost and there's no confusion about what goes where.

7 If you're working on the floor, it's possible to pull the shoes against the springs and off their mounting points, but if you're working underneath the vehicle it may be sensible to use a lever.

8 With springs and shoes out of the way, the slides can be extracted from the adjuster. Note the amount of rust that's started to form – a precursor to seizing up.

9 The adjuster body is held to the backplate with a pair of machine screws.

10 Use a spanner to screw the adjuster pin inwards as far as it will go...

11 ...then finish removing it by hand and clean both components thoroughly in solvent to remove all traces of ancient grease.

12 Four machine screws hold the backplate in place. At the same time, two of them also fix the oil catcher – held here by Don's left hand – to the backplate assembly.

13 When you remove the slides from the operating mechanism take careful note that each slide has a hardened steel roller at the end of it. Retrieve both of them.

14 Don had removed the slides and rollers to prevent them dropping out when lifting off the backplate.

15 From the rear of the backplate Don carefully pulled out the operating plunger.

16 After removing the fixing clip, these two retainers can be slid off in opposite directions after first ensuring that they're no longer locked against each other.

17 The adjuster body was now taken away from the front of the backplate.

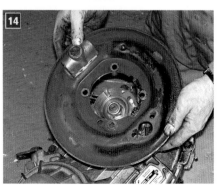

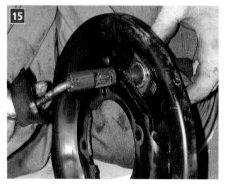

18 These are the components of the adjuster body and the three clips that hold it in place while allowing it to slide as necessary on the backplate.

19 If you're replacing the transfer box you'll need to swap over the operating lever. We were extremely concerned that the bolt holding the lever in place would shear before it came out. Here a heat gun is being applied to the boss into which the box was screwed.

20 This shot was taken later when it had all cooled down again. Note the correct positions of the washers and the retaining bolt. The arm contains a bearing that should be cleaned out and thoroughly lubricated before being refitted.

21 These are the components as removed and after having been washed clean ready for reassembly. If the rubber gaiter (arrowed) on the back of the operating mechanism is split or damaged in any way, renew it. Note how the backplate around the aperture where the operating mechanism will fit has been smeared with copper grease.

22 When the operating mechanism is pushed through the backplate, the two locking plates are slid against each other until the tabs – one of them being pointed out here with the end of the screwdriver – have sprung into place.

23 To fit the outer locking plate requires a little bit of effort and determination. You need to make sure that the operating mechanism is pushed into the backplate fully, and that the two interlocking plates are held tight against the backplate with a screwdriver while the outer plate is slid into the groove in the tube of the operating mechanism.

24 With lots more copper grease, the operating plunger, rollers and slides can be refitted.

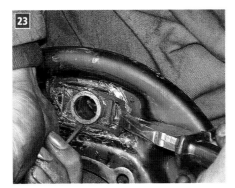

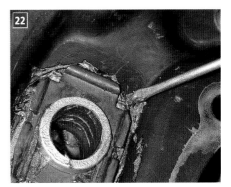

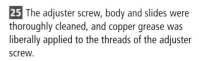

25 The adjuster screw, body and slides were thoroughly cleaned, and copper grease was liberally applied to the threads of the adjuster screw.

26 More copper grease was wiped on to the slides...

27 ...and when the adjuster was reassembled, both the adjuster and the operating mechanism slides were held in place with elastic bands to prevent them from slipping apart.

28 The screws connecting the brake drum backplate to the rear output housing were refitted and tightened to a torque of 73Nm.

29 Before refitting the shoes, make sure that the adjuster is screwed out so that the slides are touching each other.

30 Refit the shoes with the springs in place and make them reasonably central...

31 ...before refitting the brake drum and the two retaining screws.

32 You'll now need to reassemble the operating linkage using new split pins.

33 Adjust the handbrake as follows:

- Turn the adjuster screw (5) clockwise until the brake shoes are fully expanded against the drum.
- Back off the adjuster until the drum is free to rotate.
- Turn the adjustment thumb wheel (7) below the handbrake lever until the parking brake operates fully on the third notch of the ratchet.
- IMPORTANT NOTE: The adjuster at the handbrake (7) must ONLY be used for the initial setting or to compensate for cable stretch. It MUST NOT be used to take up brake shoe wear, which must be adjusted at the brake drum adjuster (5).
- Operate and release the handbrake several times and then recheck that the parking brake is fully operational on the third notch of the ratchet. Readjust if necessary.

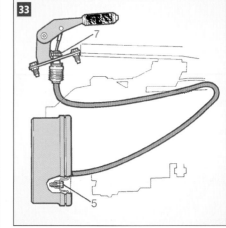

Front shock absorber, tower, coil spring replacement

Although this section shows uprated components being fitted, the procedure is exactly the same as standard. The work was carried out by Ian Baughan of IRB Developments.

1 You won't need to raise and lower the axle at the front end, so Ian used axle stands before undoing the bottom mounting nut. Note that the body has first been supported with the suspension fully extended.

2 Pay attention to how the bushes and retaining washers fit together so that the new ones can be correctly fitted.

3 After removing the coolant reservoir from this side of the engine bay and the rubber cover on the inner wing top, Ian used a long extension on his ratchet to remove the four nuts...

4 ...holding the suspension tower in place. Note that the axle has been supported with the suspension fully extended so that there's no pressure on the spring as these four nuts were undone.

5 The air-driven ratchet gun made short work of removing the top shock absorber nut without having to lock the shock absorber to prevent it from turning...

6 ...and again, it pays to take note of the correct orientation of bushes and washers.

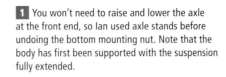

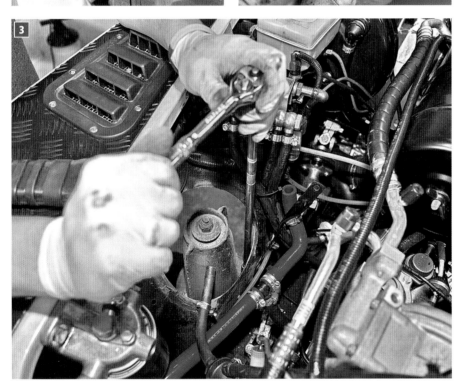

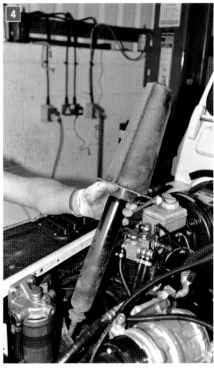

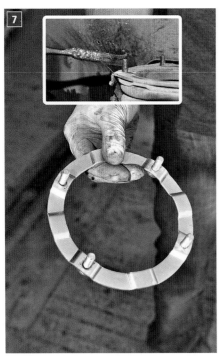

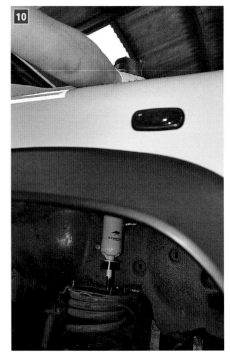

7 In many cases, as vehicles get older, you can expect to have to replace components such as rusty suspension towers, and more often than not you'll have to replace the bolt plate because bolts shear off. Ian supplies galvanised ones but also adds a wipe of copper grease to the threads before fitting.

8 Remembering the correct order of fitting, the new washers and bushes supplied with this kit were fitted to the top of the new shock absorber after it had been pushed into the tower.

9 After a wipe of copper grease, the smaller washer and lock-nut were fitted...

10 ...before offering up the new shocker with its tower and with the upper washer and bush fitted to the bottom of the shock absorber so that it could be pushed right down into its locating hole.

11 Once in situ the lower bush and washer were fitted and all of the fixings fully tightened.

Front and rear suspension bushes, Panhard rod and anti-roll bar

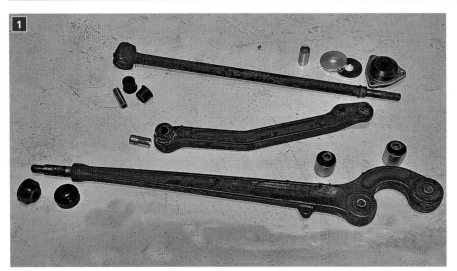

This work was carried out by Ian Baughan at IRB Developments. Modified (polyurethane) bushes were fitted, but apart from rubber bushes needing to be pressed in, as well as pressed out, as shown here, the process is the same.

1 Here's a selection of suspension and steering arms from the left side of the vehicle, waiting to receive their new bushes.

RADIUS ARM

2 Off came the steering arm, removed by Ian's mate Ada, to allow the radius arm to be detached from the vehicle.

3 The front of the radius arm is detached by removing the two bolts, one each side of the axle.

4 At its rear end, the radius arm passes through part of the chassis. Its threaded end has bushes, washers and a large lock-nut holding it in place while cushioning shocks from the front axle.

5 Ada and Ian remove the radius arm from the vehicle.

6 At the front end of the radius arm, through which the bolts were removed earlier, is a pair of bushes, and at the rear you can see the arrangement of washers and bushes demonstrated by Ian.

7 As a general rule, bushes at the chassis ends can be pulled off by hand whereas those at the axle ends need pressing out. Here, Ada pumps Ian's hydraulic press to remove the front radius arm bushes. They can take a lot of pressure to shift. If you don't own a hydraulic press you'll invariably save yourself a lot of time and grief by taking the bushes to an agricultural or mechanical engineer or a garage with a suitable press.

8 Using lots of the lube supplied with the kit, Ian used the press to insert the bush…

9 …making sure that the outer part of the bush was fitted centrally in the radius arm. With most polyurethane bushes the centre tube can be fitted separately later.

10 The bushes at the axle end are a simple push-fit.

11 Again, it's essential to use the correct lubricant. Regular grease or oil will rot rubber. Silicone lubricant would be a good alternative. Some recommend washing-up liquid, but it might cause corrosion.

12 On our example the bushes are already in, of course, but this is a reminder about which way round the bolts (B) should fit, according to the manual.

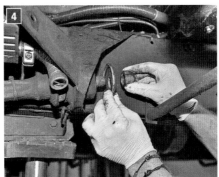

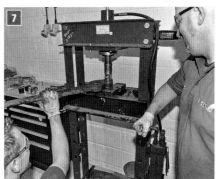

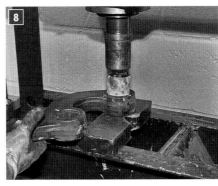

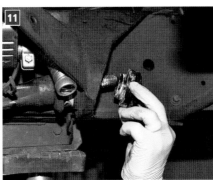

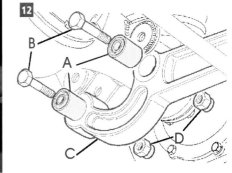

13 However, it can't possibly matter which way round they go and you'll find that you'll be able to push them in more easily from this side. Note that a fair bit of levering will be required in most cases.

14 Ada used the air tool to spin nut and bolt together. They must be tightened later with a torque wrench to the correct torque – and no tighter.

REAR SUSPENSION LINK ARM

15 It's best to slacken the large nut holding the link arm to its mounting while it's on the vehicle so that it's held firmly and can't turn. Next, Ian slackened and removed the three sets of nuts and bolts holding the mounting to the chassis.

16 At the other end, Ada removed the nut from the pin…

17 …and then had a battle to get the pin out of the mounting bracket…

18 …allowing the link arm to drop free.

19 These are the old mounting bracket and bushes from the front end of the arm.

20 At the rear of the link arm you can see that conventional bushes (right) are in one piece and have to be pressed in from one side, whereas polyurethane bushes are invariably in two sections and are inserted by hand.

21 The centre tube of the polyurethane bushes can sometimes be a very tight fit. Ian used the hydraulic press, though a vice or woodworker's cramp would be sure to do the job.

22 Ian fitted the new mounting and finger-tightened the lock-nut…

23 …before offering up to the vehicle and loosely fitting the three nuts and bolts (positions arrowed) holding it in place.

24 At this point the axle almost certainly won't line up properly. You could use a ratchet strap to pull it in whichever direction it needs to go…

25 …until the re-bushed arm slides easily into its mounting position.

26 It's good practice to always use lots of copper grease on bolt shanks and threads.

27 After fitting the axle end Ian tightened the three chassis mounting bolts followed by the large lock-nut.

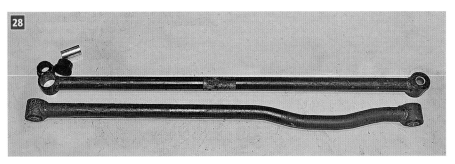

PANHARD ROD

28 The Panhard rod prevents excessive lateral movement of the front axle. The LHD Panhard rod (at bottom, with the clearance kink in it) looks different to the RHD rod, but they're exactly the same length.

29 Ada removed the pins…

30 …and levered the rod out, ready to be re-bushed.

ANTI-ROLL BARS

31 Anti-roll bars, when fitted, are also located with rubber-type bushes as standard.

32 New polyurethane bushes, lubricated as before, are split (like their standard counterparts) and are simply pushed over the anti-roll bar…

33 …and are retained by their mounting brackets.

34 At the axle end there are more new bushes at the anti-roll bar links.

35 Ian later used a torque wrench on these and all other mounting bolts to ensure that all were tightened correctly.

36 Following top engineering practice, he marked each nut or bolt with a paint pen immediately after each had been checked and tightened. The idea is that you then go around the whole vehicle after you've finished, making sure that each threaded connection is marked.

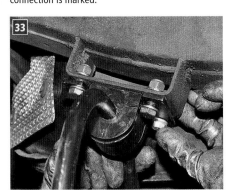

Rear shock absorber and coil spring replacement

This work was carried out at Ian Baughan's IRB Developments. Modified springs and shock absorbers were fitted, but the process is the same.

1 Ian Baughan's brother Chris turned up to lend a hand, and once my Defender was off the ground he used a transmission hoist to support the weight of the rear axle. You'll see why later.

2 Ian started by slackening the nut holding the rear shock absorber top mounting in place...

3 ...and removed the nut and backing washer.

4 Next, Ian turned his attention to the bottom shock absorber nut.

5 You need to grip the shock absorber to prevent it from turning as you undo its central nut. Invariably the shaft will have a flat on it, and, while this is enough to stop the shaft from turning while you're tightening the nut on a brand new unit, you won't stand a chance of locking it when undoing one that's been on for a while. If it doesn't matter about marking the shock absorber body, you could use a Stillson's wrench (left) or, if you don't want to damage it, an oil-filter removing tool with rubber strap.

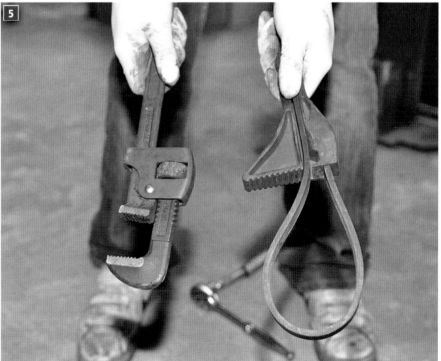

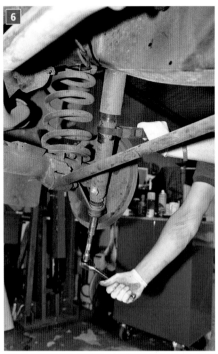

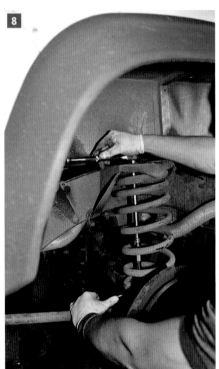

6 Here, Ian grips one of the shock absorber bodies while removing its bottom nut.

7 The rear shock absorber can now be removed, but note how you have to take care that the flexible brake hose (inset) isn't stretched as the axle is allowed to drop. This is why Chris fitted the transmission hoist earlier on.

8 Because the rear springs were also to be replaced, Ian used a long extension on the ratchet to loosen the spring clamp nuts and bolts. Note that you need a second spanner to prevent the bolt from turning.

9 Without fully removing the clamp plate, Ian rotated the spring to 'unscrew' it, making sure that the axle was low enough to allow the spring to clear the top of the housing.

10 This is how the spring plate should look if corrosion isn't too bad. Usually components will need replacing.

11 Ian removed, cleaned off and loosely refitted the spring seat and clamp.

12 The new, uprated spring was slightly longer than the original, so as Ian rotated the new spring into

position he also had to encourage it to fit the top mounting.

13 You mustn't use grease on rubber bushes, though it's OK to do so with polyurethane. These bushes were wiped with silicone grease, but, even so, they couldn't be pushed in by hand. Ian used his hydraulic press but a vice or woodworker's cramp would be almost as good.

14 Ian pushed the top end of the shock absorber on to its mounting pin and loosely fitted the retaining washer and lock-nut.

15 This is the arrangement of the bushes and upper and lower washers you'll need in all cases. Whether or not you use the dished washers will depend on whether or not your Defender has them built in to the bracket on the axle. Earlier Defenders don't, but being a 2006 model this one did, so the supplied, shaped washers weren't needed.

16 With the upper large washer and upper bush in place, the bottom of the shock absorber was lined up with the hole in the bracket...

17 ...and the axle was raised until it became possible...

18 ...to fit the lower bush, plus large and small washers followed by the lock-nut. The inset shows the original bush and the way it appears not to have been correctly seated when the vehicle was manufactured. Try not to make the same mistake!

19 After Ian had fully tightened the bottom nut (you need to just compress the bushes, but not so much that they become flattened or heavily distorted)...

20 ...he turned his attention to the top nut and fitted that, too.

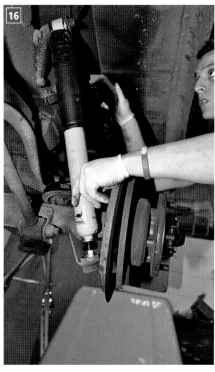

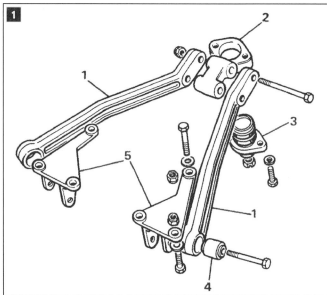

Most Defenders have just one ball joint at the A-frame, but those with self-levelling rear suspension have two more. Here's how to replace all types, plus hints and tips on how to make this a slightly less horrible job than it otherwise might be!

Eventually the A-frame ball joint wears, leaving too much play in it. Therefore one symptom of a worn A-frame ball joint is that, as you apply the brakes or throttle, you'll hear a distinct 'clunk' from the rear.

1 The main ball joint (2 and 3) in the A-frame (1) is in an awkward position, with restricted access, though it's in an exposed position for the road elements, so it's almost certain to be rust-welded in place.

2 The self-levelling unit, though fitted to relatively few Defenders, has two more ball joints, one each at top and bottom.

3 First give the large nut and split pin (red) a really

good soak with penetrating fluid and, while you're at it, the two retaining bolts (B). Using first a flat screwdriver then pliers, remove the split pin. Using a 30mm socket on a long extension bar, loosen the castle nut then remove the nut and washer.

4 Use 19mm spanners to remove the two lock-nuts and bolts (arrowed) that hold the A-frame arms to the fulcrum (the ball joint housing). You'll need to use a hammer and drift to knock out the fulcrum and ball joint.

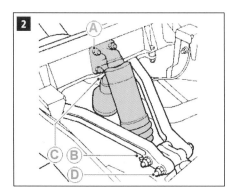

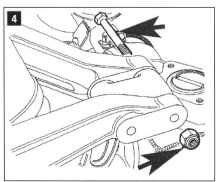

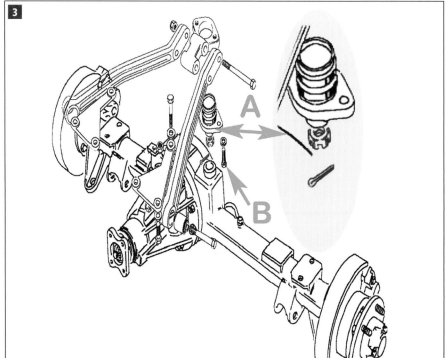

5 Theoretically, you can next remove the two 13mm bolts that hold the ball joint to the fulcrum, and start to remove the ball joint. However – and bearing in mind that the old ball joint is scrap – you may well be better off cutting your losses (literally) and using an angle grinder to cut off some of the ball joint base. You can see how even this was rusted in place.

6 Clean off around the joint at the back, give it another good soaking with releasing fluid and then try to drive the ball joint out with a hammer. However, in all likelihood you'll need the services of a heavy-duty hydraulic press. Most of us don't own one, so a trip to your friendly neighbourhood garage or engineering shop will save you an awful lot of grief.

7 The idea will be to remove the ball joint from the fulcrum bracket, leaving it ready for a good clean-up and paint, before...

8 ...applying copper grease and fitting the new ball joint. Note how the ball joint body, where it enters the fulcrum bracket, is splined – meaning you'll need another trip to the owner of the hydraulic press or the services of something like an old hub nut spanner with a block of wood on top and a lot more hammering. You have to temporarily fit two longer-than-standard 13mm bolts to ensure the ball joint lines up to the fulcrum as it goes in. Once the ball joint is fully home you can fit the new 13mm bolts of the proper length.

9 Having said all that, here's a plan: you can purchase, from Land Rover specialists, a new ball joint ready fitted to a new fulcrum bracket, so all you need to do is remove the old assembly from the A-frame and bolt in the new. It'll save you hours,

much pain and anguish – not to mention the beer tokens you'll no longer have to provide to the owner of the hydraulic press. Compare prices and do your own calculations.

10 Whichever way you go, you can refit the ball joint assembly loosely back on to the axle, using the new washer and castellated nut, before refitting the two bolts to the A-frame arms. Tighten them up and then torque up the castellated nut. Turn it by the minimum amount so that a castellation slot aligns with the hole in the ball joint pin, and refit the split pin.

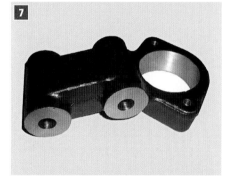

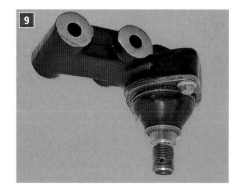

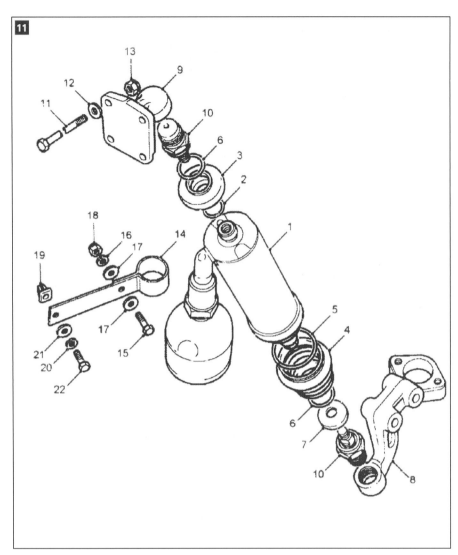

11 These are the components of the self-levelling unit, when fitted. Not all parts are currently available and prices are impossible to predict, because they're often old stock – when they're available at all.

1	NRC7050	Control unit – self levelling
2	NRC7066	Spring ring
3	NRC5707	Gaiter – self levelling unit, ball joint – upper
4	NRC6561	Gaiter – self levelling unit, ball joint – lower
5	577703	Spring ring
6	90577704	Spring ring
7	NRC8007	Seal
8	90575878	Bracket – rear axle fulcrum – to (V) KA 930263
8	ANR3036	Bracket – rear axle fulcrum – metric fixing – from (V) KA 930264
9	NRC8375	Mounting assembly – rear suspension
10	575882	Joint – self levelling unit ball
11	BH110351	Bolt
12	NRC5758	Washer
13	NY110041L	Nut – hexagonal head-nyloc-M10
14	NRC6320	Strap – retaining levelling 3 holes
14	NRC8518	Strap – retaining levelling 2 holes
15	SH106301	Screw – hexagonal head M6 x 30 – long
16	WL106001L	Washer – sprung M6
17	2215L	Washer – plain
18	NH106041L	Nut – hexagonal nyloc-M6
19	NN106011	Nutsert – blind – to (V) VA 999222
19	AWR6715	Nutsert – blind M6 – from (V) VA 999223
20	WL106001L	Washer – sprung M6
21	22151	Washer – plain
22	FS106201L	Screw – flanged head M6 x 20

WARNING: The levelling unit contains pressurised gas and must not be dismantled, nor the casing screws removed. Repair should not be attempted – replace complete unit only.

12 With self-levelling unit removed, this is a typically disintegrated top ball joint gaiter. Once a gaiter is breached the ball joint will rapidly fail.

13 The ball joint is unscrewed from the self-levelling unit.

14 To remove the ball joint from its housing, the retainer (right) has to be unscrewed.

15 With the addition of lots of grease, a replacement ball joint and, if available, retainer are easily fitted.

16 Original self-levelling boots (centre) are no longer to be had, it seems. Slide-a-Boot Small Ball Joint Boot replacements are shown here on each side of the original, displaying their top and bottom holes.

17 The top hole of the original was found to be 22.2mm in diameter. The Slide-a-Boot Small Ball Joint Boot (A) is designed to cover 11–15mm, but was easily opened out (B) with a Dremel-type tool, used on a slow speed, to make it a slightly stretchy fit.

18 The size of the larger hole on the original is 34.9mm and the Slide-a-Boot replacement (large hole: 25–30mm) can be opened out accordingly or stretched to fit.

19 Incidentally, Slide-a-Boot's replacement gaiters can be used to replace those on the self-levelling unit, if necessary.

20 The modified boot was pushed firmly on to the top of the self-levelling unit. There's no facility for clipping it in place, as with the original, but the natural springiness in its height is sufficient to hold it in position when assembled.

21 The ball joint was screwed back into the unit and tightened.

22 The large end of the boot was then stretched into place on the ball joint housing...

23 ...and secured with one of the spring clips supplied with the new boots.

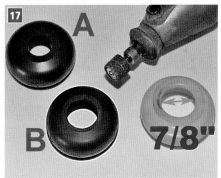

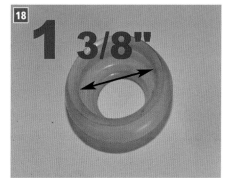

Self-levelling unit

Defender self-levelling suspension is an option that was dropped by Land Rover a good few years ago. However, it works very well, and if you've got it and want to keep it – though replacement parts can be very expensive – here's how it goes together.

Look between the propshaft and the exhaust pipe in the main picture and you'll see the 'levelling unit' (all other manufacturers, as far as I can tell, call it 'self-levelling') made by Boge, and fitted as an expensive option to older 110s and also to some 'Classic' Range Rovers, though without the large bulb protruding from the top of the casing on the Defender version seen here.

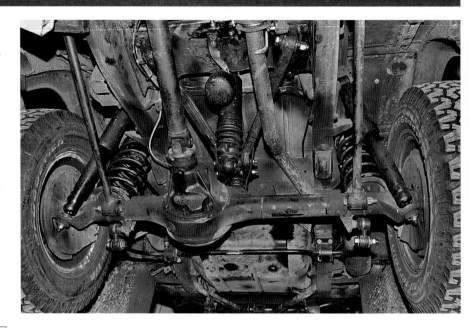

SPRING TYPES

According to the excellent and useful information shown on the www.land-rover-parts-shop.com website, these are the various part numbers of OE road springs available for Defenders. In each case, the driver's-side spring is shown first.

Land Rover 90
Standard front: NRC9446 and NRC9447
Standard rear: NRC9448 and NRC9449
Heavy duty front: NRC9448 and NRC9449 (which are standard spec 90in rear springs)
Heavy duty rear: RKB101230 and RKB101240

Land Rover 110
Standard front: NRC8044 and NRC8045
Standard rear: NRC6389
Self-levelling rear: NRC6388 and NRC7000
Heavy duty front: NRC9448 and NRC9449 (which are standard spec 90in rear springs)
Heavy duty rear: NRC6904

130 (possibly also 127)
Front: NRC9448 and NRC9449 (which are standard spec 90in rear springs)
Rear: NRC6389 and NRC6904

HD 130 and some Camel Trophy 110s
Inner helper springs: RRC3266

Note that springs are also colour-coded – refer to the relevant workshop manual for details.

1 The springs used with self-levelling are softer than standard, the idea being that the unit stiffens the suspension when the vehicle is laden but you enjoy a softer ride (if that's what you enjoy) when lightly laden.

2 These are the main elements of the self-levelling unit.
a   Top ball joint and bolts that pass through chassis crossmember x 4.
b   Pressurised Boge unit that restores the standard

ride-height when the vehicle is loaded. Presumably the large bulb not found on the equivalent Range Rover version is to account for the extra load capacity of the Defender.
c   Leather check strap.
d   Bottom ball joint and assembly for mounting to standard location on axle.

3 This is how the parts appear 'in the flesh'. At IRB Developments, Ian Baughan first pulled out the split pin, then the nut holding the ball joint in place.

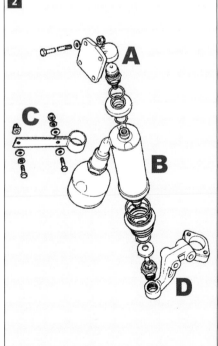

4 As you can see, the ball joint has a Morse taper and you may need to use a splitter or to shock the female part of the taper with a hammer, in the same way as you would when removing a steering ball joint. Two long through-bolts attach the ball joint to the A-frame.

5 The replacement ball joint (top) is identical to the standard one except that it has an extension on the casting, joined to the self-levelling unit.

6 To refit, Ian lifted the complete assembly into place, dropping the tapered end of the ball joint into the axle casing and reinserting the two through-bolts.

7 We'd received some NORD-LOCK washers (top) from Würth, and used them with some new plain washers. NORD-LOCK washers are said to provide superb self-locking qualities because of the wedge-shaped interlocking sections inside the washers. They're said to be reusable and unaffected by lubrication. Do they work? Since Würth sell them, I think we can assume they do.

8 Ian used the air wrench to zip up the fixing nuts, finishing off with a torque wrench later.

9 Next came an interesting challenge. I'd been pre-warned that the fixing bolts were designed to be fitted and removed after raising the body. Another common approach used to be to cut holes in the floor toeboard through which the bolts could be passed. But neither of those would do at all! We found that the top bolts can just be inserted by first sliding them into the self-levelling unit mounting plate then inserting them into the holes in the chassis.

10 For the bottom bolts, you could dismantle the top end of the self-levelling unit so that the bolts could be inserted from the front. Or you could do as we did, and insert the bolts from the rear.

11 You can see the lower bolt protruding forward (it's non-standard – they don't usually protrude this far) while Ian's wrench is on the head of the bolt at the top, facing backwards.

12 The job of the check strap is to prevent the unit from swinging full-stretch to the left or right, where it could bang on the A-frame arms.

Front and rear bump-stops

Each of the four bump-stops – there's one mounted above each end of each axle – is held in place with nuts, washers and bolts. The biggest difficulty is likely to arise in removing corroded nuts and bolts. If this is the case, you may be well advised to use a nut splitter, or cut through the nut with a hacksaw, from top to bottom, fitting a new nut and bolt with the new bump-stop.

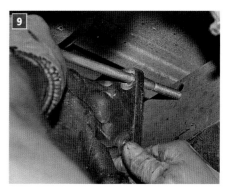

1 It helps to understand how the Land Rover's steering system works! This engine bay, sans engine, helps you to see the components. The steering column with its two universal joints (A) runs from the bulkhead to the steering box (B). The drop arm (C) connects to the cross-rod (D) which joins to the left-hand steering arm on the front of the hub. The track rod (E) connects the steering arms on the rears of the hubs on both wheels.

2 This schematic view also shows power steering components (RHD models).
a   Steering column (upper)
b   Universal joints
c   Compression joint
d   Lower column
e   Steering box
f   Hydraulic pump
g   Fluid reservoir
h   Hydraulic fluid hoses
i   Drag link
j   Drop arm

3 The ball joint on the end of the cross-rod (front of left wheel)...

4 ...and the track rod ball joint at the rear of the same wheel.

5 The opposite end of the track rod at the back of the right wheel.

6 For further information on these areas, see sections Steering box replacement.

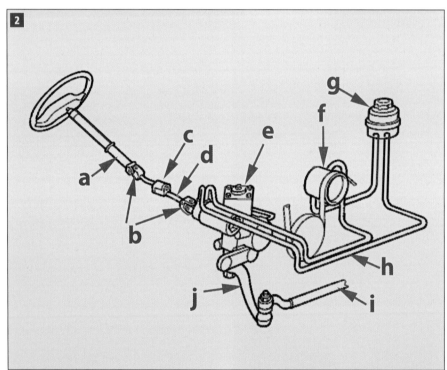

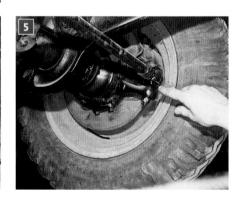

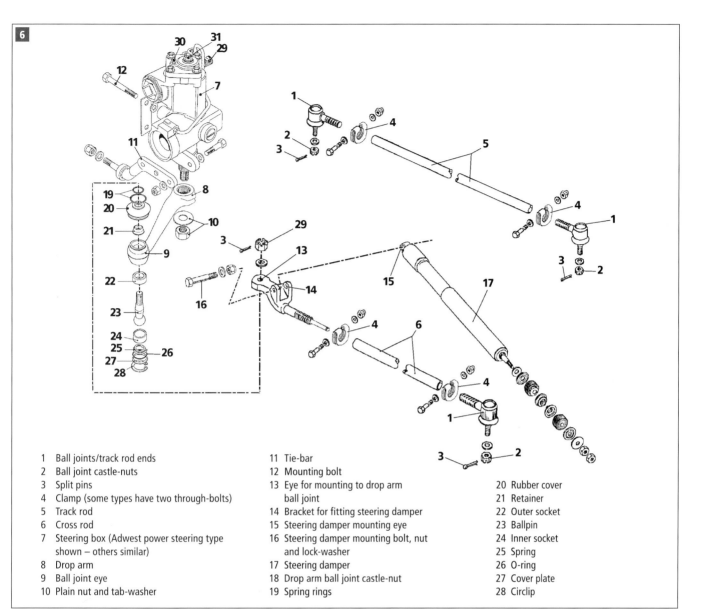

6

1 Ball joints/track rod ends
2 Ball joint castle-nuts
3 Split pins
4 Clamp (some types have two through-bolts)
5 Track rod
6 Cross rod
7 Steering box (Adwest power steering type shown – others similar)
8 Drop arm
9 Ball joint eye
10 Plain nut and tab-washer

11 Tie-bar
12 Mounting bolt
13 Eye for mounting to drop arm ball joint
14 Bracket for fitting steering damper
15 Steering damper mounting eye
16 Steering damper mounting bolt, nut and lock-washer
17 Steering damper
18 Drop arm ball joint castle-nut
19 Spring rings

20 Rubber cover
21 Retainer
22 Outer socket
23 Ballpin
24 Inner socket
25 Spring
26 O-ring
27 Cover plate
28 Circlip

Track-rod and cross-rod ball joint replacement

1 First, straighten out the split-pin (3) and pull it out of the castle-nut (2) with a pair of pliers.

2 Unscrew the castle-nut and remove the washer from beneath it.

3 Use a ball joint separator to free the ball joint. This is a Sykes-Pickavant tool, available from most auto-accessory stores. Be sure to buy one large enough! If the taper on the ball joint is particularly stubborn use a pair of hammers,

and hit simultaneously on each side of the eye. You stand a strong chance of splitting the ball joint rubber, but if you intend replacing it in any case that doesn't matter.

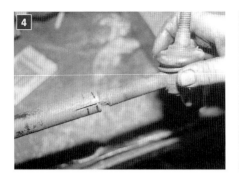

4 Each track-rod has a left-handed and a right-handed thread ball joint for adjustment to the rod. Make sure you're getting the right one started and make sure the slot in the track-rod tube is clear, as there's a clamp that goes on to squash the rod tight against the shoulder of the track-rod joint. Ensure it's a good fit and use lots of grease. The clip isn't shown in the photograph.

5 The steering tube clamp and bolt are seen here, ready to go on to the steering tube. Later models have double clamps, with double bolts.

6 A new split-pin goes into the castle-nut – a small but vital point to remember! Some non-original track-rod ends use self-locking nuts, but many experts prefer the split-pin arrangement.

A Undo the clamp bolt holding the clamp (4) in place...

B ...and unscrew the ball joint (1) from the track-rod or cross-rod, counting the *exact* number of turns before the ball joint comes free. Write down the number of turns so that you won't forget it later!

C Screw in the replacement ball joint and refit as a reversal of the removal procedure, but note the following important points:

i The angle of the ball joint must be turned so that the threaded pin, going into the eye, is centralised in the ball joint and isn't tipping to one side or the other, otherwise it'll wear out quickly.

ii Be sure to screw in the replacement ball joint by exactly the same number of turns as it took to remove the old one.

iii Be sure to have the track checked by a garage with track setting equipment before using the vehicle again on the road (other than driving it to the garage), otherwise the steering could be dangerous in use and you could suffer from rapid tyre wear.

Steering damper removal and replacement

1 Remove the nut and lock-nut on the end of the old steering damper, though, as always, severely rusted components can take a lot longer to detach.

2 A new damper should be primed by working it in and out a couple of times before fitting it, in order to get rid of any trapped air. (It'll work its way out in use, but this gets there first!)

3 Make sure you have the assembly order properly organised before refitting.

4 Apply copper grease to the steering damper threads. You can see the inner bush already fitted.

5 Naturally enough, the outer bush and shaped washer go on once the damper has been inserted into the hole in the bracket. You tighten the inner nut sufficiently to put the bush under the right amount of tension (without squashing it too much), using a filter wrench if necessary to stop the damper from turning. Then, gripping the inner nut with one spanner, you fit and tighten the outer lock-nut.

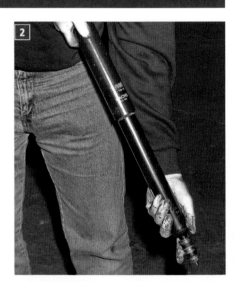

Drop arm ball joint overhaul

1 Take out the split pin (3) and remove the castle-nut (29) from the top (arrowed) of the drop arm ball joint (23).

2 Use a ball joint separator, as described for track-rod and cross-rod ball joints, to free the drag link (13) from the drop arm (8).

3 Knock back the tab on the lock-washer and remove the drop arm retaining nut. Make an alignment mark on the bottom of the splined shaft, and on the drop arm (8), so that the drop arm can be replaced in exactly the same location. Pull the drop arm off the splines on the bottom of the steering box.

4 You'll now have the drop arm off the vehicle, complete with the ball joint mounted in it. Clean it all off ready for dismantling. Take off the spring rings (19) and lever off the dust cover (20).

5 You now have to compress the cover plate (27) with a clamp and remove the circlip (28) from the underside of the ball joint (9).

6 SAFETY NOTE: It's important that the cover plate is compressed, otherwise as the circlip is removed the force of the spring beneath could cause injury.

7 You can now remove the spring (25), socket (24) and O-ring (26).

8 Use a soft-faced mallet to tap the ball joint (23) out of the drop arm.

9 You can now drive the cup socket (22) from the housing, but note that you may have to heat the housing in boiling water to expand it before the housing will come out.

10 The overhaul kit will include a new ballpin and sockets, and all of the other minor components that you removed from the drop arm. After cleaning out all of the old grease from the socket, fit the components in the reverse order of removal, but pack the inside of the socket with grease after fitting the cup socket.

11 Note the following important points:
a When refitting the spring, the small diameter must be towards the ball.
b When refitting the circlip, you'll have to compress the cover plate with a clamp.
c When refitting the components to the vehicle, use new lock-washers, lock-nuts and split pins, as appropriate.

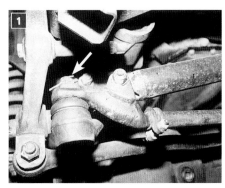

Steering box adjustment

A small amount of adjustment can be made to the steering box to compensate for wear. However, the problem is that most wear takes place in the straight-ahead position, with very little wear at the outer 'edges'. Therefore, when you adjust out the wear in the straight-ahead position you're likely to end up with stiff steering the more you turn the wheel – an extremely dangerous condition if the steering is reluctant to self-centre, or even jams, when turning a corner. So take very great care to check the steering very carefully at the two extremes of steering lock before driving the vehicle on the road, and if in doubt have a specialist carry out this work for you.

It's MOST IMPORTANT that there's no free play in any of the joints in the steering system before attempting to adjust the steering box. Wear is more likely to take place in steering joints than in the box itself, so check these first!

Raise the front of the vehicle off the ground and chock the rear wheels in front and behind. Gently rock the steering wheel at the straight-ahead position and feel the amount of free play in the steering wheel. This shouldn't be more that 9.5mm (⅓in) at the rim of the steering wheel.

1 If necessary, have an assistant slacken the (outer) lock-nut on the adjuster on the top of the steering box and, while continuing to rock the steering wheel, have the (inner) adjuster screw gradually tightened until the free play in the rim of the steering wheel is no more than the prescribed amount.

However, you must now check that there's no tightness whatsoever in the steering when it's turned from lock to lock. If there is, you'll have to compromise by backing off the adjuster screw, because the first priority is not to have stiff steering! This is so even if you have too much free play in the steering wheel. If the problem can't be overcome through adjustment, and if you've checked that there are no loose or worn joints in the steering system, have a specialist check the system for you and, if necessary, renew the steering box.

When the free play has been satisfactorily adjusted, retighten the lock-nut and check once again that there's no excessive tightness at either lock. As a final check, take the vehicle to a safe, open space, such as a deserted car park, and drive the vehicle slowly, turning from lock to lock. The steering should self-centre; in other words, it must be free enough to return to the straight-ahead position without any stiffness.

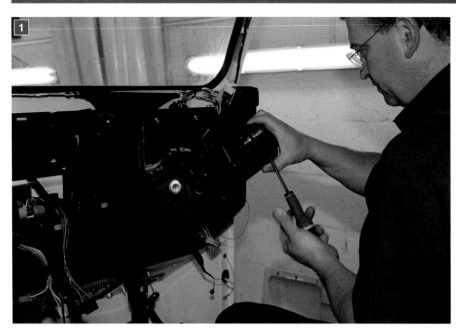

1 A shroud covers the indicator stalk.

2 Unique plugs and sockets carry the wiring for the indicator stalk assembly.

3 Nene Overland's Michael removed the lock by taking out these 'impossible to remove' bolts. Replacement bolts are called shear bolts and, when fully tightened, the head shears off, which makes them ... well, obviously not impossible, but darned difficult to remove.

4 Steering column components fit together with splines and pinch bolts.

5 Engine bay access is immeasurably improved without an engine! The top steering joint is disconnected...

6 ...followed by the connection to the steering box.

7 With bulkhead mounting bolts removed, the steering column can be taken away from the vehicle for reuse later.

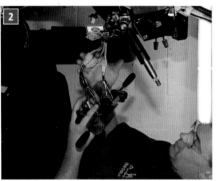

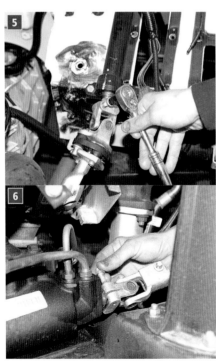

Steering wheel removal and refitting

With the ignition key removed, turn the steering wheel so that the steering lock is engaged. This is so that the steering column will be locked in the same position when you come to refit the steering wheel later. Expose the steering wheel retaining nut by removing the centre cover.

LATER MODELS

1 Carefully lever the badge out from the centre of the wheel.

EARLY MODELS

2 Take out the retaining screw (8) and lift off the trim cover (6). (Illustration courtesy Land Rover)

On all vehicles, remove the steering wheel retaining nut (4) and washer (5), mark the position of the steering wheel on the shaft so that it can be replaced in the same position and lift off the steering wheel.

If, as is likely, the wheel sticks on the splines, put the retaining nut back on by no more than one turn,

and pull hard towards you on the steering wheel or hit the back of the rim with your hands. The retaining nut will stop the wheel from flying off into your face!

When refitting, note the following points:

i Before refitting the wheel, make sure that the indicator cancelling ring (3) is in good condition – if not, replace it. Turn the ring so that the slots are vertical and the lug with the arrow points to the left, in the direction of the indicator switch.

ii Make sure that the finisher attachment lug is at the bottom of the steering wheel when refitting it (early models), and make sure that the indicator cancelling forks are located properly in the cancelling ring slots.

iii With the steering wheel back in place, and the shake-proof washer underneath the retaining nut, tighten the nut to the correct torque and refit the finisher.

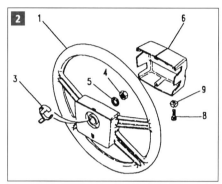

Steering column bearing replacement

1 If you have a lot of up and down play in the top of the steering column, start by disconnecting/ checking the upper steering column clamp (18) and checking that the rubber seal (25) beneath is intact. If the mounting is OK, and you need to replace the bearings, start by disconnecting the intermediate shaft and remove the steering wheel, as described in earlier sections. Take off the steering column shroud and disconnect all the electrical wiring from the switchgear. Disconnect the column from its lower bracket by taking out the mounting bolts (19) and disconnect from the upper

brackets (11). Remove the column. (Illustration courtesy Land Rover)

2 Needle roller bearings are fitted to the top (a) and bottom (b) of the steering column (c), and if they're very badly worn these bearings could break up and need replacement. If so, proceed as follows. (Illustration © Lindsay Porter)

A Take off the circlip (d) from the lower end of the steering column and drift out the inner shaft (e) downwards, working from the top end of the

column, complete with its lower bearing (b).
B Drift out the roll-pin (f) from the bearing retaining collar (g)...
C ...and carefully tap the bearing (b) and collar (g) from the lower end of the inner shaft.
D Remove the needle bearing (a) from the top end of the outer column.
E Fit new bearings and refit the components in the reverse of the removal sequence, but make sure that the new bearing at the top end of the outer column is fitted to a depth of 10mm from the end of the column, as shown.

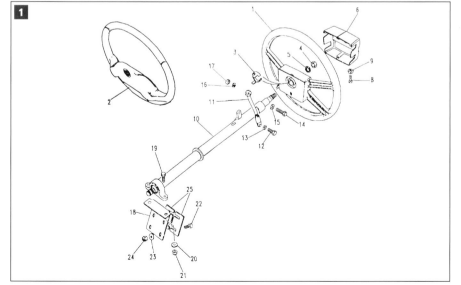

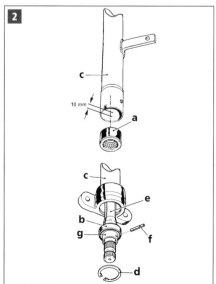

Steering lock-stop adjustment

1 If the tyres rub or there's insufficient lock on one side or the other, the steering lock in each direction is adjusted by slackening the lock-nut (a) and adjusting the position of this stop-bolt (b), before retightening the lock-nut. Simple but effective, in the Land Rover tradition!

Steering box replacement

1 The steering box fixings are removed from the chassis rail.

2 Nene Overland's Michael collected all fittings for the replacement steering box before reassembly...

3 ...and reused the fixings from the other side to bolt it in place. It makes sense to start with the 'box because all of the steering components radiate out from it.

4 This new steering box came without a drop arm, so Michael transferred the one from the old box. Once tight, the tab washer has to be knocked down and over one of the flats on the nut, and another up and over a flat on the drop arm itself.

5 Both the steering arm and the steering damper are simply refitted.

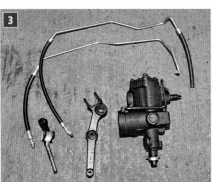

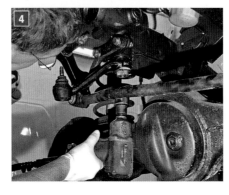

Bleeding the power steering system

1 Top-up the fluid reservoir to the MAXIMUM mark, have an assistant run the engine and be prepared to add more fluid very quickly if the level drops as the engine starts up. Once the level stabilises, turn the front wheels to the straight-ahead position. Now leave the engine running until it reaches its normal running temperature, allow it to run on tick-over and don't turn the steering.

2 Push a length of clear plastic pipe on to the bleed nipple (see arrow) on top of the steering box, allowing it to drain excess fluid into a jar. Slacken the bleed screw and watch until a steady flow of fluid, free from air bubbles, comes out of the bleed screw, while your assistant tops up the reservoir as necessary.

Turn the steering to full left-lock, then full right-lock, holding it in each position from five to ten seconds. It is MOST IMPORTANT that the steering isn't held at full lock for more than 30 seconds at a time, because otherwise the hydraulic system could be damaged.

Now check that there are no leaks anywhere in the hydraulic system, and if all is clear slacken the bleed screw once more to check that no more air will come out of the system. Remember to finish off by topping-up the hydraulic fluid to the correct level.

Power steering pump replacement

See page 212 for component schematic drawing.

1 From beneath the vehicle, slacken the two adjustment clamp bolts and the pivot bolt (but don't remove them), release the tension from the belt and remove it. This is the type fitted with a supplementary tensioner pulley (3).

2 Clamp the flexible hydraulic hoses near to the pump (A) to minimise fluid loss, but be prepared to catch such fluid as will be spilled. Disconnect the hydraulic hoses from the pump (B). (Illustration © Lindsay Porter)

Now continue as follows:

A Remove the tension/adjustment bolts slackened earlier and take off the pump complete with its adjustment plate and pulley.

B Clean the surfaces, then use paint or something similar to mark the position of the pump on the plate. Remove the four attachment bolts and separate the pump from the plate.

C When refitting the pump, be sure to align the pump and adjustment plate as they were when previously fitted, and tension the drive belt so that there's 12mm (½in) of deflection, using thumb pressure in the mid point of the belt run.

D It's IMPORTANT that you don't lever against the pump casing when tensioning the belt, because this will easily damage and ruin the pump.

E Top-up and bleed the system as described above.

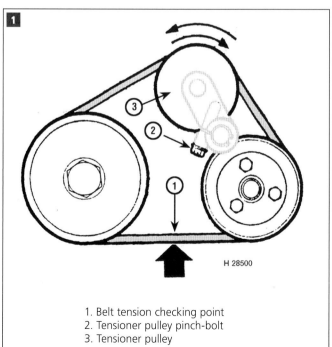

H 28500

1. Belt tension checking point
2. Tensioner pulley pinch-bolt
3. Tensioner pulley

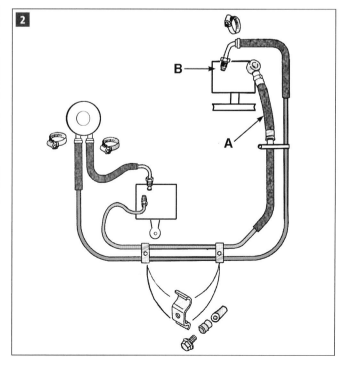

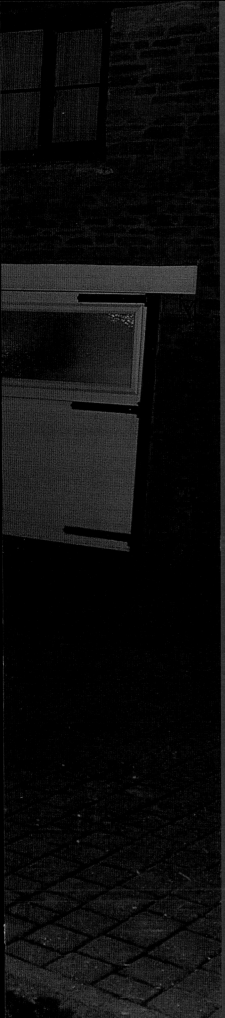

Electrical equipment

When things go wrong with the charging circuit, the easy solution is to trade-in the (assumed) faulty component for an exchange item. But there's a tendency for people to assume that a major component has failed when in fact the fault is a much more minor one, and there are still a number of areas where the enthusiast can carry out repairs without writing off the whole component. For instance, it's entirely feasible to change worn alternator brushes and, in so doing, save yourself a whole lot of money! However, there have been several different types of alternator fitted to Defenders over the years, for which see the following details.

COMMON FAULTS
Most Defender models, regardless of year, seem to suffer from a similar problem of bad earths ('grounds') on both starter motors and alternators. Before assuming that a component is faulty, check the condition of all engine-bay earth connections.

ALTERNATOR CHECKS AND OVERHAUL
Alternators can be checked for a number of faults, but there are several precautions to be taken. It's essential that good electrical connections are maintained at all times, including those at the battery. You should never disconnect battery cables or break any connections in the alternator control or charging circuits while the engine is running, otherwise the alternator may well be irreparably damaged.

Whenever a basic rapid charger is used on the battery, it must be disconnected from the vehicle so as not to damage the alternator. Better battery chargers have protection built in – check first!

Battery voltages apply to the alternator even though the ignition is switched off. It's essential that the battery is disconnected before carrying out any work on the alternator, and also before carrying out any arc or MIG welding on the vehicle.

ELECTRICAL CONNECTIONS
Apparent alternator faults may be caused by no more than poor electrical connections. Disconnect, clean up and remake all of the charging and control circuit electrical connections, including main earth straps.

IGNITION WARNING LIGHT
Because the ignition warning light is connected in series with the alternator circuit, bulb failure on early Defenders will prevent the alternator from charging. DON'T replace the alternator just for the price of a replacement bulb – check the bulb first!

TD5 ALTERNATORS
Before replacing what appears to be a faulty alternator, note that on TD5 models the alternator is fused through the brake/stop light circuit. If the fuse for the brake lights blows, the alternator won't charge, so check the brake/stop light fuse before assuming there's a component fault.

PRE-TD5 ALTERNATOR REMOVAL
After disconnecting the battery, disconnect all of the electrical connections from the back of the alternator, making a careful note so that you know what goes where. Remove the alternator by slackening off all of the pivot and tensioning nuts and bolts, taking the tension off the belt, removing the belt and then taking out all of the bolts.

TD5 ALTERNATOR REMOVAL
After disconnecting the battery, disconnect all of the electrical connections from the back of the alternator, making a careful note so that you know what goes where.

1 After removing the cooling fan, use a 15mm ring spanner to release the drive belt tensioner and

remove the belt from the pulleys. Remove the LH thread bolt (arrowed) and remove the auxiliary drive belt tensioner.

2 Remove the bolt securing the support stay to the alternator (a).
i   Remove the clip holding the lubrication drain hose to the vacuum pump (rear of photograph).
ii   Disconnect the vacuum pump lubrication pipe (c), and discard the 'O' ring.
iii Remove the bolt (d) and release the alternator from the mounting bracket.
iv   Disconnect the hose from the vacuum pump (b).
v   Remove the alternator – take care not to damage the radiator cooling fins.
vi   Four bolts hold the vacuum pump to the alternator. Plug all open connections.

LUCAS A115 AND A113 ALTERNATOR OVERHAUL

3 These are the components of these two alternator types.
i   Pull out the wiring plug (a), take out the interference suppression capacitor screw (b) and remove the suppressor. (Illustration courtesy Lucas)

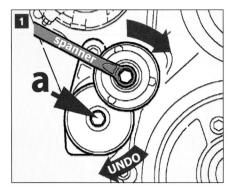

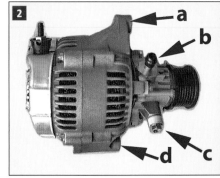

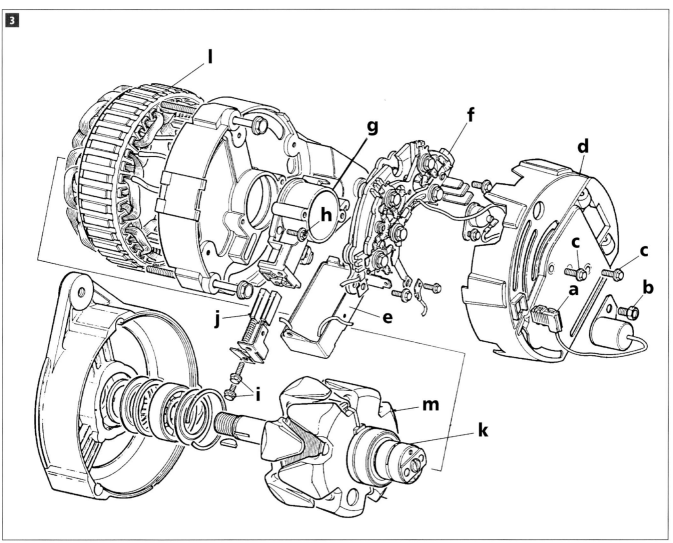

3

ii   Take out the two screws (c) and remove the cover (d).

iii Make a careful written note of the positions of all the wires to the regulator (e), the rectifier (f) and the brush box components (g).

iv   Disconnect the wires from the rectifier and the regulator, then take out the screws holding the regulator in place and remove it. Note that one of the brush mounting plates is also held in position by one of the screws.

v   The two screws (h) holding the brush box in place can be taken out and the brush box (g) removed.

vi   Take out the two screws (i) and lift out the brush set from the brush box. If the carbon part of the brush is less than 5mm (0.20in), they should be renewed.

vii The slip rings, on which the brushes bear, can be wiped clean with a spot of solvent on a rag. If they're very heavily covered in deposits, use very fine glass paper to clean them before wiping them clean with solvent.

viii When reassembling the components, make absolutely sure that the brushes can move freely in the brush box.

ELECTRICAL TESTS

Rotor field winding

4 Connect a battery-operated ohmmeter between points A and B on the alternator slip ring. This enables you to check that there's continuity in the field winding (*ie* there are no breaks), and also that the resistance is about 3.2ohm.

Stator windings

Because of the very low resistance of the stator windings, specialist equipment is needed to check them. However, if you see obvious signs of the varnish on the stator windings (see illustration above), the stator assembly is ripe for renewal – and this is probably a good indicator that you need an exchange alternator.

Bearings

If there are any signs of rubbing between the rotor (m) and the stator windings (l), it's fairly certain that the bearings are worn and you'll need an exchange overhauled alternator.

No other checks can be carried out on the alternator without specialist equipment.

4

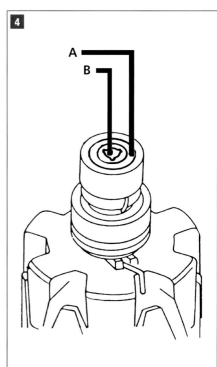

5

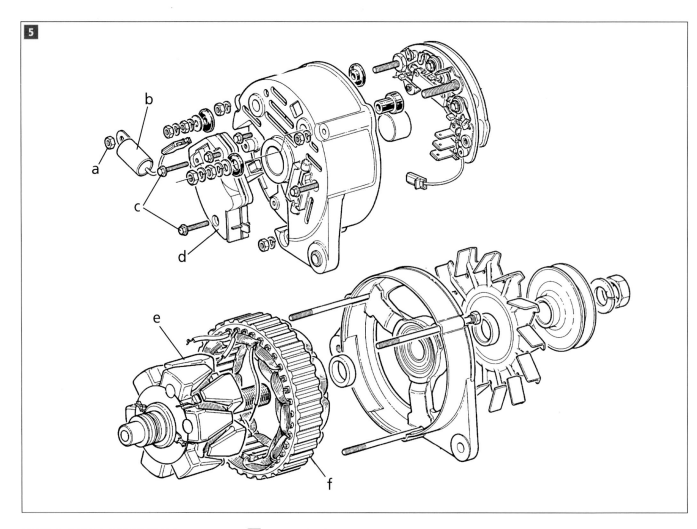

LUCAS A127 ALTERNATOR OVERHAUL

5 Remove the alternator as described in the previous section. These are the component parts of a typical A127 alternator. (Illustrations courtesy Lucas)

a Remove the nuts and washers (a) holding the suppressors (b) – there are two rectangular units fitted to some models – and then remove the suppressors after pulling the electrical plugs out of their sockets in the back of the alternator.

b Remove the three bolts (c) holding the voltage regulator/brush box assembly (d) to the back of the alternator, tip the outside edge of the assembly upwards and remove it.

6 You'll now be able to see the protrusion of the brushes (A), which should be 5mm (0.2in) or more. If not, the brushes by themselves can't be changed and the voltage regulator/brush box assembly must be replaced as a unit. Clean up the slip rings as described in the previous section.

Rotor field windings
7 Connect a battery-operated ohmmeter to the slip rings as shown. If there's no reading, there's a break in the wiring. You can also check for excessive resistance – you should obtain a reading of 3.2ohm.

Stator windings
See illustration 3, part f. If the stator windings are burned or damaged, the stator will need to be replaced,

which is usually a sure sign that the alternator should be exchanged for an overhauled replacement.

Bearings
If there are any signs of rubbing between the rotor (e) and the stator windings (f), it's fairly certain that the bearings are worn and you'll need an exchange overhauled alternator.

No other checks can be carried out on the alternator without specialist knowledge or equipment.

TD5 ALTERNATORS
No information is currently available on availability of components for rebuilding the Denso alternators fitted to TD5 diesels.

6

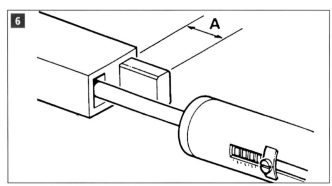

7

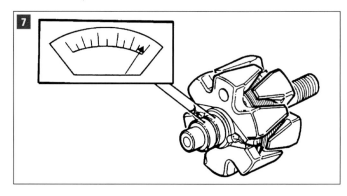

Starter motors

There are many checks you can carry out to a starter motor, but the great majority of starter motor 'faults' fall into one of three categories:

A Battery condition, leads and connections – ie not starter motor faults at all! Very many starter motors are replaced every year even though the fault lies elsewhere. Check all of the main terminals first, especially those at the battery and the main cables leading to earth. Check also that the earth from the engine to the chassis is sound, and then check all of the connections on the starter motor itself.

B Solenoid faults. The simplest way to find out if the solenoid is working is to listen to it while an assistant operates the starter switch. If it's working, you should be able to hear the click of the contacts closing. If you can't, it may be a faulty solenoid – but do check the wiring, as mentioned above.

C Worn brushes. For the starter motor to

be faulty because of worn brushes, the brush length will have to be considerably less than the minimum shown in the specifications. Don't just replace the old brushes on a whim; a set of brushes will typically cost around 20% of the price of an exchange starter motor, so only replace them if you think it'll really help.

If the starter motor is faulty in any other way, you're probably better off cutting your losses and going for an exchange starter motor. Replacement bush sets are available, and replacement isn't too difficult except on the quite rare, early diesel engines' Lucas 2M113 starter motor, so we include that here. In practice, if the bushes are worn the rest of the starter motor may also be badly worn.

LUCAS 2M113

1 These are the components of the Lucas 2M113 starter motor fitted to very early diesel engines. (Illustration courtesy Lucas)

Solenoid removal
Disconnect the link to the starter motor (a), then take out the two hex-head screws (b) and withdraw the solenoid (c), lifting the front end of the plunger (d) to release it from the top of the engagement lever (e).

Brush replacement
Take out the two brush-box securing screws (f) and the two long through bolts (g). The end plate (h) and seal (i) – if fitted – can now be removed. The brushes can now be seen and should be removed from under their spring clips. If the brushes have worn down to 8mm (5/16in) or less, they should be replaced.

Wedge the earth brushes (j) in the open position in their housings (l) using the brush spring. Fit the field coil brushes (k) into position in the brush box as it's offered back up into position. Now make sure that the brushes move freely in their holders. The rest of the reassembly process is the reverse of dismantling.

Bearing bushes
There are three bushes, and replacement of the centre bush involves rather more dismantling on this type if the centre bearing is to be replaced.

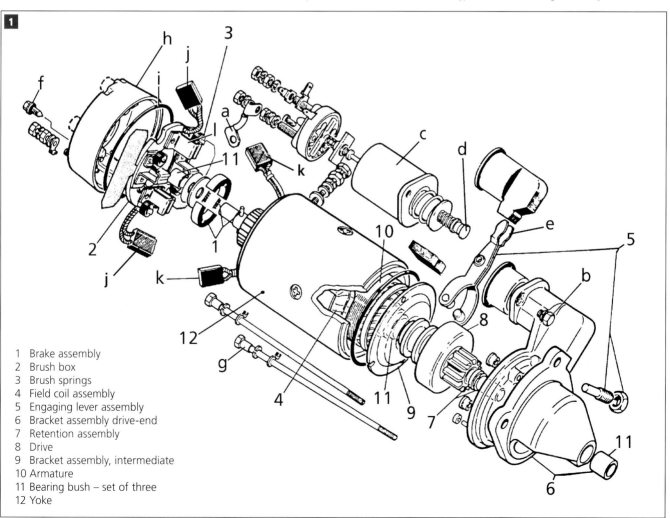

1 Brake assembly
2 Brush box
3 Brush springs
4 Field coil assembly
5 Engaging lever assembly
6 Bracket assembly drive-end
7 Retention assembly
8 Drive
9 Bracket assembly, intermediate
10 Armature
11 Bearing bush – set of three
12 Yoke

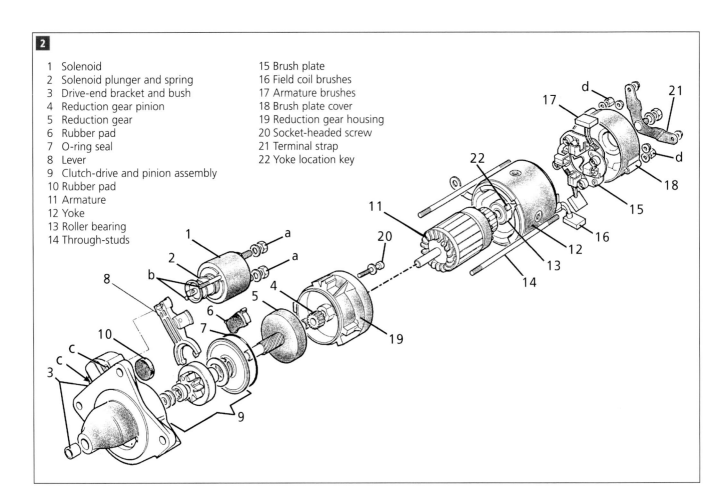

2

1 Solenoid
2 Solenoid plunger and spring
3 Drive-end bracket and bush
4 Reduction gear pinion
5 Reduction gear
6 Rubber pad
7 O-ring seal
8 Lever
9 Clutch-drive and pinion assembly
10 Rubber pad
11 Armature
12 Yoke
13 Roller bearing
14 Through-studs
15 Brush plate
16 Field coil brushes
17 Armature brushes
18 Brush plate cover
19 Reduction gear housing
20 Socket-headed screw
21 Terminal strap
22 Yoke location key

TURBO DIESEL AND 200 Tdi ENGINES (NOT 300 Tdi) PARIS RHONE/VALEO STARTER MOTOR

2 These are the components of the Paris Rhone starter motor. (Illustration © Lindsay Porter)

Solenoid removal
Remove the lead that goes from the solenoid wiring connection (a) to the starter motor. Take off the two nuts from the mounting bolts (b) at position (c), and lift away the solenoid (1).

Brush replacement
Take off the terminal strap (21), remove the two nuts (d) on the end of the through studs (14) and take off the brush plate cover (18). No information is available from Land Rover regarding the minimum length of the brushes. Refitting the brush box must be carried out in exactly the same sequence as described for the Lucas 2M113 starter motor. See above.

Glow plug testing

When overhauling an engine, you should test the glow plugs and replace any that aren't in perfect condition. Faulty glow plugs will lead to poor diesel engine starting, and it's useful to know what to look for.

GLOW PLUGS OUT OF ENGINE
With the glow plugs unscrewed from the cylinder head, start by checking their physical condition. If the tips have been burnt or eroded, the injectors should be checked for a bad injector spray pattern. If they're OK, hold the glow plug in a clamp or vice and apply a 12V current with jump leads from a 12V battery. If the glow plug is in good condition, it'll start to glow red at the tip after about five seconds or so. If it starts glowing in the middle instead of the tip, or if it takes much longer than five seconds to

warm up, the glow plug is defective. Be sure to leave the glow plug for several minutes so that it cools down completely before handling it. Don't apply current to the glow plug for more than about 20 seconds – especially if it fails to glow at all – because it's then probably faulty and there could be a short circuit. Don't apply 12V directly to the early series-wired glow plugs – see below.

GLOW PLUGS IN VEHICLE
Early vehicles were fitted with glow plugs that were wired in series, which means that if one plug fails, the supply to all of the plugs will fail. It also means that if you apply 12V directly to one of these early series-wired glow plugs it'll burn out.

You can test the supply to the plugs by connecting a test light between the glow

plug supply cable and a good earth on the bodywork or engine. With the 'ignition' turned on, the light should illuminate. You can test each individual glow plug by connecting a 12V test light in series with the glow plug, after first disconnecting it from its normal wiring connections. The connections would go: 12V feed to bulb; bulb to glow plug wiring connection; engine earth to battery earth. If the light illuminates, the plug is working. You may be able to rig up a 3V feed and a suitable bulb to test the early type of series-wired glow plug without burning it out.

If you still suspect glow plugs of inadequate performance, remove them from the vehicle and take them to a diesel engine specialist, who'll be able to test them properly and pronounce them well, ill or dead at a very moderate charge.

Headlight replacement

1 To get at the Defender headlight, you have first to remove the sidelights...

2 ...and then the trim. This applies both to the standard trim and the KBX Upgrades trims I've got fitted.

3 Remove the screws (one shown) holding the headlight to the vehicle, but not the headlamp ring screws, shown later.

4 The halogen unit, complete with bulb, unplugs from the trailing lead inside the housing.

5 There are three screws into three clips...

6 ...that hold the headlamp rings to the glass bowls. Remove all three and keep them safe – don't let them escape across the floor!! Defender headlamp rings are notoriously rust-prone. (Doesn't anyone make stainless steel ones?) You'll want to clean them up and rust-proof them, or even fit new ones if necessary. I recommend a smear of copper slip on the inside faces.

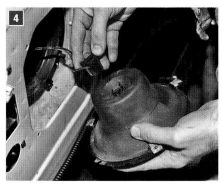

Dashboard lights

Before attempting to replace any of the warning lights, DISCONNECT THE BATTERY.

In its typically thorough way, Land Rover ensure that warning lights and instrument lights can be replaced very easily. To replace warning lights, you simply take out the two screws and remove the warning light module from the front of the instrument panel. The plug connector is detached from the back of the module and this gives access to the warning light bulbs. Each bulb is twisted and then withdrawn from its socket.

In the case of later Defenders, the lights are built into a printed circuit board. There are different versions available for different models and specifications of Defender.

The instrument panel is easily accessed after removing the four screws holding the panel in place, after which the panel is pulled forwards. You may need to disconnect the drive cable from the back of the speedometer to allow you to pull the panel sufficiently far forwards.

Wiper mechanism overhaul

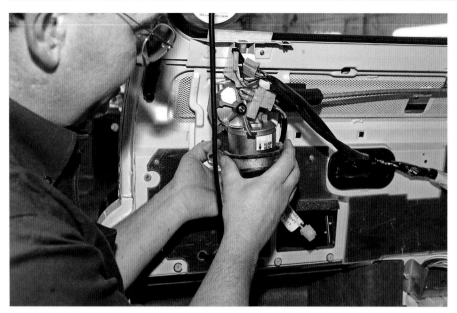

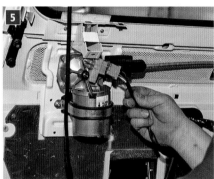

The wiper motor is located on one side or other, behind the dash, depending on whether the vehicle is LHD or RHD. To remove the wiper motor, after disconnecting the battery and removing the wiper arms:

1 Carefully lever the Land Rover decal from the grab handle and remove the screw beneath (RHD only).

2 Remove the lower screw and lift the handle from the fascia.

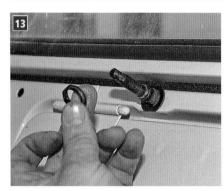

3 Remove the screw holding the finisher to the wiper motor cover (RHD only).

4 Remove the door check strap cover, (three screws), and take off the wiper motor cover.

5 Disconnect the multi-plug from the wiper motor and (earlier models only) disconnect the wiper motor earth lead.

6 Lift the rubber sleeve and slacken (don't detach) the wiper motor drive tube nut.

7 Remove the strap retaining screws and release the wiper motor.

8 You can now fully unscrew the tube nut and remove the wiper motor and drive rack.

LEFT-HAND DRIVE VEHICLES WITH AIR CONDITIONING

You also need to:
- Remove the centre and LH fascia top crash rail support bracket fixings.
- Remove both demister vents from ducts.
- Remove the RH demister vent hose from duct.
- Remove the RH vent demister vent fixing and pivot the vent and hose to one side.

TO CONTINUE DISMANTLING

9 Remove the demister vent top duct, instrument housing, fascia crash pad and the ventilator grille panel.

10 Slacken the steering column support rod lower fixing.

11 Remove the steering column upper support fixing.

12 Slacken the nuts holding the backplates to the wheel boxes and remove the drive rack tubes.

13 Slacken the grub screws and remove the wiper arm adaptors, then remove the wheelbox spindle nuts.

14 Take off the wheel box assemblies.

15 These are the wiper components ready for examination.

WIPER MOTOR OVERHAUL

The wiper motor is easily dismantled and checked. The drive gear needs to be properly lubricated and undamaged and the motor brushes need to be in usable condition. The motor can only be dismantled once it's been removed from the vehicle.

After removing the screws, the cover plate can be removed. Lever off the circlip (3) and washer that holds the connecting rod (4) in place. Take off the connecting rod and the washer from beneath it (5). (Illustration courtesy Lucas)

Turn the unit over and take off the circlip and washer (6) from the gear shaft, then turn it back again and lift out the gear shaft and the dished washer (8).

Make alignment marks on the yoke and on the gear body (9) so that they can be reassembled in exactly the same location. Take out the yoke securing bolts (10) and remove the yoke and armature assembly. The screws holding the brush gear assembly (12) can be taken from the gear drive body.

Remove the brushes, and if they're worn to 4.8mm (0.19in) or less fit new ones.

When reassembling the motor, be sure to thoroughly soak the yoke bearing felt washer with oil. When fitting the brushes, be sure to push the brushes apart so that they'll fit over the armature. Reassemble the armature and yoke to the gearbox, using the alignment marks you made earlier, and retighten the bolts. If a new armature has been fitted, slacken the thrust screw (14) before tightening the bolts.

Lubricate metal bearing surfaces in the conventional way, but be sure to only lubricate the gearwheel teeth, the armature shaft wormgear, the connecting rod and pin, cable rack and wheel box gearwheel with lubricant which is suitable for plastic. Land Rover recommend Ragosine Listate grease. If a new armature shaft has been fitted, hold the unit so

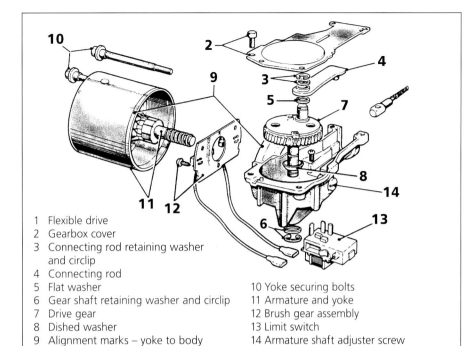

1 Flexible drive
2 Gearbox cover
3 Connecting rod retaining washer and circlip
4 Connecting rod
5 Flat washer
6 Gear shaft retaining washer and circlip
7 Drive gear
8 Dished washer
9 Alignment marks – yoke to body
10 Yoke securing bolts
11 Armature and yoke
12 Brush gear assembly
13 Limit switch
14 Armature shaft adjuster screw

that the armature shaft is in a vertical position with the adjuster screw (14) uppermost. Turn the adjuster screw inwards carefully until resistance is just felt, then unscrew it by a quarter turn.

Land Rover recommend that the motor should run, within one minute of being started from cold, at from 42 to 48rpm (low speed) and between 62 and 68rpm (high speed), although they don't state whether this is loaded or unloaded. Don't allow the windscreen wipers to rub across a dry screen.

Wiring tips

You must ALWAYS use the correct grade of wire for the application. Take a section of the piece you want to replace (or consult your Land Rover specialist) when buying replacement cable.

1 In addition, you should ALWAYS properly solder wiring joins. Insulation tape isn't adequate. This is Würth shrink-fit tube, which is pushed over the join...

2 ...and shrinks tightly in place when heated. Superb!

3 For stripping wire, either use a purpose-made wire stripper that guarantees the right result every time... (Illustration courtesy Würth)

4 ...or use a multi-purpose tool that's a touch slower to use but can cut wire or crimp connections, as shown here.

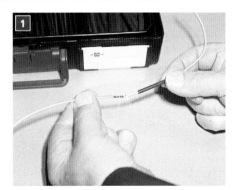

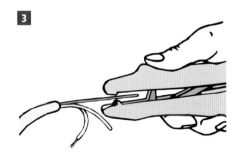

CHAPTER 8

Interior

Front seat removal and refit

There are several types of front seat fitted to 90s, 110s and Defenders, and although the removal procedures are similar there are differences.

1 The basic type of seat, used up until about 1987, is very similar to those fitted to earlier Land Rovers. These are the seat base mounting arrangements.

2 The far more common type has a seat base that pulls upwards off its clips. It's then a matter of removing the nuts and bolts holding the seat frame to the seat base in each of its four corners. With the seat cushion out of the way, the access plate from beneath the cushion is removed and you then have access to the separate nuts (when appropriate) inside the seat base. Some types have two bolts at the front location shown here.

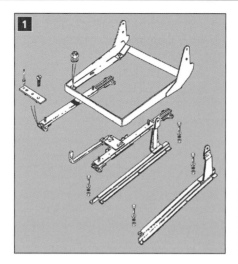

Rear seats, centre-row, front-facing, removal and refit

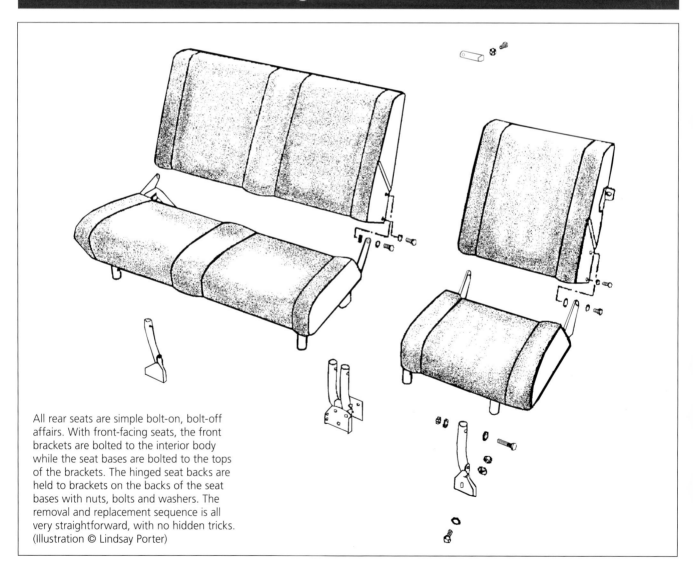

All rear seats are simple bolt-on, bolt-off affairs. With front-facing seats, the front brackets are bolted to the interior body while the seat bases are bolted to the tops of the brackets. The hinged seat backs are held to brackets on the backs of the seat bases with nuts, bolts and washers. The removal and replacement sequence is all very straightforward, with no hidden tricks. (Illustration © Lindsay Porter)

Here we show the fitting of a full set of Britpart's folding individual rear seats and matching lap seat belts.

1 Each seat comes as a self-contained Britpart box of parts. Mechanic Stuart began by laying out the parts and comparing them with the single drawing on the instruction sheets. He didn't follow the exact same sequence of events described in the instructions, but it all worked out perfectly in the end.

2 Before starting to fit the seats, Stuart worked out, by offering up the seat bases, where the seat belts were going to be fitted.

3 It's important to drill the mounting holes for the seat belts – or at least the ones in the rearmost corners of the floor – before fitting the seats, because otherwise there'll be a real risk of damaging the seats with the electric drill. In practice, you're strongly recommended to follow the approach carried out by Stuart: drill holes for the seat belts only after marking out their positions with the seats temporarily fitted into position. Then, take the seats out again, drill for the seat-belt mountings and then fit the seat belts or the seats in the order you prefer.

4 Each seat back and base has captive nuts built in. Locations are clearly indicated with red dots stuck on to the surface of the trim. You need to use a sharp knife to cut the trim so that mounting bolts can be entered cleanly, but you also have to take great care not to cut too much material away. You really don't want to see jagged, cut edges of trim protruding from underneath the surfaces of the brackets.

5 The backrest brackets have to be fitted the correct way round as shown in the instructions. It's vitally important that each bolt has its thread started in its captive nut carefully, by hand, before starting to tighten it up. If you accidentally cross a thread you'll almost certainly break the captive nut free inside the trim, making it impossible to bolt the frame in place.

6 In this installation, the brackets on the seat backs lined up with existing holes in the bodywork. In addition, there are slotted holes strategically placed in the body side rails to enable you to insert the relevant washers and fixings.

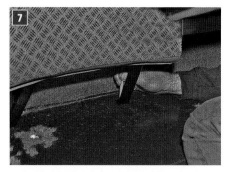

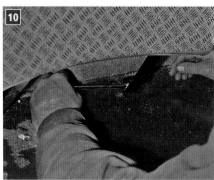

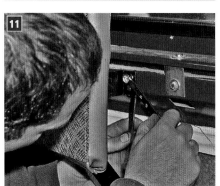

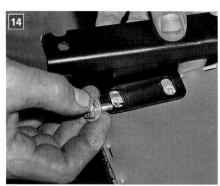

7 With the top brackets in place, the bottom ends of the brackets can be pushed back or forth until they're parallel with the body sides. The positions of the mounting holes can then be transferred to the top surface of the wheel arch box.

8 To centre-punch aluminium, you use a sharp centre punch and give it a single, crisp tap with the hammer. If you hammer too hard or give too many blows you'll dent the surrounding aluminium. Remember that it's significantly softer than steel!

9 Stuart then drilled clearance-sized holes...

10 ...before fitting the bolts into the wheel arch box, not forgetting to use substantial flat washers to spread the load on the underside of the box.

11 Stuart used the slotted holes you can see here in the bodywork rail to tighten the upper seat backrest mounting bolts.

12 This Britpart drawing illustrates the swivel bracket that needs to be fitted to the seat base in the position arrowed. It's also the drawing referred to earlier, showing you which way round the seat back brackets have to be fitted.

13 Stuart prepared to cut the trim fabric...

14 ...so that the brackets could be bolted into position remembering, as before, to start each bolt by hand, ensuring its clean entry into the captive nut secreted away behind the trim.

15 A thin black strip has to be screwed down to the outer edge of the underside of each seat base...

16 ...but bear in mind that the front two bolt holes are also there to enable the swivel bracket to be bolted down.

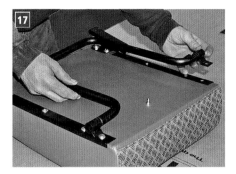

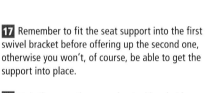

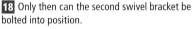

17 Remember to fit the seat support into the first swivel bracket before offering up the second one, otherwise you won't, of course, be able to get the support into place.

18 Only then can the second swivel bracket be bolted into position.

19 The next job was to offer up the seat base and mark out the hole positions for the seat base swivel brackets. Note that it's most important that the seat backrest is already in place at this stage so that you can be sure to check the correct position of the base both when folded away and when laid flat.

20 Off with the seat base. In with the electric drill. Create clearance-sized holes for bolting down the seat base.

21 Now, what holds the seat base up when it's not in use? This strap does. It clips on to the underside of the seat base having previously been screwed permanently on to the back of the backrest. And did we forget to fit the first one?

22 We did! So Stuart removed the first backrest, but remembered to fit the strap to the rears of all the other backrests before fitting their brackets. Ah well, we're only nearly perfect...

23 Stuart was really chuffed with the first seat he fitted and quite rightly so.

24 But before going any further, he fitted the first of the lap seat belts.

25 You'll need an assistant when tightening both the seat bases and the seat belts. Either that, or 3m-long arms!

26 Once the first seat belt was in place, Stuart couldn't resist trying out the first seat for size. This made him even more chuffed than he'd been before!

27 With all the seats and belts in place, you can see the extra versatility that a set of Britpart individual folding rear seats brings to the back of both long-wheelbase and short-wheelbase Defenders. And don't they look right, too!

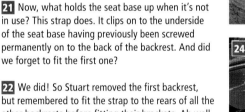

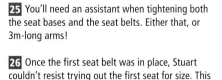

REAR SEATS, SIDE-FACING, REMOVAL AND REFIT

SEAT BACKREST RE-COVERING

You can buy replacement Defender seat covers and foams. Matt Morgan, Britpart's Trim Shop manager, shows how to re-cover the Defender's seats.

There are two types of Defender seat shown here. The earlier type, with a moulded plastic back on the backrest, was made in relatively small numbers, and there are no like-for-like replacements available at the time of writing. Instead, Matt shows how to strip down the early type of seat back. The options are to try to use a later type of cover with the early type of back and foam, have a new cover made by a bespoke trimmer, or fit a new later-type back.

EARLY-TYPE SEAT BACKS

1 Matt pointed out that Britpart's seat backs are different from the originals in that the originals had sewn stitching which (a) didn't match the base and (b) caused the seat to split along the seam over a period of time, rather like 'Tear here' perforated paper. The replacements have heat-formed vertical sections to match the appearance of the originals without matching their weakness.

2 Matt used a pointed bradawl to lever out the start of the rubber strip…

3 …which holds the back cover in place on the earliest seats.

4 This released the plastic cover and allowed it to be lifted away.

5 He removed the two screws holding the headrest bezel in place.

6 At the back, the seat cover is clipped on to these metal tabs (arrowed).

7 The steel rod holding the back of the cover in place was now free.

8 Matt released the two ends of the string holding the sides and front of the cover in the channel around the frame.

9 Next, he freed the cover from the base…

10 …and unclipped the foam from the base frame.

11 The foam was also glued down to the frame and had to be peeled away.

IMPORTANT NOTE: For fitting the later-type back to the early-type base, see picture 38.

LATER-TYPE SEAT BACKS

12 Matt tapped off the adjuster knob…

13 …before removing the adjuster cover. It's meant to be held on with a screw through the hole shown here, but it's frequently broken or missing.

14 The centre of the cover is held in place with this clip, which means that it must be levered off.

15 The later type of seat back is joined beneath the base, front-to-back, with a plastic clip that's simply peeled apart.

16 Matt pulled back the backrest cover to its fullest extent…

17 …then removed the rod holding the trim clips in place.

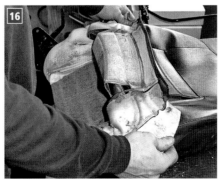

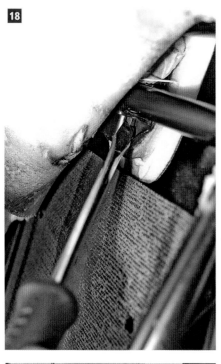

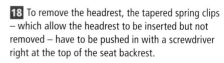

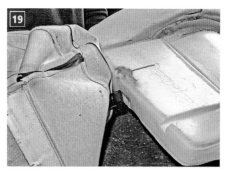

18 To remove the headrest, the tapered spring clips – which allow the headrest to be inserted but not removed – have to be pushed in with a screwdriver right at the top of the seat backrest.

19 This enabled Matt to remove the seat cover and headrest complete.

20 The glued-on foam was then peeled away.

21 New seat foams are almost always fitted unless the old ones are in unusually good condition. Matt sprayed contact adhesive on to the base in Britpart's glue spraying booth.

22 He then placed the backrest frame in place, into the recesses in the foam…

23 …before gluing and folding over the tab of foam shown here.

24 This is the new seat back cover being offered up.

25 The rod (A) has to be passed through the hole in the foam (B) and then, on the other side…

26 …held in place with a professional's hog ring (and these are the specially made hog ring pliers).

27 Alternatively, a top tip is to use a pair of strong cable ties after making suitable holes in the canvas support panel.

28 Matt recommends that you always start by lining up the headrest hole in the cover with that in the frame.

29 He says that the upper corners then need to be aligned…

30 …and the cover pulled down like a tight T-shirt on a chubby child…

31 …making sure that the seams on the cover align with the corners of the backrest frame.

32 Matt showed how the cover is pulled tight and taut, smoothing out the wrinkles until it fitted perfectly.

33 Matt fitted the extra piece of foam supplied with the kit at this stage…

34 …between the centre panel of the cover and the main foam section, tucking it into place at the base…

35 …before clipping together the two halves of the cover, front and rear, rather like a resealable plastic bag.

36 The replacement adjuster cover was fitted…

37 …followed by the adjuster knob, which had to be tapped on, taking care not to damage the plastic end of the knob.

38 NOTE: If fitting the late back to the early base this spring (seen here on a later-type back) has to be bent to fit. It locates on a peg on earlier types.

39 Matt stands by his newly re-covered backrest, while in the background the Britpart shop turns out more pallet-loads of trim ready for despatch.

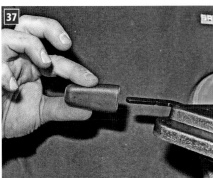

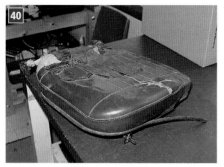

SEAT BASE RE-COVERING

40 It's not unusual to see a Defender seat base looking as bad as this. This base is clean, but even the duct tape repairs have worn through and it looks well past its sit-by-date.

41 The first job is to remove the rubber fillet from the open-sectioned frame around the base of the seat.

42 At the back of the underside of the seat, there are two metal tabs (arrowed), which need to be levered up…

43 …allowing this section of the trim to be released.

44 A number of plastic pegs are pushed through the trim at the rear and have to be carefully levered out with a screwdriver. Replacements are supplied with the kit.

45 Matt has lifted the edge of the trim out of the channel (arrowed) and is now freeing it all the way round.

46 With the trim free from the base you can also see that the base foam is starting to disintegrate, and that the cells in many places have collapsed and the foam has become flattened.

47 The foam has to be replaced, so Matt pulls it away from the steel base using the rolling action shown here.

48 There's absolutely nothing wrong with this steel base and it would be a simple matter to remove the remainder of the old adhesive and foam with cellulose thinners (work out of doors and away from any sources of ignition) and to repaint the frame if there are any signs of rust.

49 We started with a new base.

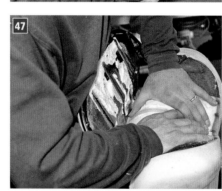

50 Matt stuck these two strips of vinyl on to the back of the foam using contact adhesive. The base of the foam inside the two strips of vinyl also has to be coated in contact adhesive…

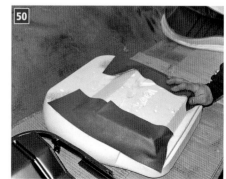

51 …and so must the upper surface of the steel seat base.

52 When the adhesive has begun to go tacky, the two items can be placed together. Here you can see Matt ensuring that the foam is pressed fully down into the seat base.

53 With base and foam turned over, you can see that the strips of vinyl glued earlier to the foam base give the correct finish to the underside of the seat.

54 Behind Matt's spray gun (most of us would use an aerosol can, of course) you can see the seat base trim turned inside out. The matching surfaces of the foam and trim have been 'painted' with contact adhesive, but only as far as the point shown here. Matt likes to allow movement on the outer edges and the front roll of the seat base.

55 You can see Matt carefully positioning the trim on the seat base foam so that the seams along the centre section line up precisely with their counterparts on the foam base.

56 Before the adhesive has fully dried, it's best to turn the seat base over and ensure that the front corners are both in their correct locations while folding the edges down over the sides of the foam. The round-edged seam at the base of the cover is tucked into the channel seen earlier.

57 Matt next fitted the rubber fillet into the channel to hold the cover in place all the way around. It's essential that the cover is symmetrical at this stage.

58 The round edge at the base of the cover is made by having a piece of upholsterer's string sewn into it, and tails of string (arrowed) can be seen at the back of the seat base. These are used to pull the cover taut.

59 Matt used an awl to find the holes in the steel seat base and push corresponding holes through the vinyl…

60 …so that the plastic pegs can be tapped through the vinyl and into the steel frame.

61 At the back of the seat, Matt inserts the steel rod supplied in the retrimming kit into the seam in the flap of fabric found there.

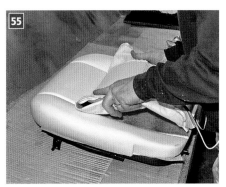

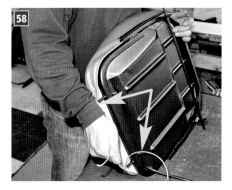

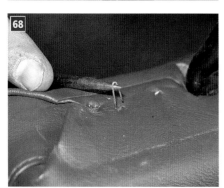

62 After folding the flap of fabric over the two locating pins on the back of the seat, Matt levered up the two tags of steel on the seat base…

63 …folded the tags through the cut-outs and, when they were neatly tucked around the steel rod, hammered them flat again.

64 This completed seat base is now, of course, brand new.

65 When the hinge pin of the backrest is pushed through the hole in the base, the two are held in place with a C-clip. This is rather a clever way of springing the C-clip into position. The ring spanner fits naturally over the outer circumference of the clip while the hammer springs it over the pin. It stops them making the usual bid for freedom.

66 The seat base that Matt has just re-covered slots into place on the seat frame. It's worth pointing out that the two plastic receptacles into which the pins are fitted often break or become lost, and it's worth replacing them so that the seat fits correctly.

67 Headrests can only be removed from seat backs when the backrest cover is off, so it makes sense to re-trim them now. The steel cover plate on the bottom of the headrest is taken off after removing the two self-tapping screws (arrowed).

68 Underneath, the folded-over trim is held down with staples, which have to be levered out.

69 The old cover is simply peeled away.

70 If you need a new foam – and you don't usually – it's simply slid off its support plate and a new one slid on in its place. Note the sheet of plastic that's been placed over the top of the foam to help the replacement trim slip over the clinging surface of the foam.

71 The base of the headrest is folded around like wrapping a Christmas parcel, the edges first and front and back last, before gluing and/or stapling the flaps into position. If you really want to go to town, you'll repaint the base with satin black aerosol paint, and the completed headrest will look much like this one.

NOTE: You might have spotted extra cables sticking out of these seats as Matt re-trimmed them. This is because we took the opportunity to fit seat heaters and lumbar supports.

Dash panel removal and refit

The battery had already been removed as part of the bulkhead replacement that formed the backdrop to this work. See 'Bulkhead replacement' in chapter 4. Also, note that the work photographed here was for a LHD to RHD conversion, so you'll see a left-hand-drive dash being removed and a right-hand-drive one going back on again. The work was carried out by workshop foreman Michael at Nene Overland.

WHAT'S IN A NAME?
Land Rover don't use the popular term 'dashboard'. In Solihull-speak, it's the 'fascia', and that's what you'll find in the official parts and workshop manuals.

DISMANTLING

1 Inside the vehicle, the fascia top rail was unscrewed...

2 ...and lifted away.

3 This provides access to the centre switch panel on later models. You can't get at these top screws without having taken the top rail away first.

4 All those differently shaped and colour-coded plugs in the back of the switch panel make reassembly so much easier!

5 These fascia screws are permanently visible...

6 ...but these can only be seen with the top rail removed.

7 Michael lifted the plastic fascia panel away from the dash.

8 Back over to the driver's side of the vehicle again and Michael unscrewed the heater fan controller.

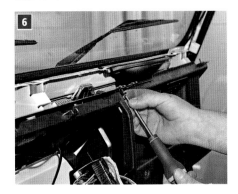

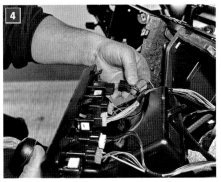

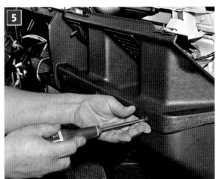

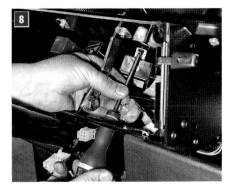

9 Land Rover do love using a wide variety of fixings, and this cable is held on with a spring clip that has to be levered off.

10 Both heater controllers were removed from their trims without first having to remove the knobs on the ends of the levers.

11 Digging deeper, Michael unscrewed and removed the screen vents and their convoluted tubing.

12 Next, the support for the instrument panel was removed.

13 The screws holding its lookalike on the other side went into the fascia panel at the front...

14 ...and the dash panel at the rear.

15 Isn't this what we love about Land Rovers? Look at the strength of that supersized support bracket!

16 The ventilator flaps' operating mechanisms need to be detached by opening the flaps and taking out the two screws holding them to their operating levers.

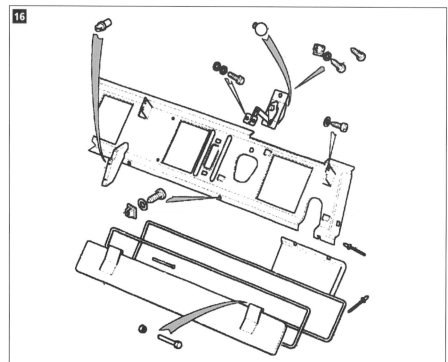

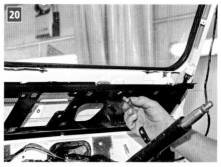

17 Next, this top-most steel panel was unscrewed and lifted away.

18 The large, plastic lower fascia trim was then unscrewed...

19 ...and lifted away.

REASSEMBLY

20 The fascia needs plastic inserts pushed into the square holes ready-punched into it. They're like 'captive nuts' for securing screws.

21 Once in place, Michael continued to fit the fascia panels.

22 Here you can see some of those plastic inserts being used as screws are refitted.

23 You'll find there are several places where there's no room to use a conventional screwdriver. A screwdriver bit in a ¼in drive ratchet can often be a lifesaver.

24 As you can see, if you've stripped out the entire dash area, there are dozens of components and some have to be fitted before others. In practice, most of it's obvious if, like Michael, you work in a logical fashion. However, you'll almost certainly have to go back once or twice when you find that fitting Part A prevents you from fitting Part B. Just resist the temptation to throw Hammer C through Window D...

25 Next, Michael offered up the ventilator flap adjuster, prior to fitting it into position.

26 He followed this up with the instrument panel back...

27 ...then inserted the screen vent outlet. He quickly realised that the vent would have to be fitted later and removed it again. This is typical of what you must do in order to make logical progress with such a complex job.

28 On TD5-type dashboards, there's a centre support panel that Michael screwed into place in yet more of those plastic inserts.

29 Here's a good example of various question marks beginning to resolve themselves. On the dash

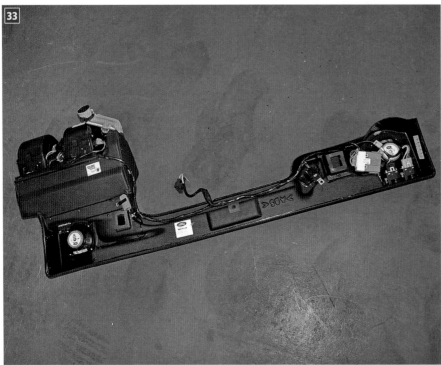

top is a piece of hose for the vent. Can it be fitted now? Not yet. And in the background, various wiring connections have been laid out approximately where they have to go. Confident that nothing will have to go over it later, Michael screwed the knob back on to the blower adjustment lever, using the tiny grub screw that has to be carefully inserted into the side of the knob.

30 Inner dash components are remarkably fiddly on later Defenders. Michael set about swapping the minor parts on to the major assemblies...

31 ...including these heater flaps.

32 The upper mounting panel had already been fitted, and finally Michael received some assistance to offer up the lower fascia panel.

AIR CONDITIONING MODELS ONLY

33 Vehicles with Land Rover air conditioning also have a sub-assembly beneath the fascia, carrying the cockpit a/c components. This is the rear view of the factory-fit dashboard assembly. It contains the fans, ducting and electrical control gear. Disconnect according to workshop manual.

34 The sub-assembly is held on with these pairs of fixing screws...

35 ...and more beneath the speaker bezels…

36 …plus a large one in the centre.

37 At this stage, the assembly can be carefully extracted from the vehicle.

Seat belts and Station Wagon trim

SEAT BELT REMOVAL AND REFIT

All seat belt mountings are tightened to captive nuts in the bodywork. Seat belt mountings are covered with trim caps, which are first levered off before undoing the mountings. It's essential that all spacers and spring washers are replaced in exactly the correct order when seat belts are being refitted.

1 If the seat belt webbing and connector have to be passed through the aperture finisher, the trim will have to be moved out of position.

Rear seat belt mountings may be of the inertia reel or fixed type (early models only), and their mounting brackets are similar to the types also used at the front.

B-POST TRIM: 110 MODELS FROM 1988 ON

2 As well as removing the top seat belt mounting as described earlier, you'll need to use a forked trim removal tool to lever out the plastic trim button. You can now remove the trim. When refitting, the button is just carefully pushed back in.

REAR QUARTER-LIGHT TRIM

3 Grasp the trim panel near its top and bottom at the door aperture and pull it towards the centre-line of the vehicle to release the spring clips. As you pull it away, the two metal clips (inset) will free themselves.

When refitting, make sure that the two metal lugs are located behind the side trim and then bang the two spring clips on to the vertical rail adjacent to the door opening, using your hand.

GRAB HANDLES

4 Two fixing screws are easily removed from each end of the grab handle once the plastic finisher has been carefully levered away.

REAR SIDE-WINDOW TRIM: STATION WAGONS FROM 1988 ON

You must first remove the rear seat and frame, the upper and lower seat belt anchorage bolts and the upper seat belt aperture finisher from the trim panel. You must also remove the rear quarter-light trim. All of these are obvious or are described in earlier sections.

5 Lever the trim panel cap fastener from the C-post.

6 Remove the lower fixings, which on some versions consist of a Phillips-head machine screw, two washers and a nut at the front, and Phillips-head machine screws, single washers and nut plates at the centre and rear. As these screws are removed, the nut plates will fall into the box section, from where they can be retrieved.

7 Three spring clips hold the top edge of the trim to the bodywork. Lift or, if necessary, strike the trim upwards to release it.

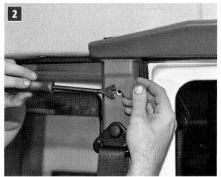

Feed the seat belt through its aperture, and the trim can now be removed from the vehicle.

Refitting is the reverse of removal, but note that on 90 models the front-most bushed hole in the trim – the one nearest the B-post – is NOT used.

UPPER SIDE-TRIM PANEL: 110 MODELS

8 This is simply lifted away – it clips behind the A-post trim – once the grab handle and other retaining trim panels have been removed.

TRIM (LINING) OVER REAR DOOR

9 Use a trim removal tool to lever out the six sturdy trim studs securing the lining to its mounting brackets.

10 Remove the lining. Take care to align holes and brackets when refitting.

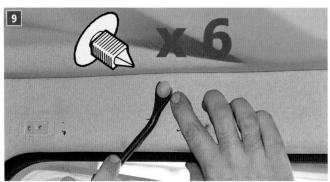

DOOR CARDs (TRIMS)

See pages 52–53.

Headlining

If you have both front and rear headlining, the rear has to be removed – or at least detached at the front as shown below – first.

**REAR HEADLINING:
STATION WAGON**

Remove the side trim panels and rear end lining – see separate sections.

1 Remove the rear interior lamp.

2 Carefully lever out the five or six (depending on model) trim studs…

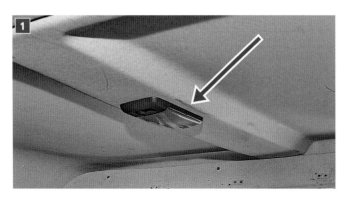

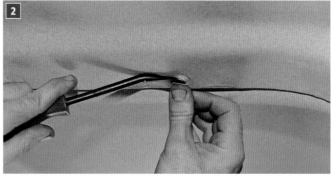

3 ...securing both the rear and front headlining sections to the roof mounting brackets.

4 Release front corners of headlining from the cantrail on both sides and pull the headlining forwards sufficiently to clear the rear end lining mounting brackets.

NOTE: The Land Rover manual advises to take care not to bend the headlining when removing or refitting. In practice, we found this amount of bend to be necessary, and in this case no damage ensued.

5 Release the rear corners of headlining from the cantrail on both sides.

6 Lower the rear headlining from the roof and remove it from the rear of the vehicle.

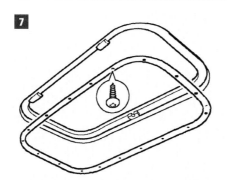

FRONT HEADLINING

Remove the A-post trims, front seat belt fixing bolts from the B-posts, and the side trim panel cap fastener from the B-posts – see separate sections.

7 When fitted, remove the screws holding the sun roof headlining finisher.

8 Remove the sun visors.

9 Remove the interior lamp.

10 Remove the interior mirror and unscrew the mounting plate.

11 Carefully lever out all the fasteners securing front and rear headlinings to the roof and above the door aperture.

12 Pull both sides of the side trim panel inwards (if still fitted) enough to release rear corners of front headlining. Lower the headlining and remove it from the vehicle through a side door.

NOTE: I take care not to bend the headlining more than absolutely necessary when removing/refitting.

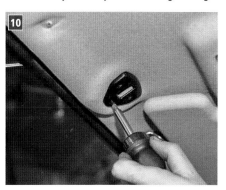

Specialists & Suppliers

ARB Corporation Ltd
42-44 Garden Street, Kilsyth, VIC 3137,
Australia
Tel: 03 9761 6622
www.arb.com.au
ARB's products are distributed in the UK by
GKN Driveline. See www.gkndriveline.com

Ashcroft Transmissions Ltd
Units 5 & 6, Stadium Estate,
Cradock Road, Luton,
Beds, LU4 0JF
Tel: 01582 496040
www.ashcroft-transmissions.co.uk

Autoglass Ltd
Ring Freephone 0800 36 36 36 for details of
your local branch.
www.autoglass.co.uk
Autoglass operate the well-known, nation-
wide call-out service for emergency glass
replacement.

Autoland 4x4 Services
Unit 8, Houghton Regis Trading Centre,
Cemetery Road, Houghton Regis,
Dunstable, LU5 5QH
Tel: 01582 866680
www.4x4service.co.uk

Britpart
Email: sales@britpart.co.uk
www.britpart.com

Clarke International Ltd
Hemnall Street, Epping,
Essex, CM16 4LG
Tel: 01992 565 300
www.clarkeinternational.com

Fertan UK
14 Broadwater Way,
Worthing,
West Sussex, BN14 9LP
Tel: 02380 456 600
www.fertan.co.uk

Holden Vintage & Classic
Linton Trading Estate, Bromyard,
Hfds, HR7 4QT
Tel: 01885 488 000
www.holden.co.uk

Illbruck Sealant Systems UK Ltd.
Trade Division, Coalville, Leicester, LE67 3JJ
Tel: 01530 835 722
www.illbruck.com

IRB Developments
Ian Baughan, near Sutton Coldfield,
Birmingham
Tel: 0121 288 1105, Mob: 0773 092 0431
(Please be aware that Ian is incredibly busy
during the working day, so you may need to
be patient when contacting him.)
www.irbdevelopments.com

Kitek
The Old Chapel, The Green, Ingham,
Lincoln, LN1 2YW
Tel: 07767 690 105

LaSalle Interior Trim
Roughburn, Dundreggan, Glenmoriston,
Inverness, IV63 7YJ
Tel: 01320 340220
www.lasalle-trim.co.uk

MJA Land Rover
Unit BH8 Buntsford Hill Business Park,
Buntsford Park Road, Bromsgrove, B60 3DX
Tel: 01527 873058
www.mjalandrover.info
Contact Mark or Paul Allard.

MM 4x4
Martin Hussingtree, Worcs, WR3 8TE
Tel: 01905 451 506.
www.mm-4x4.com

Morris Lubricants
Castle Foregate, Shrewsbury, Shropshire,
SY1 2EL
Tel: 01743 232 200
www.morrislubricants.co.uk

Pentagon Auto-Tint (Reading)
Unit 3B, 175/177 Cardiff Road,
Reading, RG1 8HD
Tel: Freephone 0800 107 5518
www.tintyourglass.co.uk
You can speak to fellow Land Rover nutcase
and regular off-road competitor Kevin
Thomas. He just loves talking Land Rovers!

Richards Chassis
Unit F2, Swinton Bridge Industrial Estate,
Whitelee Road, Swinton, Mexborough, S64 8BH
Tel: 01709 577477
www.richardschassis.co.uk

R T Quaife Engineering Ltd
Vestry Road, Otford, Sevenoaks, Kent, TN14 5EL
Tel: 01732 741144
www.quaife.co.uk

Screwfix Direct
Freepost, Yeovil, BA22 8BF
Freephone: 0500 41 41 41
www.screwfix.com

**Slide-a-Boot. P & A Auto
Products Ltd**
89 Westoning Road, Harlington,
Dunstable, Beds. LU5 6PB
Tel/Fax: 01582 754775
www.cvbootclips.co.uk

Stig Fasteners
19 Leith Road, Darlington,
Co. Durham, DL3 8BE
Tel: 01325 464243
E-mail: sales@a2stainless.com
www.a2stainless.co.uk

Turner Engineering
Churchill House, West Park Road,
Newchapel, Lingfield, Surrey, RH7 6HT
Tel: 01342 834 713
E-mail: sales@turner-engineering.co.uk
www.turner-engineering.co.uk

U-PO
Head Office, 1 Totteridge Lane,
London, N20 0E
Tel: 020 8492 5900
www.u-pol.com

Wards of Rugby
3A Earl Street, Rugby, CV21 3SS.
Tel: 01788 54 39 00
Contact Richard Campbell

Würth UK Ltd
1 Centurion Way, Erith,
Kent, DA18 4AF
Tel: 03300 555 444
www.wurth.co.uk

X-Eng
Unit 5c & 5d Sumners Ponds,
Chapel Road, Horsham,
West Sussex, RH13 0PR
Tel: 01403 888 388
E-mail: Enquiries@x-eng.co.uk
www.x-eng.co.uk

YRM Metal Solutions Ltd
Ravensford Farm House,
Bishop Auckland,
Co. Durham, DL13 3NH
Tel: 01388 488150
www.yrmlandrover.com